The Princeton Review®

Cracking the

SAT
Subject Test™
in Spanish

16th Edition

The Staff of The Princeton Review

PrincetonReview.com

Penguin
Random
House

The Princeton Review
555 W. 18th Street
New York, NY 10011
E-mail: editorialsupport@review.com

Published in the United States by Penguin Random House LLC,
New York, and in Canada by Random House of Canada, a division
of Penguin Random House Ltd., Toronto.

ISBN: 978-1-5247-1082-8
eBook ISBN: 978-1-5247-1098-9
ISSN: 1558-3406

SAT Subject Tests is a trademark of the College Board, which is
not affiliated with The Princeton Review.

The Princeton Review is not affiliated with Princeton University.

Editor: Meave Shelton
Production Artist: Deborah A. Silvestrini
Production Editor: Ali Landreau

Printed in the United States of America on partially recycled
paper.

10 9 8 7 6 5 4 3 2 1

16th Edition

Editorial
Rob Franek, Editor-in-Chief
Casey Cornelius, VP Content Development
Mary Beth Garrick, Director of Production
Selena Coppock, Managing Editor
Meave Shelton, Senior Editor
Colleen Day, Editor
Sarah Litt, Editor
Aaron Riccio, Editor
Orion McBean, Associate Editor

Penguin Random House Publishing Team
Tom Russell, VP, Publisher
Alison Stoltzfus, Publishing Director
Jake Eldred, Associate Managing Editor
Ellen Reed, Production Manager
Suzanne Lee, Designer

Acknowledgments

The Princeton Review would like to extend special thanks to George Roberto Pace, Michael Giammarino, and Claudia Landgrover for their contributions to previous editions; Anne Goldberg for her contributions to this edition; and to Jonathan Chiu, National Content Director for High School Programs, for his expert oversight.

Special thanks to Adam Robinson, who conceived of and perfected the Joe Bloggs approach to standardized tests and many of the other successful techniques used by The Princeton Review.

We are also, as always, very appreciative of the time and attention given to each page by Ali Landreau and Debbie Silvestrini.

Contents

Get More (Free) Content

1 Go to **PrincetonReview.com/cracking.**

2 Enter the following ISBN for your book: 9781524710828.

3 Answer a few simple questions to set up an exclusive Princeton Review account. (If you already have one, you can just log in.)

4 Click the "Student Tools" button, also found under "My Account" from the top toolbar. You're all set to access your bonus content!

Need to report a potential **content** issue?

Contact **EditorialSupport@review.com.**
Include:

- full title of the book
- ISBN number
- page number

Need to report a **technical** issue?

Contact **TPRStudentTech@review.com** and provide:

- your full name
- email address used to register the book
- full book title and ISBN
- computer OS (Mac/PC) and browser (Firefox, Safari, etc.)

The Princeton Review®

Once you've registered, you can...

- Access your listening drills for extra practice

- Take a full-length practice SAT and/or ACT

- Get valuable advice about the college application process, including tips for writing a great essay and where to apply for financial aid

- If you're still choosing between colleges, use our searchable rankings of *The Best 382 Colleges* to find out more information about your dream school

- Access comprehensive study guides and a variety of printable resources including additional bubble sheets, score conversion tables, and chapter summary pages

- Check to see if there have been any corrections or updates to this edition

- Get our take on any recent or pending updates to the SAT Subject Test in Spanish

Look For These Icons Throughout The Book

ONLINE ARTICLES

ONLINE AUDIO

PROVEN TECHNIQUES

APPLIED STRATEGIES

STUDY BREAK

MORE GREAT BOOKS

COLLEGE ADVISOR APP

Part I
Orientation

Chapter 1
Introduction

The SAT Subject Test in Spanish is an hour-long, multiple-choice exam intended for students who have had a minimum of two years of high school-level Spanish or the equivalent. In this chapter, we explain why you've made a wise decision to prepare with The Princeton Review and discuss the reasons you should take this exam. We also present the structure of the exam.

YOU'RE ON YOUR WAY—¡VAMOS!

Congratulations! By purchasing this book, you've taken the first step toward raising your score on the SAT Subject Tests in Spanish. Now you just have to read the book, practice the strategies, and take the practice tests. We know that taking a standardized test is about as exciting as watching paint dry, but we've done everything possible to make working through this book as painless and fun as possible.

To get the most out of this book, you should tackle it in bite-size pieces. You'll drive yourself crazy and lose interest if you try to read through the entire book in one sitting or one weekend. We recommend that you figure out how much time you have left before you take the actual test and come up with a game plan that makes sense. Just be sure to set aside a solid hour to take each one of the practice tests. You won't do yourself any good or get an accurate assessment of your performance if you take the practice tests in pieces or if you give yourself extra time to finish them.

WHAT IS THE PRINCETON REVIEW?

The Princeton Review is a test-preparation company with branches across the United States and abroad. We've developed the techniques you'll find in our books, courses, and online resources by analyzing actual exams and testing their effectiveness with our students. What makes our techniques unique is that we base our principles on the same ones used by the people who write the tests. We don't want you to waste your time with superfluous information; we'll give you just the information you need to improve your scores. You'll learn to recognize and comprehend the relatively small amount of information that's actually tested. You'll also learn to avoid common traps, think like the test writers, find answers to questions of which you're unsure, and budget your time effectively. You need to do only two things: trust the techniques, and practice, practice, practice.

WHY OUR BOOK?

The Princeton Review is on your side. We didn't create the tests, and we don't force anyone to take them. We simply help students do better on them. In this book, you'll find a thorough review of the content that will be covered on the test, test-taking strategies that will help you apply your existing knowledge, and enough practice tests for you to determine your own personal strengths and weaknesses.

Welcome
Remember—this test shows little of your knowledge of Spanish, only how well you do on this particular test.

WHAT ARE THE SPANISH SUBJECT TESTS?

There are two different Spanish Subject Tests: the traditional Spanish Subject Test and the Spanish with Listening Subject Test. Most of you will take the traditional Spanish Subject Test, and the majority of this book will be dedicated to that exam. However, for those of you who are planning to take the Spanish with Listening Subject Test, we provide some strategies to help you do your best, as well as online listening drills for realistic practice. See the "Get More (Free) Content" page at the front of this book for instructions on accessing these drills.

Both SAT Subject Tests in Spanish are hour-long, multiple-choice exams that are supposed to measure your knowledge of Spanish. Do the Spanish Subject Tests really accomplish this? Absolutely not. If you really want to know how well you speak Spanish, you should try reading a Spanish newspaper, watching a Spanish television show, or speaking Spanish with a native speaker. Each of these activities will give you a better idea of how well you speak the language than the results of the SAT Subject Tests in Spanish.

Register your book online to gain access to our free listening drills for extra practice!

WHY SHOULD YOU TAKE A SPANISH SUBJECT TEST?

There are only two good reasons to take a Spanish Subject Test. The first of these reasons is that one of the colleges to which you are applying either requires or strongly recommends you take several different SAT Subject Tests. If this is the case, you will want to make sure you pick the three subjects that best demonstrate your academic achievement. Evaluate your own strengths and weaknesses, and contact colleges to see which tests they suggest or require. The second reason you might take the SAT Subject Test in Spanish is that one of the colleges to which you're applying plans to use it as a placement exam.

Love Spanish?
Are you a Spanish aficionado? Are you enrolled or planning to enroll in AP Spanish? We also have a prep book for the Advanced Placement Exam! Check out *Cracking the AP Spanish Language & Culture Exam.*

WHEN SHOULD YOU TAKE IT?

The first thing you need to decide is whether to take one of the Spanish Subject Tests. These tests are appropriate for students who have completed a minimum of two years of high school Spanish or the equivalent, but are more often taken by students who have completed or are in the middle of their third year of high school Spanish.

The second thing you need to decide is whether to take the Spanish Subject Test or the Spanish with Listening Subject Test. If you have a lot of experience speaking Spanish, you might want to take the Spanish with Listening Subject Test. If you learned most of your Spanish from reading a book, you should probably take the Spanish Test that does not contain a listening section.

The Spanish Subject Test is given six times each year: August, October, December, January, May, and June. The Spanish with Listening Subject Test is given only once each year, in November. There is really no advantage to taking the test in a particular month, though there are plenty of rumors going around that certain administrations are easier than others. Don't pay any attention to those rumors; just take the test when you feel most ready to do so. Of course, if you decide to take the Spanish with Listening Subject Test, you don't really have much choice in the matter.

HOW DO I REGISTER FOR THE TESTS?

To register by mail, pick up the *The SAT and SAT Subject Tests Student Registration Booklet* at your guidance counselor's office. You can also register at the College Board website at **collegereadiness.collegeboard.org/sat**. This site contains other useful information such as the test date and fees. If you have questions, you can talk to a representative at the College Board by calling 1-866-756-7346.

You may have your scores sent to you, to your school, and to four colleges of your choice. Additional reports will be sent to additional colleges for—you guessed it—additional money. Scores are made available to students via the College Board's website. To find out about the timeline of when scores are made available, please visit sat.collegeboard.org.

HOW IS THE TEST STRUCTURED?

Both the Spanish Subject Test and the Spanish with Listening Subject Test contain 85 multiple-choice questions. You'll have one hour to complete each of the tests, but you do not necessarily need to finish either test to get a good score. The structure of each test is discussed in the pages that follow.

Subject Test: Spanish

The Spanish Subject Test contains three sections that measure different skills. Each section is weighted equally and contains approximately the same number of questions (about 28). The three sections are

- Part A: Vocabulary and Structure (Sentence Completion)
- Part B: Paragraph Completion
- Part C: Reading Comprehension

Subject Test: Spanish with Listening

The Spanish with Listening Subject Test consists of two sections: the Listening section and the Reading section. The Listening section (about 20 minutes) contains approximately 30 questions, and the Reading section (about 40 minutes) has around 55 questions. Each section contains questions that measure different skills.

Want to know which colleges are best for you? Check out The Princeton Review's College Advisor app to build your ideal college list and find your perfect college fit! Available for free in the iOS App Store and Google Play Store.

Listening Section

- **Part A: Pictures**—You will be presented with a series of images (approximately 10) and asked to select the sentence that best reflects what is portrayed in the picture or what someone in the picture might say. The answer choices will be spoken to you in the listening sample rather than written in your test booklet.
- **Part B: Rejoinders**—You will listen to a short conversation and/or selection and then be asked to select the answer choice that best represents the continuation of the conversation. There are no written questions, answers, or images in your test booklet. This portion requires you to listen carefully to the conversation and answer about 10 questions.
- **Part C: Selections**—You will be asked to listen to extensive selections including conversations among a group of people, advertisements, or short stories. You will then have to answer approximately 10 questions. Unlike those in Parts A and B, the questions and answers in Part C *are* written in your test booklet.

Reading Section

- Part A: Vocabulary and Structure (Sentence Completion)
- Part B: Paragraph Completion
- Part C: Reading Comprehension

HOW IS THE TEST SCORED?

Your overall score on either the Spanish Subject Test or the Spanish with Listening Subject Test is based on the number of questions you answer correctly minus $\frac{1}{3}$ of the number of questions you answer incorrectly. You get no credit and lose no points for questions you leave blank. On the Spanish Subject Test, the result of this simple calculation (number correct $- \frac{1}{3}$ of number incorrect) represents your raw score. Raw scores can range from –28 to 85. On the Spanish with Listening Subject Test, you receive several different scores: a raw score for each section, a scaled score for each section (20–80), and an overall scaled score (200–800).

Both Spanish Subject Tests are scored on a 200–800 scale. Just like with the SAT, the lowest possible score is a 200 (even if you answer every question incorrectly) and the highest possible score is an 800 (which you can get even if you miss a question or two). The only tricky thing about the scoring is on the Spanish with Listening Subject Test. On this test, the two sections are weighted differently. Because the Reading section represents about $\frac{2}{3}$ of the overall test, your raw score in that section is multiplied by 1.12. The Listening section represents about $\frac{1}{3}$ of the overall test, so your raw score in that section is multiplied by .881. The products of these two calculations are added together to determine your overall raw score. This new raw score is then converted to a scaled score between 200 and 800.

You shouldn't get too worked up over the scoring. Just do your best, and follow the techniques you learn in this book.

THE SPANISH WITH LISTENING TEST
If you're fairly comfortable listening to spoken Spanish or if you speak it regularly, consider taking the Spanish with Listening Test. If not, you may be better off taking the basic Spanish Subject Test.

The Essentials
If you plan to take the Spanish with Listening Subject Test, the most important thing you need to remember is to bring a CD player with you to the test center. That's right, even though the test administrators will hand out a CD on the day of the test, they will NOT provide you with a CD player. For your CD player to be "acceptable," it must have earphones, operate on batteries (bring your own—the test administrator will not have extras), and be able to play a standard CD. Under no circumstances will you be allowed to share your CD player with another student.

The other thing to keep in mind if you're considering taking the Spanish with Listening Subject Test is that it's offered only once each year—in November. If you're planning to take the test, be sure to register in time for the November exam.

Strategies
The good news is that the strategies that apply to the Spanish Subject Test are also appropriate for the Reading section of the Spanish with Listening Subject Test. Chapters 3 to 6 contain a thorough review of the vocabulary and grammar you need for both tests, as well as a review of the reading and test-taking strategies you need for the Spanish Subject Test and the Reading section of the Spanish with Listening Subject Test. However, you need to prepare for the Listening section of the Spanish with Listening Subject Test on your own. The following are a few ways you can do this:

- Practice speaking Spanish with your friends, classmates, or family members—by speaking Spanish with others, you will get more comfortable with understanding and responding to spoken Spanish.
- Listen to a Spanish-language radio station and practice interpreting what you hear.

- Watch a Spanish-language television program and practice interpreting what you hear.
- Be sure to take our online listening drills, which can be found by going to **PrincetonReview.com/cracking** and registering your book. Once you complete the free "Checkout" process, click on "Student Tools" to access the listening drills.

The most important thing you can do to improve your score on this section of the test is to relax, take a deep breath, and focus.

IS THERE ANY OTHER MATERIAL AVAILABLE FOR PRACTICE?

The College Board publishes a book called *Official Study Guide for All SAT Subject Tests*, which contains full-length tests in almost all the SAT subjects offered. You can also go to the College Board's website, **www.collegeboard.org,** for more information and practice questions.

> For book updates, links to more information, last-minute test changes, and access to our practice listening drills, visit this book's online Student Tools at **PrincetonReview.com/cracking.**

Pressed for time? Our free, customized study guides can help you break up the content in this book into manageable chunks depending on how much time you have available. Register your book online and download them right away!

FINAL THOUGHTS

You may be concerned that you'll be at a significant disadvantage if you're not a native speaker. This is a common concern, but remember that college admissions officers aren't stupid. They will realize that non-native speakers cannot be expected to meet the same standards as native speakers.

Preparation is the key to success—not only on this test, but also in everything you do. If you want to succeed on the Spanish Subject Test or any other test, make sure you understand the content, practice the strategies, and develop an overall plan to attain your target score. In addition to working through this book, you may want to read a Spanish newspaper (looking up the words you don't know in a dictionary), listen to Spanish-language radio stations, watch Spanish-language television programs, or engage in conversations in Spanish with your classmates, friends, or family members.

Finally, RELAX. Once you've finished preparing, there's no need to stress about the tests. Just make sure you get plenty of sleep the night before the test, eat a balanced breakfast, walk into the test center with a feeling of confidence, and do your best. In the end, your score is just a number. These tests will never be able to measure the most important aspect of your academic potential: your determination.

Summary

Did you get all that?

o   There are two different Spanish Subject Tests: the traditional Spanish Subject Test and the Spanish with Listening Subject Test. Most of you will take the traditional test, but if you have a lot of experience speaking Spanish, consider taking the Spanish with Listening Subject Test. Keep in mind that the listening test is only administered in November each year.

o   The good news is that you can use the same strategies to prepare for both exams!
   • Read articles from Spanish magazines, newspapers, and journals. Find academic articles, short stories, and pop culture articles to challenge and broaden your vocabulary.
   • Practice speaking Spanish with your friends or family.
   • Listen to Spanish radio stations or watch Spanish TV shows.
   • Use our listening drills, which can be found in Student Tools in your online dashboard. Go to **www.PrincetonReview.com/cracking** to access the drills.

o   Don't stress! By preparing the right way and taking time to relax, you'll be able to take the test with confidence.

Chapter 2
How to Take the Test: Overall Strategies

Strategy is very important when taking a standardized exam. In this chapter, we look at overall strategies for the test, such as pacing, guessing, and Process of Elimination (POE).

In Chapters 3 through 5 you will review the Spanish that you need to know (as well as some strategies) for the different question types. Right now, let's talk about how to take a standardized test.

PACING

Since your earliest days in school, you were probably taught that when you take a test, finishing is important. Standardized tests, however, are a completely different ball game. The folks who write these tests are interested in how fast you can work, and they design the tests so that it's nearly impossible to finish on time. Because you're so accustomed to the idea that finishing is crucial, you may pressure yourself to answer every question. Have you ever stopped to consider how much sense this makes? It's not as if you get a special prize for finishing! In fact, to finish, you usually have to rush through questions, and as a result you make careless errors that could have been avoided. Doesn't it make more sense to slow down a little, answer the questions of which you're sure, and leave a few blanks? Well, let's see how pacing yourself on the Spanish Subject Tests relates to actual scores.

> **Pace Yourself**
> There is no need to do the whole test, especially because it's designed so that you can't! Use the pacing chart. Not doing all the questions gives you more time to get the ones you **are** doing right. If you walk into the test without a pacing strategy, you're basically unprepared.

Pacing Chart

Structure
60 minutes, 85 questions

To Get a Score of	Answer About	Leave This Many Blank
400	13	72
450	26	59
500	38	47
550	48	37
600	58	27
650	68	17
700	78	7
750 and up	85	0

Understand that the pacing chart assumes you'll make fewer than six mistakes, and it doesn't take guesses into account. If you take your time, pick your questions carefully, and learn to guess effectively, making fewer than six errors really isn't as tough as it might sound.

You should walk into your test with a target score in mind and a pacing strategy that reflects the score you want. Remember, this is *your* test, and that means you can answer the questions you want, when you want, how you want, and still get an excellent score. If you want to leave most (or all) of the reading comprehension questions blank and concentrate on the other questions, go ahead. If you're good at reading comprehension but not so good at grammar, then do more of the reading comprehension and fewer of the grammar sentence completions. If all the other students at your test site want to race frantically to the end of the test and make careless mistakes along the way, that's their problem. You're going to be sitting there, cool and relaxed, taking your time and getting a great score.

THE GUESSING STRATEGY

Many people talk about the "guessing penalty" on the SAT Subject Tests. What they really mean is that there's no advantage to random guessing. The truth is, there really isn't a penalty either.

Each question on the Spanish Subject Test and the Spanish with Listening Subject Test has four answer choices. If you answer a question correctly, you will receive 1 raw-score point. If you get a question wrong, you will lose $\frac{1}{3}$ of a raw-score point. If you were to randomly guess on four questions with four answer choices each, odds are you would get one question right and three questions wrong. How would this affect your raw score?

1 question correct = +1 point

3 questions incorrect = $-(\frac{1}{3}) \times 3 = -1$ point

Total impact on overall score = 0

So should you guess? Sometimes. If you can eliminate one or more incorrect answer choices, the odds become more favorable. Imagine you were able to eliminate two answer choices and then randomly guess on the remaining two answer choices for four different problems. In this case, you would likely get two questions right and two questions wrong. How would this affect your raw score?

2 questions correct = +2 points

2 questions incorrect = $-(\frac{1}{3}) \times 2 = -\frac{2}{3}$ point

Total impact on overall score = $+1\frac{1}{3}$ points

The moral of this story is that if you can eliminate even one answer choice over several questions, guessing is to your advantage. If you can't eliminate any answer choices, there's no reason to guess. You'll just be wasting valuable time.

THE THREE-PASS SYSTEM

Because the test is written for students with varying levels of expertise in Spanish, the questions vary in difficulty. The questions in a section often get more difficult as you go along. That said, whether you find a question difficult is a personal thing; it's a matter of whether *you* know the words and/or grammar being tested.

The Three-Pass System Means...

- **First Pass**—Go through an entire section of the test from beginning to end, but answer only the easiest questions, that is, those for which you thoroughly understand all the vocabulary, grammar, and so on. Skip anything that looks as if it's going to give you grief.
- **Second Pass**—Go back to the beginning of the same section and take a shot at those questions for which you knew some, but not all, of the vocabulary.
- **Third Pass**—Use Process of Elimination on each remaining question in that section to eliminate some answers. Then take a guess. If you can't eliminate anything, leave the question blank.

Taking a section of the test using the Three-Pass System keeps you from getting stuck on a tough question early in the section and spending too much time on it.

Note: The Three-Pass System does not work on the Listening section of the Spanish with Listening Subject Test. For that section, you listen to a CD and must answer the questions in the order in which they appear (you can, of course, choose to leave some blank).

POE—PROCESS OF ELIMINATION

Process of Elimination is one of the gifts of a multiple-choice exam. The idea is simple: There are three wrong answers and only one right one; therefore, if you can eliminate answers you know are wrong, you eventually stumble upon the right answer because it's the only one left. Approaching questions in this manner also ensures that you avoid the traps the test writers set for students. You'll learn how this applies to each question type later on. POE varies based on question type, but the general idea is always the same.

Summary

o   You don't need to answer every question to get a good score. Use your target score as a guide for how many questions you should answer.

o   Guessing is to your advantage when you can eliminate at least one incorrect choice.

o   Process of Elimination (POE) is an extremely useful strategy on this exam. The idea behind it is to eliminate choices that you know are wrong so you can get to the right answer.

Part II
Practice Test 1

Practice Test 1

SPANISH SUBJECT TEST 1

Your responses to Spanish Subject Test 1 questions must be filled in on Test 1 of your answer sheet (at the back of the book). Marks on any other section will not be counted toward your Spanish Subject Test score.

When your supervisor gives the signal, turn the page and begin the Spanish Subject Test.

SPANISH SUBJECT TEST

PLEASE NOTE THAT YOUR ANSWER SHEET HAS FIVE ANSWER POSITIONS MARKED A, B, C, D, E, WHILE THE QUESTIONS THROUGHOUT THIS TEST CONTAIN ONLY FOUR CHOICES. BE SURE <u>NOT</u> TO MAKE ANY MARKS IN COLUMN E.

Part A

Directions: This part consists of a number of incomplete statements, each having four suggested completions. Select the most appropriate completion and fill in the corresponding oval on the answer sheet.

---

1. Si quieres ver el principio de la película, llega al teatro ------- .

   (A) más tarde
   (B) sin dinero
   (C) a tiempo
   (D) por la noche

2. Cuando vivía en Nueva York, ------- mucho tiempo escuchando conciertos y visitando los museos.

   (A) pasaba
   (B) pasé
   (C) he pasado
   (D) pasaré

3. Mi abuelo quiere vivir en un sitio bien tranquilo, porque no le gusta el ruido. Por eso se ha mudado ------- .

   (A) a una calle muy ruidosa
   (B) fuera de la ciudad
   (C) al centro del mundo
   (D) sin querer

4. ¿ ------- museo prefieres, el de ciencia o el de arte?

   (A) Cuál
   (B) Qué
   (C) Cuánto
   (D) Quién

5. ¿Qué ------- cuando me llamaste al móvil esta tarde?

   (A) quisieras
   (B) querrían
   (C) querías
   (D) quieres

6. No lo conozco muy bien, pero la gente dice que ------- un tipo muy sincero e inteligente.

   (A) estamos
   (B) son
   (C) está
   (D) es

7. La invención del teléfono por Alexander Graham Bell en 1876 ------- como la gente se comunica.

   (A) cambia
   (B) cambió
   (C) cambiaron
   (D) cambias

8. Vamos a tomar el viaje en dos días en vez de uno, porque nuestro destino está muy ------- aquí.

   (A) cerca de
   (B) lejos de
   (C) junto a
   (D) en frente de

9. Mi hermano nació tres años antes que yo; por eso es ------- .

   (A) mayor
   (B) más alto
   (C) mi hermano favorito
   (D) muy aburrido

10. Si no te gusta la ley, ¿por qué ------- los últimos cuatro años trabajando como abogado?

   (A) pasas
   (B) has pasado
   (C) pasarías
   (D) pasarás

GO ON TO THE NEXT PAGE

11. En la biblioteca se encuentran ------- .

(A) plumas
(B) esperanzas
(C) preguntas
(D) libros

12. La bandera que ondea sobre el estadio es ------- .

(A) nuestro
(B) nuestras
(C) nuestra
(D) mío

13. La sopa caliente me dio dolor de muelas.
Necesito ------- .

(A) una silla
(B) una mesa
(C) un dentista
(D) un tornillo

14. La receta que Marta le dio a Verónica era difícil de
leer por que ------- .

(A) es grande
(B) es linda
(C) estaba borrada
(D) estaba limpia

15. Para ir a México el ------- más rapido es este.

(A) camino
(B) cielo
(C) paseo
(D) suelo

16. Ayer tenía mucho dolor de espalda, pero hoy no
------- ninguno.

(A) tienen
(B) tenemos
(C) tienes
(D) tengo

17. La copa mundial de futbol es un ------- .

(A) evento para espectadores
(B) deporte local
(C) evento nacional
(D) partido

18. García es nuestro cliente más estimado; siempre
------- damos a él lo que quiera.

(A) la
(B) le
(C) lo
(D) les

19. Alberto se sienta y pide arroz con pollo y una copa
de vino. El está en ------- .

(A) un restaurante
(B) un circo
(C) un banco
(D) una zapatería

20. ¿ ------- cuándo han estudiado la historia española?

(A) Hasta
(B) Durante
(C) Desde
(D) En

21. Este otoño que viene, ------- todos juntos a mi casa
en las montanas.

(A) vamos
(B) vayan
(C) voy
(D) iremos

22. Mi tío sabe cocinar los frijoles negros
bastante ------- .

(A) bien
(B) bueno
(C) buenos
(D) baños

23. El concierto que vimos anoche fue estupendo.
¡Esa ------- de verdad sabe tocar!

(A) partido
(B) novela
(C) comida
(D) orquesta

GO ON TO THE NEXT PAGE

24. Tengo miedo de que la tormenta ------- durante la boda que vamos a tener en el patio.

    (A) llegue
    (B) llega
    (C) llegaría
    (D) llegara

25. Carlos es un muchacho muy pesado que siempre está metido en algún lío. No es milagro que todo el mundo lo ------- .

    (A) quiera
    (B) rechace
    (C) ayude
    (D) conozca

26. Los libros de la biblioteca no están en buenas condiciones. La biblioteca no tiene los ------- para comprar nuevos libros.

    (A) dinero
    (B) fondos
    (C) espacio
    (D) estudiantes

27. Después de dos años de investigaciones, el médico por fin ------- la causa de la enfermedad.

    (A) descubrió
    (B) dirigió
    (C) abrió
    (D) buscó

28. Jamás hemos bailado la samba, pero sí ------- bailar la lambada.

    (A) conocemos
    (B) conozca
    (C) sabrán
    (D) sabemos

29. Se dice que José Martí, el famoso autor cubano, empezó a escribir ------- cuando tenía solamente seis años.

    (A) lápices
    (B) alfabetos
    (C) idiomas
    (D) poemas

GO ON TO THE NEXT PAGE

Part B

Directions: In each of the following passages, there are numbered blanks indicating that words or phrases have been omitted. For each numbered blank, four completions are provided. First read through the entire paragraph. Then, for each numbered blank, choose the completion that is most appropriate given the context of the entire paragraph and fill in the corresponding oval on the answer sheet.

Desde hace 10 años en Colombia (30) presentado propuestas de telenovelas que han remplazado el melodrama tradicional, ya que el formato colombiano siempre se ha preocupado (31) representar la clase trabajadora del país. Es así como (32) de la población (33) en los personajes e historias de las teleseries su propia imagen.

Un buen ejemplo es "Yo soy Betty la fea" (1999), ya que (34) uno de los aciertos televisivos más grandes de la historia de las telenovelas. (35) la frustración de una mujer (36) que se enamora (37) su jefe, un hombre rico y (38) del negocio de la moda. (39) vive rodeado de modelos y tiene un compromiso matrimonial con una mujer que además de ser bella, pertenece a (40) mismo círculo social.

Excerpted from "Telenovelas Colombianas: Un Fenómeno Social," VeinteMundos.com.

30. (A) se han
    (B) se había
    (C) se hemos
    (D) se ha

31. (A) por
    (B) para
    (C) de
    (D) a

32. (A) el mayor
    (B) las mayorías
    (C) los mayores
    (D) la mayoría

33. (A) ha sabido
    (B) ha detestado
    (C) ha encontrado
    (D) ha saludado

34. (A) ha estado
    (B) ha sido
    (C) había sido
    (D) había estado

35. (A) Muestra
    (B) Prueba
    (C) Avisa
    (D) Oculta

36. (A) joven
    (B) alta
    (C) bella
    (D) fea

37. (A) de
    (B) con
    (C) por
    (D) a

38. (A) viejo
    (B) feo
    (C) poderoso
    (D) débil

39. (A) Este
    (B) Está
    (C) Esta
    (D) Ella

40. (A) sus
    (B) su
    (C) la
    (D) lo

GO ON TO THE NEXT PAGE

Allí estaba otra (41) ese ruido. Aquel ruido frío, (42), vertical, que ya tanto conocía pero que ahora (43) presentaba agudo y doloroso, como si de (44) día a otro se hubiera desacostumbrado a él.

Le giraba (45) cráneo vacío, sordo y punzante. Había sentido ese ruido "las otras veces", con (46) insistencia. Lo (47) sentido, por ejemplo, el día en que (48) por primera vez. Es simplemente "una muerte viva".

Excerpted from "Ojos de Perro Azul," by Gabriel García Márquez, 1947.

41. (A) primer
    (B) vez
    (C) tiempo
    (D) tal vez

42. (A) tranquilo
    (B) caliente
    (C) cortante
    (D) plácido

43. (A) se le
    (B) se lo
    (C) se la
    (D) se les

44. (A) un
    (B) una
    (C) unos
    (D) unas

45. (A) debajo de la
    (B) encima de la
    (C) detrás del
    (D) dentro del

46. (A) lo mismo
    (B) las mismas
    (C) la misma
    (D) los mismos

47. (A) había
    (B) habían
    (C) han
    (D) ha

48. (A) mordió
    (B) murió
    (C) expiró
    (D) paró

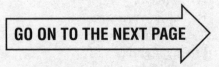

GO ON TO THE NEXT PAGE

Pepe tenía veinticinco años cuando (49) cierta ciudad del Mediodía, donde (50) , completamente resuelto (51) ministro.

Su padre (52) un empleado de diez y seis mil reales, y a la verdad que (53) muy tristes consideraciones esta pícara costumbre (54) los empleos públicos por (55) con que se retribuyen. ¿No hay los empleos públicos alguna cosa más importante, más noble, más elevada que el sueldo? ¡ (56) , no! Su padre le dio una educación (57) mediana.

Excerpted from "Querer es Poder," by Antonio de Trueba, 1922.

49. (A) abandonaron
    (B) abandonaba
    (C) abandonó
    (D) abandona

50. (A) había nacido
    (B) ha nacido
    (C) han nacido
    (D) habían nacido

51. (A) a ser
    (B) por ser
    (C) para ser
    (D) de ser

52. (A) es
    (B) era
    (C) fuera
    (D) estaba

53. (A) sugiere
    (B) sugerir
    (C) sugiera
    (D) sugerirá

54. (A) de mostrar
    (B) de decir
    (C) de contar
    (D) de clasificar

55. (A) el situación
    (B) el sueldo
    (C) el soldado
    (D) el sol

56. (A) Por lo menos
    (B) Es decir
    (C) Por lo visto
    (D) Por que

57. (A) más que
    (B) menos que
    (C) más de
    (D) menos de

GO ON TO THE NEXT PAGE

SPANISH SUBJECT TEST–*Continued*

Part C

Directions: Read the following texts carefully for comprehension. Each passage is followed by a number of questions or incomplete statements. Select the answer or completion that is best according to the text and fill in the corresponding oval on the answer sheet.

Roy sabía desde pequeño que moriría joven. No era una sensación, era una certeza. A lo largo de su infancia, cuando los demás niños relataban en forma entusiasta a qué se dedicarían de mayores, el pequeño Roy se limitaba a decir que pretendía estudiar guitarra y componer canciones. Entrada la adolescencia y acompañado seis de los siete días de la semana por su camiseta de Bono, el ahora espigado Roy contaba con una hilera de pelos en el pecho y una guitarra color caoba que cautivaba tanto como las secuencias de acordes que aquél muchacho compartía canturreando en los muros de la secundaria. Llegaron las primeras canciones dedicadas fugazmente a algunas mujeres, el primer amigo de verdad, que rápidamente influyó en letras y músicas.

Una tarde, cercano a cumplir los treinta, Roy componía la que sería su mejor canción hasta ese momento, cuando a su lado se sentó La Muerte.

Excerpted from *Cuentos de Café Corto*, by Germán Bernardez, 2016. This work is licensed under a Creative Commons Attribution-NonCommercial-NoDerivs 3.0 Unported License.

58. Al principio, ¿qué relataban los niños?

(A) Que no le gustaban a Roy
(B) Cuentos cortos que influyó la música de Roy
(C) Que morirían joven
(D) A qué se dedicarían de mayores

59. ¿Quién es el protagonista?

(A) Es un tipo triste y solo que nunca tiene amigos.
(B) Es un chico que llega a la mayoría de edad y de repente se muere.
(C) Es un tipo un poco aislado que compone canciones.
(D) Es un solitario que últimamente descubre una compañera.

60. ¿Cómo era el futuro del pequeño Roy en el pasaje?

(A) No tenía ningún futuro.
(B) Roy estaba condenado a morirse.
(C) Roy no sabía qué quiere hacerse cuando llegara a la mayoría de edad.
(D) Roy se limitaba a decir que pretendía estudiar guitarra y componer canciones.

61. Cuando Roy entra la adolescencia, ¿qué hace?

(A) Roy canta y escribe canciones originales.
(B) Roy se muere.
(C) Roy cuenta una hilera de pelos en el pecho.
(D) Roy conoce a muchos amigos verdaderos.

62. Los primeros canciones de Roy consisten de

(A) su camiseta de Bono
(B) acordes y letras de mujeres y amigos
(C) una hilera de pelos en el pecho
(D) certezas y sensaciones de su infancia

63. ¿Qué pasa al fin del pasaje?

(A) La Muerte se acerca a Roy.
(B) Roy se muera.
(C) Roy estaba soñando y al fin despierta.
(D) La Muerte es una mujer seductiva que influye a Roy.

GO ON TO THE NEXT PAGE

Desde el descubrimiento de la tumba del Apóstol Santiago, en Compostela (España), en el siglo IX, el Camino de Santiago se convirtió en la más importante ruta de peregrinación de la Europa medieval.

El paso de los innumerables peregrinos que, movidos por su fe, se dirigían a Compostela desde todos los países europeos, sirvió como punto de partida de todo un desarrollo cultural, social y económico que dejó sus huellas a lo largo del Camino de Santiago.

En la actualidad, el Camino de Santiago está considerado como uno de los principales productos de turismo cultural en España. Junto con las ciudades de Madrid y Barcelona y la Comunidad de Andalucía, esta ruta es un recurso turístico fundamental, por sus contenidos y su oferta monumental, gastronómica y de alojamiento.

Excerpted from "Camino de Santiago: Una Ruta Legendaria," VeinteMundos.com.

64. ¿Cuándo fue descubierto la tumba del Apóstol Santiago?

   (A) en el siglo V
   (B) en el siglo IX
   (C) en el siglo X
   (D) en el siglo XIV

65. ¿Por qué se pasa por el Camino de Santiago?

   (A) Es un calle principal en España.
   (B) Es una carretera entre Madrid y Barcelona.
   (C) Se pasa por el Camino de Santiago para mostrar la fe cristiana.
   (D) Algunos pasan por la fe mientras otras pasan por el turismo.

66. ¿Cómo ha servido al país el Camino de Santiago?

   (A) Ha aumentado su crecimiento cultural y económico.
   (B) Ha servido como una atracción turística a los lugareños.
   (C) No sirve para nada.
   (D) Sirve como una ruta entre países.

67. ¿Por qué se menciona Madrid, Barcelona y la comunidad de Andalucía?

   (A) Son lugares que se habían beneficiado por la popularidad del Camino de Santiago.
   (B) Son destinaciones populares para los turistas.
   (C) Son los extremos del Camino de Santiago.
   (D) Son ciudades importantes de España.

68. ¿Qué se puede decir del turismo cultural de España?

   (A) Hay turismo gastronómico y arquitectural.
   (B) Los turistas hacen daño a la economía.
   (C) Solamente las peregrinas participan en el turismo.
   (D) El turismo ha disminuido reciamente.

69. El pasaje trata de

   (A) un paisaje único y bella
   (B) un paso famoso y importante
   (C) un santo importante e influyente
   (D) un campo que fue descubierto

GO ON TO THE NEXT PAGE

Los aztecas consideraban a Quetzlcoatl como el dios de la inteligencia y del viento. Además de descubrir el maíz, dio clases de ciencia a los hombres y les enseñó la elaboración del calendario y a convivir dentro de una sociedad civilizada.

Según otra leyenda, también fue hombre. Era rubio, blanco, alto, barbudo y de grandes conocimientos científicos, que instruyó a los pobladores de lo que hoy es México a trabajar los metales, además de la orfebrería y la astrología. Eso sí, jamás se llegó a saber su nacionalidad y su procedencia.

Básicamente, Quetzlcoatl representa la dualidad propia del ser humano: es cuerpo físico y espíritu. Sus enseñanzas quedaron recogidas en ciertos documentos llamados Huehuetlahtolli o las "antiguas palabras", transmitidos por tradición oral hasta que fueron escritas por los primeros cronistas españoles.

Excerpted from "Personajes Mitología Latinoamerica," VeinteMundos.com.

70. ¿Quién es Quetzlcoatl?

(A) Es el nombre del dios cristiano en México.
(B) Es un científico y astrólogo.
(C) Es una figura mítica de los aztecas.
(D) Es un hombre alto y sabio que vive en México.

71. ¿Qué representa Quetzlcoatl?

(A) la tradición de la religión azteca
(B) inteligencia y el viento
(C) el dios de maíz y las ciencias
(D) la dualidad del ser humano

72. ¿Qué son "antiguas palabras"?

(A) parte de un poema anciana
(B) parte de una tradición oral
(C) un hechizo recitado por Huehuetlahtolli
(D) unos dichos sabios y religiosos

73. ¿De qué se trata este pasaje?

(A) Cuenta de los leyendas rodeando a Quetzlcoatl.
(B) Describe la actitud de Quetzlcoatl sobre las tradiciones orales.
(C) Ilustra por qué los aztecas rezan a Quetzlcoatl.
(D) Trata de los dificultades de describir a Quetzlcoatl.

GO ON TO THE NEXT PAGE

SPANISH SUBJECT TEST—*Continued*

Descripción del campamento

Nuestro objetivo es hacer un campamento de formación ecuestre completa, mediante el ocio y la formación ambiental en un marco incomparable como es la Esquela de Equitación Estadonidence, que hará de este campamento de verano unas vacaciones inolvidables.

Información general

- **Edad:** 3 a 18 años
- **Nivel:** Todos los niveles
- **Duración:** 7 días
- **Alojamiento:** Escuela de Equitación Estadonidence
- **Pensión Completa**
- **Profesores y Monitores Ecuestres Titulados**
- **3 horas diarias de curso ecuestre**
- **Actividades y juegos**

Transporte: No incluido. Lo ideal es que cada familia se encargue de llevar a su hijo a los campamentos por medios propios, de esta forma conocerán las instalaciones que sus hijos van a disfrutar.

Asistencia y seguro médico.

Seguro de responsabilidad civil y de accidentes. La prioridad absoluta en nuestros campamentos de verano es garantizar la salud y el bienestar de los jóvenes.

Dinero: Los jóvenes dispondrán de todo lo necesario por lo que no precisan de dinero, fomentando así la igualdad.

Lugar:
Escuela de Equitación Estadonidence
5511 Calle 13 noreste
Los Angeles, CA 90210

74. ¿Este anuncio es para qué tipo de servicio?

(A) un hospital
(B) una oficina de negocios
(C) un campamento de verano
(D) una escuela secundaria

75. ¿Cuántos años tienen los campistas?

(A) infantes y jovenes
(B) adultos
(C) jóvenes y adolescentes
(D) adolescentes

76. ¿Cómo llegan los campistas al campamento?

(A) Hay un autobús que les lleva al campamento.
(B) No hay ningún manera a llegar al campamento.
(C) Las familias les llevan por su moda preferida de transportación.
(D) Los campistas deben llegar a caballo.

77. ¿Por cuánto tiempo dura el campamento?

(A) 3 horas
(B) 3 días
(C) 7 días
(D) 18 días

78. ¿Cuánto dinero necesitan los estudiantes del campamento?

(A) No necesitan dinero para disfrutar el campamento.
(B) Necesitan dinero para comer las tres comidas del día.
(C) Pueden tomar todo el dinero que quieran.
(D) Necesitan dinero para las lecciones privadas de ecuestre.

79. ¿Cuáles medidas de seguridad hay en el campamento?

(A) Hay arneses para todos los estudiantes.
(B) Hay seguro médico y seguro de responsabilidad civil.
(C) Hay cameras de seguridad en el campamento.
(D) Hay un guardia armado que pasa por el campamento.

GO ON TO THE NEXT PAGE

El corazón le galopeaba fuertemente, la transpiración le caía a chorros y las piernas casi no se le veían, de lo rápida que corría.

Era de noche y en la calle no se veía a nadie. Ni los gatos, que siempre solían estar rondando a esas horas.

Ella corría sin saber a dónde estaba corriendo, ni se daba vuelta para ver si aquello que la hacía huir había quedado atrás o seguía ahí. Al ver una esquina, después de tremenda huida, dobló y se recostó de espaldas contra el edificio. Pero en el momento en que creyó poder respirar vio a un chico, que le cubría la boca con su mano. Mientras que con la otra le hacía una señal de que mantenga la calma. La chica soltó lágrimas que le llenaban los ojos.

Excerpted from "El viaje de Nadia," *Cuentos cortos y otras cosas II*, by Karina Zander Repetto, 2011.

80. ¿Qué hace la chica al principio del pasaje?

(A) Está confundido por su nuevo lugar.
(B) Está corriendo and tiene miedo.
(C) Está peleando con su querido.
(D) Está fatigada porque ha corrido tanto.

81. ¿Cómo es la calle al principio del pasaje?

(A) oscura y desierta
(B) congestionada y ruidosa
(C) estrecha y larga
(D) ancha y tranquila

82. ¿Por qué la chica no sabe a dónde está corriendo?

(A) No sabe si el chico sigue siguiéndole.
(B) Está en un país extraño.
(C) No puede ver el camino.
(D) Está confundida y necesita un mapa.

83. ¿Por qué el chico le hace una señal de que mantenga la calma?

(A) No le gusta el llanto de la chica.
(B) No quiere que la chica haga ruido.
(C) Ella es demasiado ruidosa.
(D) Él no sabe de dónde están.

84. ¿Qué pasa cuando ella deja de correr?

(A) Ella se cae por el suelo.
(B) Un chico la agarra.
(C) Disfruta el silencio en la calle.
(D) Descubre un edificio seguro.

85. ¿Por qué llora la chica al fin del pasaje?

(A) Porque es difícil correr tanto
(B) Porque no puede respirar
(C) Porque está triste
(D) Porque tiene miedo del chico

S T O P
**If you finish before time is called, you may check your work on this test only.
Do not work on any other test in this book.**

Practice Test 1: Answers and Explanations

- Practice Test 1 Answer Key
- Practice Test 1 Explanations
- How to Score Practice Test 1

PRACTICE TEST 1 ANSWER KEY

Question Number	Correct Answer	Right	Wrong	Question Number	Correct Answer	Right	Wrong	Question Number	Correct Answer	Right	Wrong
1	C	___	___	33	C	___	___	65	D	___	___
2	A	___	___	34	B	___	___	66	A	___	___
3	B	___	___	35	A	___	___	67	B	___	___
4	A	___	___	36	D	___	___	68	A	___	___
5	C	___	___	37	A	___	___	69	B	___	___
6	D	___	___	38	C	___	___	70	C	___	___
7	B	___	___	39	A	___	___	71	D	___	___
8	B	___	___	40	B	___	___	72	B	___	___
9	A	___	___	41	B	___	___	73	A	___	___
10	B	___	___	42	C	___	___	74	C	___	___
11	D	___	___	43	A	___	___	75	C	___	___
12	C	___	___	44	A	___	___	76	C	___	___
13	C	___	___	45	D	___	___	77	C	___	___
14	C	___	___	46	C	___	___	78	A	___	___
15	A	___	___	47	A	___	___	79	B	___	___
16	D	___	___	48	B	___	___	80	B	___	___
17	A	___	___	49	C	___	___	81	A	___	___
18	B	___	___	50	A	___	___	82	A	___	___
19	A	___	___	51	A	___	___	83	B	___	___
20	C	___	___	52	B	___	___	84	B	___	___
21	D	___	___	53	A	___	___	85	D	___	___
22	A	___	___	54	D	___	___				
23	D	___	___	55	B	___	___				
24	A	___	___	56	C	___	___				
25	B	___	___	57	A	___	___				
26	B	___	___	58	D	___	___				
27	A	___	___	59	C	___	___				
28	D	___	___	60	D	___	___				
29	D	___	___	61	A	___	___				
30	A	___	___	62	B	___	___				
31	A	___	___	63	A	___	___				
32	D	___	___	64	B	___	___				

PRACTICE TEST 1 EXPLANATIONS

Part A

1. **C**   **Translation:** If you want to see the beginning of the film, arrive at the theater ------- .

    (A) later
    (B) without money
    (C) on time
    (D) at night

    The key phrase in this sentence is **si quieres ver el principio**. If you were able to get this much, you could determine that time had something to do with the answer, and that would eliminate (B) and (D). What would make more sense in terms of seeing the beginning of something: arriving later or arriving on time? On time makes more sense, and (C) is the correct answer.

2. **A**   **Translation:** When I lived in New York, I ------- a lot of time listening to concerts and visiting the museums.

    (A) spent (imperfect)
    (B) spent
    (C) have spent
    (D) will spend

    Because the sentence refers to the past, the answer must be some kind of past tense, and because **pasaré** is the future, you can immediately scratch (D). The other three choices are all past tenses, but since the action described was an ongoing one during the time the person lived in New York, the answer must be in the imperfect tense, which is (A).

3. **B**   **Translation:** My grandfather wants to live in a peaceful place because he doesn't like noise. That's why he's moved ------- .

    (A) to a noisy street
    (B) outside of the city
    (C) to the center of the earth
    (D) unintentionally

    If you understood either the part about not liking noise or the part about wanting to live peacefully you could eliminate (A). Choices (C) and (D) are sort of ridiculous, and so (B) is your best bet.

4.   A   Translation: ------- museum do you prefer, the science one or the art one?

(A) **Which**
(B) What
(C) How much
(D) Who

Quién is used to refer to people, and since we're talking about museums, you can eliminate (D). **Cuánto** is used to inquire about quantities, so we're down to (A) and (B). **Qué** is often used in questions (**¿Qué hora es?**), but because a choice is asked for, **cuál** (A) is used instead of **qué**.

5.   C   Translation: What ------- when you called my cell phone this afternoon?

(A) would you have wanted
(B) would they want
(C) **did you want**
(D) do you want

Choice (B) can be eliminated because **me llamaste** tells us that we need a second person verb. The preterite, along with **cuando**, clues us into the need for the imperfect to express an action that was ongoing when something else occurred.

6.   D   Translation: I don't know him well, but people say that he ------- a sincere and intelligent guy.

(A) (we) are (estar)
(B) (they, you pl.) are (ser)
(C) is (estar)
(D) **is (ser)**

Since we're talking about one person (**lo** is a singular pronoun), (A) and (B) can be easily eliminated. Now for the subtle part. If you know when to use **ser** and when to use **estar**, this question is a piece of cake. Does the sentence give us any reason to suspect that this person's admirable qualities are going to change or disappear in the near future? No. Therefore, (D) is correct.

7.   B   Translation: The invention of the telephone by Alexander Graham Bell in 1876 ------- how people communicate.

(A) changes (él)
(B) **changed (él)**
(C) changed (ellos)
(D) change (tú)

The year 1876 tells us that the action (inventing the telephone) happened in the past, so we need the verb **cambiar** *(to change)* conjugated in the past (preterite) tense. Our only options are (B) and (C), and because there is only one Alexander Graham Bell, (B) is the correct answer.

8. **B** **Translation:** We're going to make the trip in two days instead of one, because our destination is very ------- here.

(A) near
(B) far from
(C) next to
(D) in front of

The meaning of this sentence gives some helpful clues. In fact, since the duration of the trip is going to be twice what was expected, the only answer that makes any sense is **lejos de** (B).

9. **A** **Translation:** My brother was born three years before I was; that's why he's ------- .

(A) older
(B) taller
(C) my favorite brother
(D) very boring

Although each of the answers is something a brother could be, *born three years before* clearly suggests (A), which is correct.

10. **B** **Translation:** If you don't like the law, why ------- the past four years working as a lawyer?

(A) do you spend
(B) have you spent
(C) would you spend
(D) will you spend

The past four years tells you that we need some type of past tense, so eliminate (A), (C), and (D). The correct answer is (B).

11. **D** **Translation:** In the library one finds ------- .

(A) pens
(B) hopes
(C) questions
(D) books

This is a very straightforward question if you know the word for *library*. The correct answer is (D). (Be careful not to confuse **biblioteca** with **librería**, the latter of which means *bookstore*.)

12. **C** **Translation:** The flag that flies over the stadium is ------- .

(A) ours (masculine, singular)
(B) ours (feminine, plural)
(C) ours (feminine, singular)
(D) mine (masculine, singular)

The wrong answers here (as on many Spanish Subject Test questions) are incorrect because they don't agree with what they're replacing, either in gender or in number. Since **la bandera** is singular and feminine, **nuestra** (C) is the correct pronoun.

13. **C** **Translation:** The hot soup gave me a toothache. I need ------- .

(A) a chair
(B) a table
(C) a dentist
(D) a screw

Toothache is the key word in this example. If you understood that much, you could easily have guessed (C), which is correct.

14. **C** **Translation:** The recipe that Marta gave to Veronica was difficult to read because ------- .

(A) it is big
(B) it is nice/pretty
(C) it was erased
(D) it was clean

The sentence tells us that the recipe was difficult to read. This would eliminate (A), (B), and (D). The only plausible answer is (C).

15. **A** **Translation:** To go to Mexico, the fastest ------- is this one.

(A) road
(B) sky
(C) stroll
(D) ground/floor

Only one of the choices is something that would be involved in going to Mexico, and that choice is (A). *Stroll* is a tricky choice because it sort of goes with *fastest,* but it makes no sense with the first part of the sentence.

16. **D** **Translation:** Yesterday I had a lot of back pain, but today I don't ------- any.

   (A) have (ellos)
   (B) have (nosotros)
   (C) have (tú)
   (D) have (yo)

Somewhere on your exam you will probably see a question whose answer is the plain present tense, like this one. All four choices are in the present tense, so you have to pay special attention to the verb ending. **Tenía** could work with **yo, él, ella,** or **Ud.**; and since the last three are not given as choices, the answer has to be (D), which uses the **yo** form.

17. **A** **Translation:** The World Cup of soccer is a ------- .

   (A) spectator event
   (B) local sport
   (C) national event
   (D) match (sport)

The World Cup of soccer is a world event, so (B) and (C) are incorrect. Choice (D) is also incorrect because the World Cup is not a single match but a series of matches. Since people from all over the world watch it, both in person and on TV, it is a spectator event. So (A) is correct.

18. **B** **Translation:** García is our most respected client; we always give ------- what he wants.

   (A) it (feminine)
   (B) him
   (C) it (masculine)
   (D) them

Direct object or indirect object: that is the question. What do we give? *What he wants*—that's the direct object. To whom? To *him*—the singular indirect object pronoun is needed, which is (B).

19. **A** **Translation:** Alberto sits down and asks for chicken with rice and a glass of wine. He is in ------- .

   (A) a restaurant
   (B) a circus
   (C) a bank
   (D) a shoe store

If you caught any of the food words in this sentence you would guess (A). The other choices aren't even in the ballpark.

20.   **C**   **Translation:** ------- when have you (pl.) studied Spanish history?

(A) Until
(B) During
(C) Since
(D) In

This is another preposition question, and once again, meaning is your savior. The only choice that really works in terms of meaning is **desde** (C). **Durante cuándo** is redundant (you would just say **cuándo**), and **hasta cuándo** does not work because of the tense of the verb: we could say *until when did you study* or *until when will you study* but not *until when have you studied*. Therefore, the correct answer is (C).

21.   **D**   **Translation:** This coming fall, ------- all together to my house in the mountains.

(A) we go (present)
(B) they go (present subjunctive)
(C) I go (present)
(D) we will go (future)

The sentence suggests *all will go together to the house in the mountains*. Since the subject is in the plural first-person tense (**nosotros**), (B) and (C) are incorrect. Furthermore, *This coming fall* indicates that the action has not yet happened, so (A) is incorrect because it is in the present tense. Choice (D) is the correct answer.

22.   **A**   **Translation:** My uncle knows how to cook black beans pretty ------- .

(A) well
(B) good (singular)
(C) good (plural)
(D) baths

Just thought we'd sneak an adjective-versus-adverb question in for fun. **Bueno** *(good)* is an adjective, and because you are describing an action (*how* the black beans are made), an adverb is used. **Baños** is thrown in there to see whether you're awake, as it resembles **buenos**. But (A) is correct.

23.   **D**   **Translation:** The concert that we saw last night was excellent. That ------- really knows how to play!

(A) game
(B) novel
(C) food
(D) orchestra

The word **concierto** points to (D), which is the correct choice.

24. **A** **Translation:** I'm afraid that the storm ------- during the wedding that we're going to have on the patio.

   (A) **arrive (subjunctive)**
   (B) arrives
   (C) would arrive
   (D) arrived

   Expressions of fear are dead giveaways that you need to use the subjunctive. Then all you have to do is check the tense of the expression to tell you which subjunctive to use. **Tengo miedo** is in the present, so this time it's present subjunctive (A).

25. **B** **Translation:** Carlos is an annoying kid who is always in some kind of trouble. It's no miracle that everyone ------- him.

   (A) likes
   (B) **rejects**
   (C) helps
   (D) knows

   There is some tough vocabulary here. Fortunately, there are many different clues that tell you Carlos isn't a particularly likable guy, and that makes (B) the best answer.

26. **B** **Translation:** The books at the library are not in good condition. The library doesn't have the ------- to buy new books.

   (A) money
   (B) **funds**
   (C) space
   (D) students

   The main ideas of these sentences are 1) the poor condition of the library's books and 2) the library's inability to buy new books. With this understanding, we can eliminate (C) and (D), which do not make sense in this context. While (A) may seem like the correct answer, the article **los** indicates a plural noun. Thus, (B) is correct.

27. **A** **Translation:** After two years of research, the doctor finally ------- the cause of the disease.

   (A) **discovered**
   (B) directed
   (C) opened
   (D) looked for

   Choices (B) and (C) don't make much sense. Choice (D) would only make sense if the doctor hadn't yet begun his research. Choice (A) is correct.

28. **D** **Translation:** We've never danced the samba, but sure ------- how to dance the lambada!

    (A) we know (conocer)

    (B) I know (subjunctive, conocer)

    (C) they will know (saber)

    (D) we know (saber)

Knowing how to do a type of dance falls under the category of facts (as opposed to people), so **saber** is the correct verb. Choice (C) is not correct because there is no reason given in the sentence either to change the subject or to change the verb to the future tense.

29. **D** **Translation:** They say that José Martí, the famous Cuban author, began to write ------- when he was only six years old.

    (A) pencils

    (B) alphabets

    (C) languages

    (D) poems

What does an author write? Well, lots of things, but out of these choices only (D) is reasonable.

Part B

Passage:

    Desde hace 10 años en Colombia <u>se han</u> presentado propuestas de telenovelas que han remplazado el melodrama tradicional, ya que el formato colombiano siempre se ha preocupado <u>por</u> representar la clase trabajadora del país. Es así como <u>la mayoría</u> de la población <u>ha encontrado</u> en los personajes e historias de las teleseries su propia imagen.

    Un buen ejemplo es "Yo soy Betty la fea" (1999), ya que <u>ha sido</u> uno de los aciertos televisivos más grandes de la historia de las telenovelas. <u>Muestra</u> la frustración de una mujer <u>fea</u> que se enamora <u>de</u> su jefe, un hombre rico y <u>poderoso</u> del negocio de la moda. <u>Este</u> vive rodeado de modelos y tiene un compromiso matrimonial con una mujer que además de ser bella, pertenece a <u>su</u> mismo círculo social.

Translation:

For 10 years in Colombia, proposals *have been* presented for soap operas that have replaced the traditional melodrama, since the Colombian format has always been concerned *with* representing the working class of the country. This is how *the majority* of the population *has found* its own image in the characters and stories of the teleseries.

A good example is "I am Ugly Betty" (1999), as it *has been* one of the biggest hits in the history of telenovelas. *It shows* the frustration of an *ugly* woman who falls in love *with* her boss, a rich and *powerful* man in the fashion business. *He* lives surrounded by models and is married to a woman who, besides being beautiful, belongs to *his* own social circle.

30.   A   (A) **have been**
          (B) would have been
          (C) we have been
          (D) has been

The subject is *proposals,* so the answer must be plural. Eliminate (B) and (D). Since the third person is used, eliminate (C). Choice (A) is correct.

31.   A   (A) **with (por)**
          (B) with (para)
          (C) of
          (D) to

This is a **por** vs. **para** question. The sentence implies *through* or *by* representing the working class, so it must be **por.** Choice (A) is correct.

32.   D   (A) the eldest
          (B) the majority (plural)
          (C) the elders
          (D) **the majority (singular)**

This sentence means to say the majority of the population, so it must be singular and feminine to match **la población.** Therefore, (D) is correct.

33.   C   (A) has known
          (B) has detested
          (C) **has encountered**
          (D) has greeted

The sentence means to say the population has *come into contact with* or *gotten to know* these characters, so (C) is the best answer. Choice (A) has to do with knowledge instead of people, (B) is the opposite meaning, and (D) is too literal here.

34.   B   (A) has been (estar)
          (B) **has been (ser)**
          (C) had been (ser)
          (D) had been (estar)

This is a **ser** vs. **estar** question masked as a verb tense question! Since this is talking about the long time that the show has been popular, use **ser** and eliminate (A) and (D). The rest of the paragraph is in the present tense, so use the present perfect instead of the past perfect. The correct answer is (B).

35. A (A) **It shows**
        (B) It tests
        (C) It advises
        (D) It hides

The sentence is describing the show, so the word needs to mean *describes*. Only (A) fits that function.

36. D (A) young
        (B) tall
        (C) pretty
        (D) **ugly**

Use the clues in the sentences surrounding. The only descriptive word for Betty is that she is **la fea,** so it must be the same meaning here. Choice (D) is correct.

37. A (A) **with (de)**
        (B) with (con)
        (C) for
        (D) to

Usually **de** means something to the effect of *of,* but this is an idiom: **enamorarse de.** Therefore, (A) is correct.

38. C (A) old
        (B) ugly
        (C) **powerful**
        (D) weak

The clues in the sentence here are **rico** and that he runs a business. The only word that fits here is **poderoso.** The correct answer is (C).

39. A (A) **He**
        (B) He/She is
        (C) This (f.)
        (D) She

This sentence is talking about the boss, so the pronoun must be masculine and referring to a person. Eliminate (C) and (D) because they are feminine. Choice (B) is a verb instead of a pronoun, so eliminate (B). The correct answer is (A).

40. **B** (A) their
     (B) his/her
     (C) the (f.)
     (D) it (m.)

The sentence is still referring to her boss, so the pronoun must refer to a person and must be singular. Eliminate (A) because it is plural. Choices (C) and (D) are not usually used for people, so (B) is correct.

Passage:

> Allí estaba otra <u>vez</u> ese ruido. Aquel ruido frío, <u>cortante</u>, vertical, que ya tanto conocía pero que ahora <u>se le</u> presentaba agudo y doloroso, como si de <u>un</u> día a otro se hubiera desacostumbrado a él.
>
> Le giraba <u>dentro del</u> cráneo vacío, sordo y punzante. Había sentido ese ruido "las otras veces", con <u>la misma</u> insistencia. Lo <u>había</u> sentido, por ejemplo, el día en que <u>murió</u> por primera vez. Es simplemente "una muerte viva".

Translation:

There it was another *time* that noise. That cold, *cutting*, vertical noise, which he already knew so well but now it seemed acute and painful *to him*, as if from *one* day to the next he had become unaccustomed to it.

It twisted *inside* his hollow skull, muffled and stabbing. He had felt that noise "the other times," with *the same* insistence. He *had* felt it, for example, the day he *died* for the first time. It is simply "a living death."

41. **B** (A) first
     (B) time (occurrence)
     (C) time (temporal)
     (D) perhaps

While (C) might be tempting, **tiempo** is not used in this context—to refer to an occurrence or happening. Choice (B) is correct.

42. **C** (A) calm
     (B) hot
     (C) cutting
     (D) placid

The other clues in this sentence are **frío** and **vertical,** so there must be something sharp or unpleasant about this sound. Choices (A) and (D) are too pleasant and mellow for this context, and (B) is the opposite of the first adjective. Choice (C) is correct.

43. **A** (A) **to him (ind. obj.)**
         (B) to him (dir. obj.)
         (C) to her (dir. obj.)
         (D) to them (ind. obj.)

This is a reflexive verb that literally means *it occurred to him,* where *him* is the indirect object. Therefore, eliminate (B) and (C) because those contain direct objects. Since it refers to the protagonist in the passage, use the singular pronoun. Choice (A) is correct.

44. **A** (A) **one (m.)**
         (B) one (f.)
         (C) some (m.)
         (D) some (f.)

The subject of this article is **día,** which is singular and masculine. The correct answer is (A).

45. **D** (A) under the (f.)
         (B) on top of (f.)
         (C) behind the (m.)
         (D) **inside of the (m.)**

The word this preposition describes is **craneo,** or *skull,* and it is masculine. Eliminate (A) and (B) because they refer to a feminine object. Between (C) and (D), it makes more sense for something to happen *inside* his skull (as a figure of speech) than *behind* his skull. Choice (D) is correct.

46. **C** (A) the same (m. sing.)
         (B) the same (f. pl.)
         (C) **the same (f. sing.)**
         (D) the same (m. pl.)

This adjective is describing **insistencia,** which is singular and feminine. The correct answer is (C).

47. **A** (A) **had (sing.)**
         (B) had (pl.)
         (C) have
         (D) has

The rest of the paragraph is in the past perfect, so eliminate (C) and (D) because those are present perfect. The protagonist is the singular subject, so (A) is correct.

48. **B** (A) bit
     (B) died
     (C) expired
     (D) stopped

The rest of the paragraph describes his "living death," so it must be something to do with death. Choice (C) may seem tempting, but it is too literal for this context.

Passage:

>   Pepe tenía veinticinco años cuando <u>abandonó</u> cierta ciudad del Mediodía, donde <u>había nacido</u>, completamente resuelto <u>a ser</u> ministro.

>   Su padre <u>era</u> un empleado de diez y seis mil reales, y a la verdad que <u>sugiere</u> muy tristes consideraciones esta pícara costumbre <u>de clasificar</u> los empleos públicos por <u>el sueldo</u> con que se retribuyen. ¿No hay los empleos públicos alguna cosa más importante, más noble, más elevada que el sueldo? ¡<u>Por lo visto</u>, no! Su padre le dio una educación <u>más que</u> mediana.

Translation:

Pepe was twenty-five years old when *he left* a certain city in the South where he *had been born,* completely resolved *to be* a minister.

His father *was* an employee of sixteen thousand reales, and in truth it *suggests* quite sad considerations, the mischievous custom *of classifying* public jobs by *the salary* with which they reward workers. Are not public jobs more important, nobler, more elevated than wages? *Apparently* not! His father gave him a *better than* average education.

49. **C** (A) abandoned (preterite, pl.)
     (B) abandoned (imperfect, sing.)
     (C) abandoned (preterite, sing.)
     (D) abandons (present)

Pepe is the singular subject, and he completed a one-time action to leave his hometown. Therefore, use the preterite instead of the imperfect. Choice (C) is the correct response.

50. **A** **(A) had been born (sing.)**
     (B) has been born
     (C) have been born
     (D) had been born (pl.)

The sentence is referring to further in the past, so use the past perfect instead of the present perfect, eliminating (B) and (C). Pepe is singular, so (A) is correct.

51. **A** (A) **to be (a)**
          (B) to be (por)
          (C) to be (para)
          (D) of being

This is an idiom: to say one *becomes a* (profession), use **a.** Choice (A) is correct.

52. **B** (A) is (ser)
          (B) was (ser)
          (C) may have been (ser)
          (D) was (estar)

This is a **ser** vs. **estar** question. His father's profession is in the past, so eliminate (A) and (C). The sentence describes an integral, long-term part of who the father was, so use **ser.** The correct answer is (B).

53. **A** (A) **suggests**
          (B) to suggest
          (C) suggest (present subjunctive)
          (D) will suggest

The subject is **la verdad,** so the verb must be singular. The verb must be conjugated, so eliminate (B), and there is no doubt expressed, so eliminate (C) as well. The sentence is in the present instead of the future, so eliminate (D), leaving (A) as the correct response.

54. **D** (A) of showing
          (B) of saying
          (C) of counting
          (D) of classifying

The sentence refers to how government workers are regarded. The only word that works in this context without being too literal or silly is **clasificar.** The correct answer is (D).

55. **B** (A) the situation
          (B) the salary
          (C) the soldier
          (D) the sun

The sentence mentions **reales,** which are a type of money, and it discusses the father's job. The only vocabulary word that works here is **sueldo.** The correct answer is (B).

56.　C　(A)　At least

(B)　That is to say

(C)　**Apparently**

(D)　Why

This is an idiom that expresses irony and surprise. The correct answer is (C).

57.　A　(A)　**more than (que)**

(B)　less than (que)

(C)　more than (de)

(D)　less than (de)

There is a comparison in the sentence, so use the idiom **que** instead of **de.** Therefore, eliminate (C) and (D). Pepe's education was better than average, so (A) is correct.

Part C

Passage:

　　　　Roy sabía desde pequeño que moriría joven. No era una sensación, era una certeza. A lo largo de su infancia, cuando los demás niños relataban en forma entusiasta a qué se dedicarían de mayores, el pequeño Roy se limitaba a decir que pretendía estudiar guitarra y componer canciones. Entrada la adolescencia y acompañado seis de los siete días de la semana por su camiseta de Bono, el ahora espigado Roy contaba con una hilera de pelos en el pecho y una guitarra color caoba que cautivaba tanto como las secuencias de acordes que aquél muchacho compartía canturreando en los muros de la secundaria. Llegaron las primeras canciones dedicadas fugazmente a algunas mujeres, el primer amigo de verdad, que rápidamente influyó en letras y músicas.

　　　　Una tarde, cercano a cumplir los treinta, Roy componía la que sería su mejor canción hasta ese momento, cuando a su lado se sentó La Muerte.

Translation:

Roy knew from an early age that he would die young. It wasn't a feeling, it was a certainty. Throughout his early childhood, while other children spoke enthusiastically about what they would do when they were older, the young Roy simply said that he would learn the guitar and compose songs. He entered adolescence and, accompanied six out of seven days of the week by his Bono t-shirt, the now lanky Roy possessed a swath of chest hairs and a mahogany-colored guitar that fascinated him as much as the chord sequences that he played while crooning from the walls of his high school. Then came the first songs dedicated fleetingly to some women, and his first real friend, who rapidly influenced him in lyrics and music.

One afternoon, close to his thirtieth birthday, Roy composed what would be his best song yet, when Death sat down beside him.

58. D **Translation:** At the beginning, what were the children telling?

(A) That they didn't like Roy
(B) Short stories that influenced Roy's music
(C) That they would die young
(D) **What they would be when they grew up**

This answer is found in the second sentence. Choice (D) is correct.

59. C **Translation:** Who is the protagonist?

(A) He is a sad and lonely guy who doesn't have friends.
(B) He is a guy who comes of age and suddenly dies.
(C) **He is a slightly isolated guy who composes songs.**
(D) He is a hermit who ultimately discovers a companion.

The passage does not say he is sad, lonely, or a hermit, so eliminate (A) and (D). He does not suddenly die when he comes of age, so eliminate (B). Choice (C) is the only choice that is supported by the passage.

60. D **Translation:** How was the future of the young Roy in the passage?

(A) He didn't have any future.
(B) Roy was doomed to die.
(C) Roy didn't know what he wanted to do when he got older.
(D) **Roy simply said that he would learn the guitar and compose songs.**

This answer is found in the second sentence of the passage. The correct answer is (D).

61. A **Translation:** When Roy enters adolescence, what does he do?

(A) **Roy sings and writes original songs.**
(B) Roy dies.
(C) Roy counts his swath of chest hairs.
(D) Roy meets many true friends.

The last half of the first paragraph describes Roy's adolescence and how he wrote songs about women and his first real friend. Choice (A) is correct.

62. B **Translation:** Roy's first songs consist of

(A) his Bono t-shirt
(B) **chords and lyrics about women and friends**
(C) a swath of chest hairs
(D) certainties and sensations from his childhood

The last sentence of the first paragraph describes his first songs as dedicated fleetingly to women, and his best friend, which match (B). His Bono t-shirt and chest hair do not describe his songs! Choice (B) is correct.

63.   A   **Translation:** What happens at the end of the passage?

(A) **Death sidles up to Roy.**
(B) Roy dies.
(C) Roy was dreaming and at the end wakes up.
(D) Death is a seductive woman who influences Roy.

All the passage says is that Death sits down next to Roy, and (A) is a paraphrase of this. It is quite mysterious and does not state any other possibilities that may happen next. Choice (A) is correct.

Passage:

Desde el descubrimiento de la tumba del Apóstol Santiago, en Compostela (España), en el siglo IX, el Camino de Santiago se convirtió en la más importante ruta de peregrinación de la Europa medieval.

El paso de los innumerables peregrinos que, movidos por su fe, se dirigían a Compostela desde todos los países europeos, sirvió como punto de partida de todo un desarrollo cultural, social y económico que dejó sus huellas a lo largo del Camino de Santiago.

En la actualidad, el Camino de Santiago está considerado como uno de los principales productos de turismo cultural en España. Junto con las ciudades de Madrid y Barcelona y la Comunidad de Andalucía, esta ruta es un recurso turístico fundamental, por sus contenidos y su oferta monumental, gastronómica y de alojamiento.

Translation:

From the discovery of the tomb of the Apostle James in Compostela (Spain), in the 9th century, the Road of St. James became the most important pilgrimage route in medieval Europe.

The passage of countless pilgrims who, moved by their faith, travelled to Compostela from all the European countries, served as a starting point for great cultural, social, and economic development that left its mark all along the Road of St. James.

Today, the Road of St. James is considered one of the main cultural tourism products in Spain. Together with the cities of Madrid and Barcelona and the Community of Andalusia, this route is a fundamental tourist resource because of the range of architecture, cuisine, and accommodations it has to offer.

64.   **B**   **Translation:** When was the tomb of the Apostle James discovered?

(A) in the 5th Century
(B) in the 9th Century
(C) in the 10th Century
(D) in the 14th Century

This answer lies in the first sentence of the passage. Choice (B) is correct.

65.   **D**   **Translation:** Why do people travel the Road of St. James?

(A) It is a main street in Spain.
(B) It is a highway between Madrid and Barcelona.
(C) One travels on the Road of St. James to show the Christian faith.
(D) Some travel because of faith while others travel for tourism.

Some are described as tourists while others are described as pilgrims in the passage. Choices (A) and (B) are silly because they treat it like an actual street with cars on it, and (C) includes only the pilgrims. Choice (D) is correct.

66.   **A**   **Translation:** How has the Road of St. James served the country?

(A) It has helped its cultural and economic growth.
(B) It has served as a tourist attraction for locals.
(C) It does not serve any purpose.
(D) It serves as a route between countries.

The second paragraph talks about how the route has been a point of growth for Spain's tourism economy. Choice (B) may seem tempting, but it is not an attraction for the locals. Choice (C) is quite opposite, as it certainly serves a tourism purpose, and (D) is untrue. Choice (A) is correct.

67.   **B**   **Translation:** Why does the passage mention Madrid, Barcelona, and the community of Andalucía?

(A) They are locations that have benefited from the popularity of the Road of St. James.
(B) They are popular tourist destinations.
(C) They are the endpoints of the Road of St. James.
(D) They are important cities in Spain.

The passage mentions these places in relation to tourism, saying that together with them, the Road of St. James is a fundamental tourist resource. Choice (A) is tempting, but these are only other tourist destinations; they are not on the route. The passage does not state that these places are endpoints, so eliminate (C), and while they are important cities in Spain, that is not the reason for mentioning them as (D) states. The correct answer is (B).

68.   A   **Translation:** What can be said about cultural tourism in Spain?

(A) **It includes gastronomic and architectural tourism.**
(B) The tourists damage the economy.
(C) Only the pilgrims participate in tourism.
(D) Tourism has declined precipitously.

This answer is found in the last sentence of the passage. The correct answer is (A).

69.   B   **Translation:** The passage talks about

(A) a unique and beautiful landscape
(B) **a famous and important route**
(C) an important and influential saint
(D) a field that was discovered

The passage talks about the Road of St. James, which is a pilgrimage route. Choice (B) is the only one that refers to a route.

Passage:

Los aztecas consideraban a Quetzlcoatl como el dios de la inteligencia y del viento. Además de descubrir el maíz, dio clases de ciencia a los hombres y les enseñó la elaboración del calendario y a convivir dentro de una sociedad civilizada.

Según otra leyenda, también fue hombre. Era rubio, blanco, alto, barbudo y de grandes conocimientos científicos, que instruyó a los pobladores de lo que hoy es México, a trabajar los metales, además de la orfebrería y la astrología. Eso sí, jamás se llegó a saber su nacionalidad y su procedencia.

Básicamente, Quetzlcoatl representa la dualidad propia del ser humano: es cuerpo físico y espíritu. Sus enseñanzas quedaron recogidas en ciertos documentos llamados Huehuetlahtolli o las "antiguas palabras", transmitidos por tradición oral hasta que fueron escritas por los primeros cronistas españoles.

Translation:

The Aztecs considered Quetzlcoatl the god of intelligence and of the wind. In addition to discovering corn, he taught science to men and taught them to devise the calendar and to live together within a civilized society.

According to another legend, he was also a man. He was blond, white, tall, bearded, and had great scientific knowledge, and he instructed the settlers of what is now Mexico to work metals as well as goldsmithing and astrology. Of course, his nationality and its origin never came to be known.

Basically, Quetzlcoatl represents the duality of the human being: he embodies the physical body and the spirit. His teachings were collected in certain documents called Huehuetlahtolli or the "ancient words," transmitted by oral tradition until they were written by the first Spanish chroniclers.

70.   **C**   **Translation:** Who is Quetzlcoatl?

(A)   It is the name of the Christian God in Mexico.

(B)   He is a scientist and astrologer.

(C)   **He is a mythical figure of the Aztecs.**

(D)   He is a tall and wise man who lives in Mexico.

Quetzlcoatl is described in different ways because he is a mythical figure of the Aztecs. Choice (B) is too specific to one description, (D) is incorrect because he is not just a guy who lives in Mexico, and (A) is never stated. Choice (C) is correct.

71.   **D**   **Translation:** What does Quetzlcoatl represent?

(A)   the religious tradition of the Aztecs

(B)   intelligence and wind

(C)   the god of corn and the sciences

(D)   **the duality of the human being**

The third paragraph describes this in the first sentence. Choice (D) is correct.

72.   **B**   **Translation:** What are "ancient words"?

(A)   part of an ancient poem

(B)   **part of an oral tradition**

(C)   a spell recited by Huehuetlahtolli

(D)   some wise and religious sayings

There is neither a poem nor a saying mentioned anywhere, so eliminate (A) and (D). Choice (C) is silly, so (B) is correct.

73.   **A**   **Translation:** What is the passage about?

(A)   **It tells of the legends surrounding Quetzlcoatl.**

(B)   It describes the attitude of Quetzlcoatl toward oral traditions.

(C)   It illustrates why the Aztecs pray to Quetzlcoatl.

(D)   It speaks of the difficulties in describing Quetzlcoatl.

Choices (B) and (C) are not supported by the passage. While (D) may seem tempting with *difficulties,* these difficulties are not in describing Quetzlcoatl, but rather in deciding which legend is correct. Choice (A) best matches this idea.

Passage:

Descripción del campamento

Nuestro objetivo es hacer un campamento de formación ecuestre completa, mediante el ocio y la formación ambiental en un marco incomparable como es la Escuela de Equitación Estadonidence, que hará de este campamento de verano unas vacaciones inolvidables.

Información general

- **Edad:** 3 a 18 años
- **Nivel:** Todos los niveles
- **Duración:** 7 días
- **Alojamiento:** Escuela de Equitación Estadonidence
- **Pensión Completa**
- **Profesores y Monitores Ecuestres Titulados**
- **3 horas diarias de curso ecuestre**
- **Actividades y juegos**

Transporte: No incluido. Lo ideal es que cada familia se encargue de llevar a su hijo a los campamentos por medios propios, de esta forma conocerán las instalaciones que sus hijos van a disfrutar.

Asistencia y seguro médico.

Seguro de responsabilidad civil y de accidentes. La prioridad absoluta en nuestros campamentos de verano es garantizar la salud y el bienestar de los jóvenes.

Dinero: Los jóvenes dispondrán de todo lo necesario por lo que no precisan de dinero, fomentando así la igualdad.

Lugar:

Escuela de Equitación Estadonidence
5511 Calle 13 noreste
Los Angeles, CA 90210

Translation:

Camp Description

Our objective is to make a comprehensive equestrian training camp, through leisure and environmental education in the incomparable setting of the American Equestrian School, which will make this summer camp an unforgettable vacation.

General Information

- Age: 3 to 18 years
- Level: all levels
- Duration: 7 days
- Accommodations: The American Equestrian School
- **Full Room and Board**
- **Certified Equestrian Teachers and Monitors**

- **3 hours daily of equestrian training**
- **Activities and games**

Transportation: Not included. Ideally, each family should take their child to the camps by their own means. This way, they will get to know the facilities that their children will enjoy.

Medical care and insurance.

Liability and accident insurance. The absolute priority of our summer camps is to ensure the health and well-being of young people.

Money: Young people will have everything they need so they do not need money, thus promoting equality.

Location:

The American Equestrian School
5511 13th Street Northeast
Los Angeles, CA 90210

74. **C** **Translation:** This advertisement is for what type of service?

(A) a hospital
(B) a business office
(C) a summer camp
(D) a secondary school

This is a vocabulary question. **Campamento de verano** means *summer camp*. Choice (C) is correct.

75. **C** **Translation:** How old are the campers?

(A) toddlers and youngsters
(B) adults
(C) youngsters and adolescents
(D) adolescents

This is in the bullet points: ages 3–18. This would be youngsters and adolescents, so (C) is correct.

76. **C** **Translation:** How do the campers arrive at the camp?

(A) There is a bus that brings them to the camp.
(B) There is no way to get to the camp.
(C) The families bring them by their preferred modes of transportation.
(D) The campers should arrive by horse.

The answer to this question is under **Transportación:** families bring them by their own means. The correct answer is (C).

77. **C** **Translation:** How long does the camp last?

(A) 3 hours
(B) 3 days
(C) 7 days
(D) 18 days

This is in the bullet points: the camp lasts 7 days. Choice (C) is correct.

78. **A** **Translation:** How much money do the students of the camp need?

(A) They don't need money to enjoy the camp.
(B) They need money to eat the three meals of the day.
(C) They can bring all the money they'd like.
(D) They need money for their private equestrian lessons.

The answer to this question is under **Dinero:** the children do not need money; not bringing any will help promote equality. The correct answer is (A).

79. **B** **Translation:** Which safety measures are there at the camp?

(A) There are harnesses for all the students.
(B) There is health insurance and liability insurance.
(C) There are security cameras in the camp.
(D) There is an armed guard who patrols the camp.

Towards the bottom of the pamphlet, it states that there is health and liability insurance at the camp. The correct answer is (B).

Passage:

El corazón le galopeaba fuertemente, la transpiración le caía a chorros y las piernas casi no se le veían, de lo rápida que corría.

Era de noche y en la calle no se veía a nadie. Ni los gatos, que siempre solían estar rondando a esas horas.

Ella corría sin saber a dónde estaba corriendo, ni se daba vuelta para ver si aquello que la hacía huir había quedado atrás o seguía ahí. Al ver una esquina, después de tremenda huida, dobló y se recostó de espaldas contra el edificio. Pero en el momento en que creyó poder respirar vio a un chico, que le cubría la boca con su mano. Mientras que con la otra le hacía una señal de que mantenga la calma. La chica soltó lágrimas que le llenaban los ojos.

Translation:

Her heart beat heavily, perspiration streamed down, and her legs were barely visible, she ran so fast.

It was night and she saw no one in the street. Not even the cats, which always used to prowl around at that hour.

She ran without knowing where she was running, nor turning to see whether that which made her flee had been left behind or was still there. Upon seeing a corner, after a tremendous flight, she turned it and leaned her back against the building. But the moment she thought she could breathe, she saw a young man who covered her mouth with his hand. With the other hand he made a signal for her to remain calm. The young woman shed the tears that filled her eyes.

80. **B** **Translation:** What does the young woman do at the beginning of the passage?

(A) She is confused by her new location.
(B) She is running and is afraid.
(C) She is fighting with her lover.
(D) She is fatigued because she has run so much.

Her heart beat heavily and she was sweating as she ran away from someone, so she was probably afraid. The passage never states that she was tired or confused, so eliminate (A) and (D). The passage does not say who the **chico** was, so eliminate (C) because it is unknown whether he was her lover (probably not!). What is clear is that she was running and that she was afraid.

81. **A** **Translation:** How is the street described at the beginning of the passage?

(A) dark and deserted
(B) congested and noisy
(C) narrow and long
(D) wide and tranquil

There was no one in the street at night, so (A) is accurate. None of the other choices are described in the passage.

82. **A** **Translation:** Why does the young woman not know where she is running to?

(A) She doesn't know whether the young man continues to follow her.
(B) She is in a foreign country.
(C) She cannot see.
(D) She is confused and needs a map.

The answer to this question is in the first sentence of the third paragraph: **ni se daba vuelta para ver si aquello que la hacía huir había quedado atrás o seguía ahí.** The correct answer is (A).

83.   **B**   **Translation:** Why does the young man signal to the young woman to remain quiet?

(A)   He doesn't like the crying of the young woman.

(B)   He does not want the young woman to make noise.

(C)   She is too noisy.

(D)   He doesn't know where they are.

Choices (A) and (D) are silly, and the passage does not say that the woman was making noise as in (C). The correct answer is (B).

84.   **B**   **Translation:** What happens when she stops running?

(A)   She falls on the ground.

(B)   A young man grabs her.

(C)   She enjoys the silence in the street.

(D)   She discovers a secure building.

The young man puts his hand over her mouth from behind, so (B) is a paraphrase. She never falls or enjoys the anything in the passage. She puts her back against a building, but it is not secure. The correct answer is (B).

85.   **D**   **Translation:** Why does the young woman cry at the end of the passage?

(A)   Because it is difficult to run so much

(B)   Because she cannot breathe

(C)   Because she is sad

(D)   Because she is afraid of the young man

She is not sad or tired from running, so eliminate (A) and (C). She is not crying because she is out of breath, so it must be out of fear. Choice (D) is correct.

HOW TO SCORE PRACTICE TEST 1

When you take the real exam, the proctors take away your exam and your bubble sheet and send it to a processing center, where a computer looks at the pattern of filled-in ovals on your exam and gives you a score. We couldn't include even a small computer with this book, so we are providing this more primitive way of scoring your exam.

Determining Your Score

STEP 1   Using the answer key, determine how many questions you got right and how many you got wrong on the test. Remember, questions that you do not answer do not count as either right answers or wrong answers.

STEP 2   List the number of right answers here.

(A) _____

STEP 3   List the number of wrong answers here. Now divide that number by 3.

(B) _____ ÷ 3 _____ = (C) _____

STEP 4   Subtract the number of wrong answers divided by 3 (C) from the number of correct answers (A). Round this score to the nearest whole number. This is your raw score.

(A) – (C) = _____

STEP 5   To determine your real score, take the number from Step 4 above and look it up in the left column of the Score Conversion Table on the next page; the corresponding score on the right is your score on the exam.

PRACTICE TEST 1
SCORE CONVERSION TABLE

Raw Score	Scaled Score	Raw Score	Scaled Score	Raw Score	Scaled Score
85	800	47	590	9	360
84	800	46	580	8	360
83	800	45	570	7	350
82	800	44	570	6	350
81	790	43	560	5	340
80	790	42	550	4	340
79	780	41	550	3	330
78	780	40	540	2	320
77	770	39	530	1	320
76	770	38	530	0	310
75	760	37	520	−1	310
74	760	36	520	−2	300
73	750	35	510	−3	290
72	750	34	500	−4	290
71	740	33	500	−5	280
70	730	32	490	−6	270
69	730	31	490	−7	260
68	720	30	480	−8	260
67	720	29	470	−9	250
66	710	28	470	−10	240
65	700	27	460	−11	230
64	700	26	460	−12	220
63	690	25	450	−13	220
62	680	24	450	−14	220
61	680	23	440	−15	210
60	670	22	430	−16	210
59	670	21	430	−17	210
58	660	20	420	−18	200
57	650	19	420	−19	200
56	650	18	410	−20	200
55	640	17	410	−21	200
54	630	16	400	−22	200
53	630	15	400	−23	200
52	620	14	390	−24	200
51	620	13	390	−25	200
50	610	12	380	−26	200
49	600	11	380	−27	200
48	590	10	370	−28	200

Part III
Content Review and Strategies

Chapter 3
Sentence
Completion:
Vocabulary

Sentence completion questions on the SAT Subject Test in Spanish are designed to evaluate your knowledge of both Spanish vocabulary and grammar. In this chapter, we focus on strategies for tackling this type of question and provide a comprehensive vocabulary review.

SENTENCE COMPLETION: AN OVERVIEW

The first section of the Spanish Subject Test and the first part of the reading section of the Spanish with Listening Subject Test consist of vocabulary and grammar questions tested in a format we call *sentence completion*. Each sentence is missing one or more words, and your job is to select the answer choice that best completes the sentence in terms of meaning. In other words, fill in the blank with the answer that makes the most sense. Like all the questions on the test, each of the questions in this section has four answer choices. Before you go any further, memorize the directions to this question type until you're so familiar with them, you never have to read them again.

Part A

Directions: This part consists of a number of incomplete statements, each having four suggested completions. Select the most appropriate completion and fill in the corresponding oval on the answer sheet.

HOW TO CRACK THIS SECTION

One of the keys to cracking sentence completion questions is to understand the vocabulary. If you know every word that appears in the section, understanding the sentences and choosing the right answers is a breeze. So, one of the things you're going to have to work on is improving your vocabulary. Later in this chapter you'll find lists of words that are most likely to appear on your test; if you think your vocabulary needs help, then start studying these lists *today*. We'll see more about vocabulary later. What else can be done to attack this question type?

To master this section, you need to combine your vocabulary and grammar reviews with some common sense. You've already read about pacing, POE, and the Three-Pass System. Now you're going to learn how these techniques, as well as some others, apply to this section in particular.

First Pass: When You Understand the Entire Sentence

It's pretty obvious that the easiest questions are the ones that don't contain unknown vocabulary words. You should do these questions first. Your approach should be to read the sentence and answer it if it's easy. If you're a little uncomfortable with some of the vocabulary, move on and come back to that question later, during your second pass.

Be careful. Just because a question is a "first-pass question" doesn't mean you should blow through it as fast as possible and risk making a careless error. Once you've decided to answer a question on the first pass, follow the steps listed on the next page.

Step 1: Think of Your Own Word   The first step after reading the sentence is to fill in the blank with your own word without peeking at the answers. Your word doesn't have to be long or difficult; in fact, short and simple is best. Your word doesn't even have to be in Spanish. If it's easier for you to think in English, then write the word in English. The important thing is to choose a word that fits in terms of meaning. After you have a word, write it down next to your sentence (or in the actual blank, if there's room). Try it on the following example:

Hoy hace mucho frío. Por eso voy a ponerme un…

What would make sense in this blank? Pretty much any article of clothing that would be appropriate in cold weather, such as a pair of gloves (**par de guantes**) or a sweater (**suéter**). You shouldn't feel that there's only one possible answer because there are usually several words that would make sense in the blank. Don't worry about picking the *right* word; just worry about picking a word that makes sense. Once you've done this, move on to the next step.

Tip:
Don't worry about picking the *right* word. Just pick a word that makes sense.

Step 2: Eliminate Answers That Are Out of the Ballpark   Now you're going to look at the answers and cross out the ones that do not fall into the same category as your word. You're not looking for the right answer; you're looking to eliminate wrong answers.

Let's say you filled in the word **suéter** in the previous example. Which of the following answer choices would you eliminate?

(A) vestido
(B) abrigo
(C) zapato
(D) lápiz

Does a dress (**vestido**), shoe (**zapato**), or pencil (**lápiz**) have anything to do with cold or a sweater? No, and so the correct choice is (B). If you don't know all of the words in the answers, then eliminate the ones you can and guess from the remaining choices.

Step 3: Avoid Trap Answers   Once you've filled in your own word, it's crucial that you don't just pick the first answer you see that reminds you of it. The people who write this test are very clever about creating answer choices that are tempting but incorrect. Knowing the types of traps they set will help you to avoid them. In this section, there are a couple of tricks that show up frequently.

• **Answers That Sound Alike**   One way the test writers try to confuse you is by having all four answers sound alike, even though their meanings are different. You can easily avoid this trap by reading carefully and not using your ear. Remember that you're picking the best answer based on its meaning, not on how it sounds.

Try the following example:

> La mamá de Pedro no le dejó salir porque
> todavía no había . . . su cuarto.
>
> (A) llamado
> (B) limpiado
> (C) llevado
> (D) llenado

Why wouldn't a mom allow her son to go out? Probably because he hadn't cleaned his room. The word for *clean* is **limpiar** and, because we're in the pluperfect, **limpiado** is the correct form (if that doesn't make sense, don't fret—the grammar review is in the next chapter, and you don't need to be an expert on Spanish grammar to do well on this test). Notice how all the other answers sound very similar to **limpiado**. This is why it's important to take your time and concentrate on meaning.

- • **Categories**   Another of the test writers' favorite tricks is to give you four choices that all come from the same category, as in the following example:

> Ricardo quiere lavarse las manos, y por eso
> necesita . . .
>
> (A) un cepillo
> (B) una cuchilla
> (C) pasta de dientes
> (D) jabón

Remember, think of the meaning of the word, and then look for a matching answer choice!

Each of the answer choices is something you'd find in a bathroom (**jabón** = *soap*, **cuchilla** = *razor*, **pasta de dientes** = *toothpaste*, **cepillo** = *hairbrush*). Although these words have very different meanings, seeing them all together like this may be confusing, especially if you're thinking in general terms (bathroom stuff) and not in terms of the specific word you chose for the blank. It's therefore very important that you fill in the blank with a specific word and not a general category.

Second Pass: When You Don't Understand the Entire Sentence

Let's say you've answered all of the easy questions. Now what? The strategy for first-pass questions works just fine when you have a clear understanding of the sentence, but unfortunately, there probably will be some words that you don't know. Will that keep you from answering these questions altogether? Absolutely not, but you *will* leave these questions for the second pass. The approach is different for these questions, but it works just as well as the approach for the first-pass questions. Not knowing some of the vocabulary is hardly a handicap if you are aggressive and use POE, so don't let these questions intimidate you.

One of These Things Is Not Like the Others One of the nice things about this question type (from your point of view) is that the answer choices are usually far apart in meaning. In other words, you *rarely* find two answers that are separated by subtle shades of meaning. Instead, you find four things that have nothing to do with one another, except perhaps a very general common category, similar to what you saw earlier in the "avoid trap answers" examples. Why is this so helpful? It allows you to eliminate answer choices even if you have only a minimal understanding of the sentence. If you can figure out the general context of the sentence by piecing together one or two words as clues, you can eliminate answers that are unlikely to appear in that context. You'll usually find that there's really only one word that makes any kind of sense in that context. Choose the answer that is *not* like the others.

Eduardo se monta en el automóvil y dice que . . .

(A) tiene hambre
(B) hace mucho calor
(C) el perro es grande
(D) necesita gasolina

What if the only word you understand in the above sentence is **automóvil**? Well, your next thought should be, "Which of the answers has a word that has something to do with a car?" Choice (A), which means *he's hungry,* doesn't seem likely. Choice (B) talks about the weather, which isn't a car-related topic. Choice (C) probably wins the prize for most ridiculous: *the dog is big.* So which answer is not like the others? Choice (D), which means *he needs gas.* Notice that if you can make out some of the key words in either the sentence or the answers, you can eliminate some of the answer choices and get the correct answer.

It's important to understand that this technique will *not* always leave you with only one remaining answer, that is, the right one. Sometimes you will be able to eliminate just one or two choices and end up taking an educated guess. However, guessing one out of two is much better than guessing one out of four. Never eliminate an answer simply because you don't understand it. If you're not sure, leave it in and deal with the choices of which you are sure. Also, the technique allows you to get around some of the tough vocabulary, but you still need to know the meanings of some of the words to use the technique: If you don't know what the answers mean, you can't determine which one is not like the others. The moral of the story is *don't neglect your vocabulary work*!

Third Pass: When You Hardly Understand Any Part of the Sentence

These questions should be left for last. Your goal on the third pass is to go back to each question that you skipped on the first two passes and see whether you can eliminate even one answer choice based on the word or words that you do know in the sentence, using the same approach that you used on the second pass. The only difference is you'll probably have less on which to base your decision. If you're unable to eliminate anything, no sweat—just move on to the next question.

You don't need to know the most difficult words in the sentence to knock off some of the answers. If you can determine only that the answer is going to be a feminine word based on its article (**la**), then that may be enough to help you get rid of one or two choices. So be aggressive!

VOCABULARY REVIEW

Why Work on Your Vocabulary?

In case you haven't already noticed, vocabulary is a very important part of this test. In fact, a sizeable portion of the exam is essentially a vocabulary test. You've already seen some ways to get around the tough vocabulary by using certain techniques, but that doesn't mean that you can blow off this section of the book. We know, we know—memorizing vocabulary words is about as much fun as watching grass grow. However, vocabulary work can translate into some easy points on the day of the test. If you know the words, the questions are that much easier. By not working on your vocabulary, you're blowing a golden opportunity to improve your score. We've narrowed down your work so that you have to deal only with the words that are most likely to appear on the test. Now it's up to you to memorize them.

How to Use These Lists

If you are taking the SAT Subject Test in Spanish, you have probably taken at least two years of Spanish. The following vocabulary lists, like the rest of the review material in this book, are meant to be used in conjunction with your accumulated classroom material. If you feel fuzzy on a concept, by all means return to your textbooks. If there seems to be a concept or a word group that you have never really mastered, then you can set up your third pass or "skip" questions accordingly.

The vocabulary in these lists is arranged by thematic category to facilitate learning the words. At the very least, you should memorize all the words in this chapter, but you may also want to review other thematic presentations in your textbooks for any categories on which you need to brush up. One of the categories contains practical words and concepts (such as prepositional phrases and conjunctions) that you'd use if you were comfortable with Spanish. Words like these frequently appear in both the paragraph completion and reading comprehension portions of the test. At the end of the chapter we also provide a vocabulary list that contains words that the test writers might use to trap you, such as false cognates. Don't forget to add any words you don't know from the practice tests to your study list! See whether you can place them into categories, as we do.

Thematic Vocabulary

Don't Forget to Use Your English Cognates

profundo	profound
participar	to participate
el automóvil	automobile
el circo	circus
el minuto	minute
el perfume	perfume
el/la dentista	dentist
la farmacia	pharmacy
la música	music
estupendo/a	stupendous
el crítico/la crítica	critic
criticar	to criticize
la ovación	ovation
el plato	plate
el programa de televisión	television program
el apetito	appetite
las vacaciones	vacation
el teatro	theater
la biología	biology
el empleado, la empleada	employee
el arte	art
el/la artista	artist
la controversia	controversy
la creación	creation
el hotel	hotel
la manifestación	manifestation
furioso/a	furious

A Cogna...WHAT?
Sounds like you may want to dance the Conga, right? Not quite! A cognate is simply a word that has the same original word or root from another language. This applies to various languages!

cordial	cordial, polite
la residencia	residence, home
practicar	to practice
la operación	operation
el estómago	stomach
falso	false, fake
decidir	to decide
el caso	case (as in *in this case,* not *suitcase*)
la clase	class (as in *school,* or *society*)
comparar	to compare
la justicia	justice
defender	to defend
la gloria	glory
misterioso/a	mysterious
la impresión	impression
plantar	to plant
servir	to serve
contemporáneo/a	contemporary
el verso	verse
el acto	act
la gracia	grace

Basic Words and Phrases You Should Know

Low-Tech Vocab Review
Make flash cards! Five minutes each day learning and reviewing words can make a huge difference.

por eso	that's why
la noticia	news
cada uno	each one
poner	to put
sentado/a	seated
dormido/a	asleep
llamar	to call
muy poco	very little
manejar, conducir	to drive
entrar (en)	to enter
¿Quién eres?	Who are you?
llevar	to take, to carry, to wear
tocar	to touch, to play (an instrument)
tocar a la puerta	to knock at the door
el correo	mail
el buzón	mailbox

sacar	to take out, to remove
dar la vuelta	to turn or flip over or around
la carrera	race (as in a *marathon*), career
el negocio	business
sin falta	without fail
terminar	to finish
la calidad	quality
la cantidad	quantity
la revista	magazine
mostrar	to show
el partido	party (as in *political*), game, match
el árbol	tree
devolver	to give back
el almacén	warehouse, store (as in *department*)
el desfile	parade, procession
advertir	to notice, observe, warn
el estilo	style
tener cuidado	to be careful
envolver	to wrap
ahorrar	to save (as in *money,* not *a life*)
algo	something
empezar	to begin
asco	disgust
falsamente	falsely
romper	to break
¿Con qué derecho?	How dare you? What gives you the right?
olvidar	to forget
sucio/a	dirty
grave	serious
a contrapelo	the wrong way

Vocabulary = Important
Make sure vocab review is a routine part of preparing for the exam. Not knowing the vocabulary is the surest way not to do as well as you could otherwise.

We Are Family

la madre	mother
el padre	father (also sometimes used for *priest*)
el hijo/la hija	son/daughter
el tío/la tía	uncle/aunt
el sobrino/la sobrina	nephew/niece
el primo/la prima	cousin

el nieto/la nieta	grandson/granddaughter
el niño/la niña	boy/girl (usually used for small children)
el muchacho/la muchacha	boy/girl (usually used for teenagers)
el abuelo/la abuela	grandfather/grandmother
el hermano/la hermana	brother/sister
el esposo/la esposa	husband/wife
el marido	husband
los gemelos	twins
el cuñado/la cuñada	brother-in-law/sister-in-law
el bisabuelo/la bisabuela	great-grandfather/great-grandmother
el padrastro	stepfather
la madrastra	stepmother
el suegro/la suegra	father-in-law/mother-in-law
el yerno	son-in-law
la nuera	daughter-in-law
la boda	wedding
el compromiso	engagement
casarse	to get married
el matrimonio, el casamiento	marriage
el divorcio	divorce

School Days

¡Despiértate!	Wake up!
¡Levántate!	Get up!
la escuela	school
a tiempo	on time
tarde	late
la tarde	afternoon
el trabajo	work
la tarea	homework
hacer la tarea	to do homework
leer	to read
el cuento	story
saber	to know
escribir	to write
la librería	bookstore
el libro	book
el número	number

tonto/a	boneheaded, silly
estudiar	to study
los estudiantes	students
prestar atención	to pay attention
el idioma	language
preguntar	to ask
la biblioteca	library

Feed Me

el apetito	appetite
tener hambre	to be hungry
comer	to eat
beber, tomar	to drink
la comida	food
el camarero/la camarera	waiter/waitress
la cuenta	the check, the bill
el arroz	rice
el pollo	chicken
gordo/a	fat
delgado/a	thin
el vaso	glass
el pescado	fish
la ensalada	salad
las legumbres	vegetables
las verduras	vegetables
el queso	cheese
el postre	dessert
la taza	cup
la cuchara	spoon
el cuchillo	knife
el tenedor	fork
el helado	ice cream
el olor	smell, odor, aroma
el sabor	flavor
el desayuno	breakfast
el almuerzo	lunch
la cena	dinner

The Neck Bone's Connected to the...

los dientes	teeth
las encías	gums
la muela	molar
el estómago	stomach
las manos	hands
la cintura	waist
la cabeza	head
las piernas	legs
los brazos	arms
los pies	feet
la espalda	back
el pelo/el cabello	hair
los ojos	eyes
la boca	mouth
la nariz	nose
el pecho	chest
el cuerpo	body
la rodilla	knee
la muñeca	wrist
la barba	beard
el dedo	finger
la garganta	throat
la nuca	nape of the neck
la mejilla	cheek
el hueso	bone
las caderas	hips
el cuello	neck
el codo	elbow
el cerebro	brain
el hombro	shoulder
el rostro	face
las uñas	nails
las cejas	eyebrows
los labios	lips
la lengua	tongue

Shopping Is My Life

comprar	to buy
ir de compras	to go shopping
la ropa	clothes
la camiseta, la playera	T-shirt
la cartera, la bolsa	purse
la zapatería	shoe store
la corbata	tie
el pañuelo	handkerchief
el calcetín	sock
el vestido	dress
el abrigo	coat
la billetera	wallet
el dinero	money
los zapatos	shoes
los pantalones	pants
la camisa	shirt
la blusa	blouse
la falda	skirt
las medias	pantyhose/stockings
los dólares	dollars
de lujo	expensive, luxurious
gastar dinero	to spend money

An Apple a Day

la úlcera	ulcer
diagnosticar	to diagnose
la operación	operation
la extracción	extraction
pálido/a	pale
la herida	injury, wound
enfermo/a	sick
sufrir	to suffer
el dolor	pain
el yeso, la escayola	arm or leg cast
urgencias	emergency room
el médico/la médica	doctor

el/la dentista	dentist
la salud	health
sano/sana	healthy
la receta	prescription
las muletas	crutches
la silla de ruedas	wheelchair
la aguja	needle
la vacuna	vaccine
la cicatriz	scar
la enfermedad	illness
la sangre	blood
las lesiones	cuts
las píldoras	pills
estornudar	sneeze
enfermarse	to get sick
mejorarse	to get better
respirar	to breathe

Mi Casa Es Su Casa

la casa	house
el piso	floor (a level of a building)
el suelo	floor (in a house), ground
la alfombra	rug, carpet
los muebles	furniture
la butaca	armchair, easy chair
salir (de)	to leave
volver	to return
el espejo	mirror
el jabón	soap
la silla	chair
el sillón	rocking chair, armchair
lavar	to wash
el fregadero	sink (kitchen)
el cesped, la grama	lawn
limpiar	to clean
el cuarto/la sala	room

la cocina	kitchen
el dormitorio	bedroom
el baño	bathroom
las llaves	keys

What's Your Job?

el abogado/la abogada	lawyer
el médico/la médica	doctor
el enfermero/la enfermera	nurse
el contador/la contadora	accountant
el/la comerciante	businessman/businesswoman
el banquero/la banquera	banker
el profesor/la profesora	professor
el maestro/la maestra	teacher
el/la periodista	journalist
el presentador/la presentadora	newscaster
el escritor/la escritora	writer
el ingeniero/la ingeniera	engineer
el científico/la científica	scientist
el psicólogo/la psicóloga	psychologist
el antropólogo/la antropóloga	anthropologist
el bombero/la bombera	firefighter
el vaquero/la vaquera	cowboy/cowgirl
el/la soldado	soldier
el/la marinero	sailor
el/la socorrista	lifeguard
el entrenador/la entrenadora	trainer
el pintor/la pintora	painter
el escultor/la escultora	sculptor
el sastre/la sastra	tailor
el cocinero/la cocinera	cook
el panadero/la panadera	baker
el peluquero/la peluquera	hairdresser
el vendedor/la vendedora	salesperson
el cajero/la cajera	cashier

Comparatively Speaking

antes	before
después	after
demasiado/a	too (as in *too much, too late, too funny,* and so on)
mayor	older
menor	younger
mejor	better
peor	worse
mediocre	mediocre
bien hecho	well done
(me) da igual	it doesn't matter (to me)

The Meaning of Life

la vida	life
cambiar	to change
con cariño	with affection
los chistes	jokes
reír	to laugh
regalar	to give as a gift
ganar	to win, to earn *(money)*
saber	to know *(facts, how to do things)*
la sabiduría	knowledge, wisdom
jugar	to play
aceptar	to accept
ofrecer	to offer
querer	to want, to love (**te quiero** = *I love you*)
amar	to love
tranquilo/a	peaceful, tranquil
reposar, descansar	to rest, relax
desear	to want
esperar	to wait
odiar	to loathe, hate
decir	to say
es decir	that is,…
tener	to have
buscar	to look for, search for
hacer	to do, to make

sentir(se)	to feel
¿Cómo te sientes?	How do you feel?
pésame, condolencias	with deepest sympathy
la pena	sorrow, trouble, pain
escoger	to choose
conocer	to know (*people, places*—indicates familiarity)
prestar	to lend
empeñarse	to pledge or devote oneself

Too Much Time on My Hands

la última vez	last time
el siglo	century
el centenario	centennial
despacio	slow, slowly
en cuanto	as soon as
inmediatamente	immediately
durante	during
empezar, comenzar	to begin
terminar, acabar	to finish
hace un rato	a little while ago
próximo/a	next
el próximo día	the next day
media hora	half hour
la hora	hour, time
¿Qué hora es?	What time is it?
de la noche	P.M. (after sunset)
de la tarde	P.M. (afternoon)
de la mañana	A.M.
apurarse	to hurry oneself
en marcha	on the move, on the go
ahora mismo	right now
la fecha	date (as in *calendar*)
hoy	today
mañana	tomorrow
la mañana	morning
la madrugada	early morning
ayer	yesterday

cada vez	each/every time
el año	year
en seguida	right away
de buena gana	gladly (I'd be happy to)
a eso de	around (**a eso de las ocho** = *around 8:00*)

Places to Go, People to See

ir	to go
la esquina	street corner
la playa	the beach
la obra de teatro	the play
la taquilla	box office
cerca de	near
la calle	street
el viaje	trip
aquí	here
allí	there
el mapa	map
dondequiera	wherever
la ciudad	city
el país	country
la película	movie
el banco	bank, bench
el camino	path, route
el señor	gentleman
la señora	lady
la mujer	woman
el hombre	man
el torero	bullfighter
el cartero/la cartera	mail carrier

How's the Weather?

hacer frío	to be cold out
hacer calor	to be hot out
caliente	hot
caluroso/a	warm, hot
llover/la lluvia	to rain/rain
mojado/a	wet

oscuro/a	dark
nevar/la nieve	to snow/snow
el sol	the sun
el viento	the wind

Music Soothes the Savage Beast

la música	music
la orquesta	orchestra
tocar	to play *(an instrument),* to touch
cantar	to sing
practicar	to practice

Beggars and Choosers

nada más	no more, nothing more
¡De ninguna forma!	No way!
nadie	no one
¡Ya lo creo!	Absolutely! For sure!
ningún/ninguna	none, neither
tener culpa	to be at fault, guilty
sin querer	unintentionally, against your will
el mendigo/la mendiga	beggar
pedir limosna	to beg
quemar	to burn
rechazar	to push away, repel, reject
quejarse	to complain
distraído/a	absentminded
poner fin a	to put an end to
de mala gana	reluctantly
de mal humor	in a bad mood
inconveniente	unsuitable, inappropriate, inconvenient

Life's a Bowl of Cherries

perfumado/a	scented, sweet-smelling
cómodo/a	comfortable
lleno/a	full
por favor	please
el premio	prize
premio gordo	grand prize

¡Cómo no!	Of course! I'd be glad to!
empeñarse	to pledge or vow
¡Felicitaciones!	Congratulations!
cortés	courteous
cordial	cordial
estar de acuerdo	to be in agreement
Que Dios lo bendiga.	May God bless you.
el regalo	gift
el regalo de cumpleaños	birthday gift
bastante	enough
gracioso/a	cute, funny

Planes, Trains, and Automobiles

el avión	airplane
el tren	train
el carro, el coche	car
el crucero	cruise
el equipaje	luggage
la maleta	suitcase
el pasaporte	passport
la tarjeta de embarque	boarding pass
el portón	gate
la aduana	customs
la seguridad	security
el pasajero	passenger
el piloto	pilot
el/la agente de viajes	travel agent
la azafata	flight attendant (feminine)
el aeromozo/la aeromoza	flight attendant
el asiento	seat
el cinturón de seguridad	seatbelt
la cabina	cabin
el pasillo	aisle
el boleto, el billete	ticket
de ida solamente	one way
de ida y vuelta	round trip
el vuelo	flight
la tarifa	fare
hacer las maletas	to pack the suitcases

embarcar	to board
despegar	to take off
aterrizar	to land
arrancar	to start
la carretera	highway
el parabrisas	windshield
la llanta	tire
el volante	steering wheel

Reflexive Verbs

ponerse	to put on, to become (with verbs of emotion)
hacerse	to make oneself, to become (with nouns: **Me hice abogado.** *I became a lawyer.*)
acostarse	to go to bed
involucrarse	to involve oneself with
lavarse	to wash oneself
peinarse	to comb one's hair
vestirse	to get dressed
sentarse	to sit down
divertirse	to have fun
quitarse	to take off
bañarse	to bathe oneself
ducharse	to shower

Other Prepositions, Conjunctions, Adverbs, and Phrases to Remember

hacia	toward
enfrente de	in front of
frente a	in front of
dentro de	inside of
fuera de	outside of
a la derecha de	to the right of
a la izquierda de	to the left of
debajo de	underneath
encima de	above, on top of
alrededor de	around, surrounding
en medio de	in the middle of

hasta	until
tras	behind, after
cerca de	close to, near
lejos de	far from
detrás de	behind
delante de	in front of
al lado de	next to
sin	without
contra	against
junto a	next to
respecto a	in regard to
a pesar de	in spite of
en vez de	instead of
en cuanto a	as to, as regards
mientras que	while, meanwhile
aunque	although
sin embargo	nevertheless
a menos que	unless
de antemano	beforehand
ni siquiera	not even
apenas	barely
a no ser que	unless
siempre que	as long as
por más que	no matter how (much)
también	also
de repente	suddenly
en seguida	immediately
por desgracia	unfortunately
al azar	by chance
de todos modos	in any case
tarde o temprano	sooner or later
de nuevo	again
despacio	slowly
acaso	perhaps
tampoco	neither, either
mientras tanto	meanwhile
de una vez	once and for all
en fin	in short

por supuesto	of course
por lo menos	at least

Practical and Useful Nouns

el rincón	corner
el sacapuntas	pencil sharpener
el incendio	fire (as *natural disaster*)
el seguro	insurance
la herencia	inheritance
la inversión	investment
el salvavidas	lifejacket
el socorrista	lifeguard
la acera	sidewalk
los impuestos	taxes
el guión	script
la red	line, Web, network
el recado	message (as in *leave a…*)
el despacho, la oficina	person's office
el escritorio	desk
el equipaje	luggage
la huelga	worker's strike
la superficie	surface
el silbido	whistle
la moda	fashion
el marco	frame
las joyas	jewelry
la mochila	backpack
la factura, la cuenta	bill (for services rendered)
la fecha	date
el estreno	debut
la empresa	company
el esfuerzo	effort
el/la periodista	journalist
el ordenador (in Spain)	computer
la computadora (in Latin America)	computer
la impresora	printer
el orgullo	pride
la misericordia	mercy
la temporada	season

el descubrimiento	discovery
el peso	weight
la pantalla	screen
los recursos	resources
la propina	tip
la contraseña	password

Verbs: Actions to Take

recuperarse	to recover
respirar	to breathe
dirigir	to direct
encabezar	to lead, head
superar	to overcome
lanzar	to launch
ampliar	to broaden, expand
repasar	to review
encargarse	to take charge of
imprimir	to print
fortalecer	to strengthen
resplandecer	to shine
sostener	to sustain
dar a luz (a)	to give birth (to)
negociar	negotiate
caer en cuenta, dar(se) cuenta	to realize
tener en cuenta	to take into account
hallar	to find
reciclar	to recycle
tranquilizarse	to calm (oneself) down
amueblar	to furnish (a room)
enjuagar	to rinse
rescatar	to rescue
traducir	to translate
viajar	to travel
agradar	to please
madrugar	to get up early
despegar	to take off (said of an airplane)
llevar a cabo	to finish
atreverse	to dare
acertar	to guess correctly

Traps

Different Genders, Different Meanings

el editorial	editorial
la editorial	publishing house
el mañana	the future
la mañana	morning
el orden	order
la orden	religious order
el coma (en estado de)	coma
la coma	comma
el corte	cut
la corte	court
el frente	front (as in a war)
la frente	forehead
el guía	guide
la guía	phonebook
el policía	police officer (masculine)
la policía	police force; police officer (feminine)
el capital	capital (as in *money*)
la capital	capital (of a country)

Feminine Nouns with Masculine Articles

el hambre	hunger
el habla	speech
el ancla	anchor
el aula	classroom
el hacha	ax
el arma	weapon

el alma	soul
el águila	eagle
el alba	dawn
el agua	water

False Cognates and Other Pitfalls

actualmente	at the present moment
sensible	sensitive
embarazada	pregnant
el éxito	success
insólito	uncanny
aterrizar	to land (said of an airplane)
el vidrio	glass (window, bottle)
grabar	to record
el desenlace	climax, denouement, finale
el frenesí	frenzy
el collar	necklace
los parientes	kin
el ámbito	field of activity, environment
cazar	to hunt
la informática	computer science
la tormenta, la tempestad	storm
estornudar	to sneeze
la tos	cough
rendirse	to surrender

Drill 1: Process of Elimination

In the following drill, each sentence is missing all but a few key words. Eliminate answers that aren't related to the words in the sentence. If you're left with more than one answer, guess the one that fits best with the words in the sentence. Answers and explanations can be found in Part IV.

1. Cristina *blah blah blah* limpia *blah blah* . . .

   (A) libro
   (B) casa
   (C) huesos
   (D) lluvia

2. *Blah blah blah* revistas *blah blah blah* . . .

   (A) vacaciones
   (B) obras de teatro
   (C) conciertos
   (D) artículos interesantes

3. No *blah* salir porque *blah* mucha . . .

   (A) comida
   (B) dinero
   (C) nieve
   (D) hambre

4. *Blah* postre me *blah blah* que . . .

   (A) el agua
   (B) las vitaminas
   (C) el helado
   (D) arroz con pollo

5. La película *blah blah blah* miedo porque *blah blah* . . .

   (A) violenta
   (B) graciosa
   (C) corta
   (D) tremenda

6. La niña *blah blah* llora por que *blah blah* . . .

   (A) feliz
   (B) silla
   (C) sueño
   (D) corriendo

Drill 2: Sentence Completion

Answers and explanations can be found in Part IV.

1. La camisa de mi novia es hecha de ------- .

   (A) rosas
   (B) algodón
   (C) madera
   (D) azul

2. Buscaba las medicinas para mi abuelo en la -------
   de la esquina.

   (A) librería
   (B) farmacia
   (C) oficina
   (D) panadería

3. Estaba ------- porque mis empleados llegaron tarde
   por cuarta vez en la misma semana.

   (A) furioso
   (B) encantado
   (C) contentísimo
   (D) abierto

4. Una buena manera de mejorar las notas en la
   escuela es ------ mucho.

   (A) enseñar
   (B) entender
   (C) hablar
   (D) practicar

5. Es un hombre sumamente vanidoso; siempre se está
   mirando en el ------- .

   (A) espejo
   (B) cristal
   (C) gafas
   (D) mismo

6. Los viejos tienen más ------- que los jóvenes,
   porque han tenido más experiencias.

   (A) tiempo
   (B) que comer
   (C) sabiduría
   (D) apetito

7. Es bastante evidente que a Alejandro le gusta hacer
   sus tareas; siempre las hace ------- .

   (A) de mala gana
   (B) con entusiasmo
   (C) muy despacio
   (D) sin gusto

8. Pedro ------- muy contento cuando nació su hijo.

   (A) se cambió
   (B) se dio
   (C) se hizo
   (D) se puso

9. Quiero que ------- apuntes sobre la lectura.

   (A) tomas
   (B) tomes
   (C) tomabas
   (D) tomaste

Summary

○ First Pass: When You Understand the Entire Sentence
- Fill in your own word (short and simple, but specific).
- Eliminate answers that are not in the same category as your word.
- Beware of the little traps: Concentrate on meaning, not sound.
- Out of the remaining choices, pick the answer that's closest to your word.

○ Second Pass: When You Don't Understand the Entire Sentence
- Determine the meanings of as many individual words as you can.
- Put these words together to try to determine the general context of the sentence.
- Eliminate any choices that don't make sense in that context.
- Pick the choice out of the remaining choices that is most likely to appear in that context (it should be the only one left).

○ Third Pass: When You Hardly Understand Any Part of the Sentence
- Try to locate sentences in which you know at least one or two words.
- See whether any of the answers seem impossible based on those words.
- Eliminate those answers and guess.

○ Never…
- eliminate an answer choice because you don't know its meaning—just because you don't know it doesn't mean it's wrong! Use POE on choices that have words you *do* know.
- leave a question blank if you can eliminate even one answer—the odds are in your favor if you can eliminate one or more of the choices, so guess!

○ Vocabulary is an essential component of the Spanish Subject Tests, which is why you should make a concerted effort to learn new words.

○ The vocabulary lists in this chapter make up some of the most frequently tested words on the exam. Test yourself on all the words by covering the translations and see how many words you know; eventually, you will learn them all.

Chapter 4
Sentence
Completion:
Grammar

Grammar is another very important part of the SAT Subject Test in Spanish. In this chapter, we review the most important grammar rules you should know for the exam and give you sample questions to test your knowledge of these rules. We cover basic terms, pronouns, essential verb forms, prepositions, and more.

Memorize All Directions
Reading the directions
when you take the test is
a waste of precious time.
Know them beforehand.

GRAMMAR QUESTIONS: AN OVERVIEW

Now we're going to take a look at the grammar portion of the sentence completion questions that you'll find in Part A of the Spanish Subject Test and the first part of the reading section of the Spanish with Listening Subject Test. The good news is that you don't need to review everything you've ever learned about grammar, because only a small portion of Spanish grammar is actually tested, and our review will focus on that portion. The even better news is that the techniques you've learned in this book work very well on this section, and by combining them with a brief review of grammar, you will increase your chances of doing well on the exam. Before you get into strategies or review, memorize the instructions for this question type.

Part A

Directions: This part consists of a number of incomplete statements, each having four suggested completions. Select the most appropriate completion and fill in the corresponding oval on the answer sheet.

Each question will be followed by four answer choices. These differ from the vocabulary sentence completion questions because the answer choices will all have the same or very similar meanings, but only one of them will fit the blank and make the sentence grammatically correct. It's not about vocabulary; it's about verbs, pronouns, prepositions, and idioms, but don't let that scare you! After you get through this chapter, you'll know everything you need to know to master this section.

HOW TO CRACK THIS SECTION

The key to succeeding on this section is to focus specifically on the grammatical concepts that are being tested, and to spend a little time relearning them. Contrary to what the test writers would like you to believe, this section doesn't test everything you learned in Spanish class, but instead sticks to a few grammatical ideas and tests them over and over again. You probably already know and are comfortable with many of them, and even if you're not right now, you will be once you invest a little time studying.

In addition to reviewing the grammar, you will use Process of Elimination and the Three-Pass System to beat this section. You'll supplement both of these with what may be your best friend on these questions: your ear. Remember how your ear could easily steer you wrong on vocabulary sentence completions because of the way the wrong answers sometimes sounded like the right ones? Well, on this section, your ear, or the way the answers sound, can actually help you to eliminate answers right off the bat without having to worry about grammar at all. This won't work on all questions, but it certainly will on some, and you're going to take full advantage of it.

Applying the Three-Pass System

First Pass: I'm Sure I've Seen This Somewhere Before

Again, the questions are not arranged in any particular order of difficulty, but the level of difficulty of the different questions varies tremendously. Your goal on the first pass is to locate the questions that test the verb tenses, pronouns, prepositions, and idioms that you know like the back of your hand. Find the easiest questions, and do them first. How do you tell whether a question is easy? Read it, and if the structure looks familiar, go for it. If it looks as if it's going to take a little POE to crack it, leave that question for the second pass.

Second Pass: Haven't I Seen This Somewhere Before?

If you read a question and the answer doesn't immediately jump off the page at you, don't be discouraged: Just because you don't immediately know what the answer *is* doesn't mean you can't tell what the answer *isn't*. Work backward from the answer choices and eliminate answers you know are wrong. If you understand some of the answer choices and know they're wrong, it's just as effective as knowing which ones are right.

Third Pass: I've Never Seen This Anywhere

If the grammar in both the sentence and answers is a complete mystery to you, chances are you won't be able to find the right answer using POE. Eliminate any of the choices that you can and then guess. The most important thing about the third pass (on any section) is that you don't spend too much time on these really tough questions.

Tip:
Remember—you don't have to do the questions in the order in which they're presented. Do the easiest first—no matter where they are in the lineup.

GRAMMAR REVIEW

Although we won't lie and tell you that reviewing grammar rules will be fun, we can promise you that spending a little time on this material will mean easy points for you on the day of the test. Grammar is merely a bunch of rules, and once you've learned those that are tested, you'll be ready for this question type.

Basic Terms

While you won't be tested on these definitions, the following terms are important because they will come up later in the chapter. Knowing them allows you to understand the rules of grammar that you're about to review.

Grammar Refresher
While you don't need to know specific grammar terms or rules for the Spanish Subject Test, having a basic grasp of grammar can be helpful. If you have the time and want to brush up on your grammar skills, pick up a copy of *Grammar Smart.*

Noun:	a person, place, or thing EXAMPLES: Abraham Lincoln, New Jersey, taco
Pronoun:	a word that replaces a noun EXAMPLES: Abe Lincoln would be replaced by *he*, New Jersey by *it*, and taco by *it*. You'll learn more about pronouns later.
Adjective:	a word that describes a noun EXAMPLES: cold, soft, colorful
Verb:	an action word; the main action being done in a sentence EXAMPLE: Ron *ate* the huge breakfast.
Infinitive:	the original, unconjugated form of a verb EXAMPLES: to eat, to run, to laugh
Auxiliary Verb:	the verb that precedes the past participle in the perfect tenses EXAMPLE: He *had* eaten his lunch.
Past Participle:	the appropriate form of a verb when it is used with the auxiliary verb EXAMPLE: They have *gone* to work.
Adverb:	an adverb describes a verb, adjective, or another adverb, just like an adjective describes a noun EXAMPLES: slowly, quickly, happily (Adverbs often, but don't always, end in *-ly*.)
Subject:	the thing (noun) in a sentence that is performing the action EXAMPLE: *John* wrote the song.

Compound:	a subject that's made up of two or more subjects or nouns
	EXAMPLE: *John and Paul* wrote the song together.

Object:	the thing (noun or pronoun) in the sentence to which the action is happening, either directly or indirectly
	EXAMPLES: Mary bought *the shirt*. Joe hit *him*. Mary gave *a gift* to *Tim*.

Direct Object:	the thing that receives the action of the verb
	EXAMPLE: I see *the wall*. (The wall "receives" the action of seeing.)

Indirect Object:	the person who receives the direct object
	EXAMPLE: I wrote the letter to *her*. (She receives the letter.)

Preposition:	a word that marks the relationship (in space or time) between two other words
	EXAMPLES: He received the letter *from* her. The book is *below* the chair.

Article:	a word (usually a very small word) that precedes a noun
	EXAMPLES: *a* watch, *the* room

That wasn't so bad, was it? Now let's put all those terms together in a couple of examples.

Dominic	spent	the	entire	night	here.
subject	verb	article	adjective	dir. obj.	adverb

Margaret	often	gives	me	money.
subject	adverb	verb	indir. obj.	dir. obj.

Alison and Rob	have	a	gorgeous	child.
compound subject	verb	article	adjective	dir. obj.

Once you've spent a little time with these terms, review the grammar on which you'll actually be tested.

PRONOUNS

You already learned that a pronoun is a word that takes the place of a noun. Now you'll review what pronouns look like in Spanish, and learn how they are tested on the Spanish Subject Test.

If you can tell the difference between subject, direct object, and indirect object pronouns, you are in very good shape. Beyond those different types, there are a few odds and ends that may show up. Still, the majority of questions that test pronouns focus on these three basic types.

Subject Pronouns

These are the most basic pronouns, and probably the first ones you learned. Just take a moment to look them over to make sure you haven't forgotten them. Then spend some time looking over the examples that follow until you are comfortable using them.

yo	I	nosotros/nosotras	we (mas./fem.)
tú/usted (Ud.)	you (familiar/formal)	vosotros/vosotras/ustedes (Uds.)	you (pl.) (mas./fem.)
ella/él	she/he	ellas/ellos	they

Note that **vosotros** is a form mainly used in Spain and almost never appears on the Spanish Subject Test.

When to Use Subject Pronouns

A subject pronoun (like any other pronoun) replaces the noun that is the subject of the sentence.

> *Marco no pudo comprar el helado.*
> Marco couldn't buy the ice cream.

Who does the action of this sentence? Marco, so he is the subject. If we wanted to use a subject pronoun in this case, we'd replace **Marco** with **él**.

> *Él no pudo comprar el helado.*
> **He** couldn't buy the ice cream.

Subject Pronouns

Subject pronouns aren't always necessary in Spanish sentences, because the form of the verb gives us a clue as to the subject's identity. They are used, however, for emphasis or clarification.

Direct Object Pronouns

A direct object pronoun replaces (you guessed it) the direct object in a sentence.

me	me	nos	us
te	you (*tú* form)	os	you (*vosotros* form)
lo/la	him, it (mas.)/her, it (fem.)/ you (*Ud.* form)	los/las	them (mas./fem.)/ you (*Uds.* form)

When to Use Direct Object Pronouns

Now let's see what it looks like when we replace the direct object in a sentence with a pronoun.

> *Marco no pudo comprar el helado.*

What couldn't Marco buy? Ice cream. Because ice cream is what's receiving the action, it's the direct object. To use the direct object pronoun, you'd replace **helado** with **lo**.

> *Marco no pudo comprar**lo**.*   or   *Marco no **lo** pudo comprar.*

When the direct object pronoun is used with the infinitive of a verb, it can either be tacked on to the end of the verb (the first example) or it can come before the conjugated verb in the sentence (the second example). Another example:

> *Voy a ver**lo**.*   I'm going to see **it**.

> ***Lo** voy a ver.*   (Both sentences mean the same thing.)

The direct object pronoun also follows the verb in an affirmative command, for example:

> *¡Cóme**lo**!*   Eat **it**!

> *¡Escúcha**me**!*   Listen to **me**!

Indirect Object Pronouns

An indirect object pronoun replaces the indirect object in a sentence. The indirect object is easy to spot in English because a preposition often comes before it. However, *this is not the case in Spanish*. In Spanish, when the object is indirect, the preposition is often implied, not explicitly stated. So how can you tell the difference? In general, the indirect object is the person who receives the direct object.

Finding the Direct Object

I throw the *ball*.
What do I throw?
Ellen knew the *answer*.
What did she know?
We will see the *bus*.
What will we see?
What received the action of the verb?
The answer is always the direct object.

me	me	nos	us
te	you (*tú* form)	os	you (*vosotros* form)
le	him/her/you (*Ud.* form)	les	them/you (*Uds.* form)

When to Use Indirect Object Pronouns

This might seem a little strange, but in Spanish the indirect object pronoun is often present in a sentence that contains the indirect object noun.

> *Juan le da el abrigo al viejo.*

> Juan gives the coat to the old man.   *or*   Juan gives the old man the coat.

Notice that the sentence contains the indirect object noun (**viejo**) and the indirect object pronoun (**le**). This is often necessary to provide clarification of the identity of the indirect object pronoun or to emphasize that identity. Typically, an expression of clarification is needed with the pronouns **le** and **les** and **se** (see below) but is not obligatory with other pronouns.

> *María **nos** ayudó.*   María helped **us**.
> *Juan **me** trae el suéter.*   Juan brings **me** the sweater.

The identity of the indirect object is obvious with the choice of pronoun in these examples, so clarification is not necessary. An expression may be used, however, to emphasize the identity of the indirect object:

> *No **me** lo trajeron a **mí**; **te** lo trajeron a **ti**.*
> They didn't bring it to **me**; they brought it to **you**.

Indirect Object
I will write a letter to *her*.
Who will get the letter?
We tell *him* the truth.
Who hears the truth?
He suggested changes to *me*.
Who got the changes?
Essentially, who gets the noun? The answer is always the indirect object.

We would change our intonation to emphasize these words in English. This doesn't happen in Spanish; the expressions **a mí** and **a ti** serve the same function.

Se is used in place of **le** and **les** whenever the pronoun that follows begins with l.

> *¿**Le** estás contando la noticia a María?*   Are you telling Maria the news?
> *Sí, **se** la estoy contando a María.*   Yes, I'm telling it to **her**.

> *¿**Les** prestas los guantes a los estudiantes?*   Do you lend gloves to the students?
> *No, no **se** los presto a ellos.*   No, I don't lend them to **them**.

Notice that **le** changes to **se** in the first example and **les** to **se** in the second because the direct object pronouns that follow begin with l. Notice also the inclusion of **a María** and **a ellos** to clarify the identity of **se** in each example.

Prepositional Pronouns

As we mentioned earlier, there are some pronouns that take explicitly stated prepositions, and they're different from indirect object pronouns. The prepositional pronouns are as follows:

mí	me	nosotros/nosotras	us
ti/Ud.	you (fam./formal)	vosotros/vosotras/Uds.	you (plural)
él/ella	him/her	ellos/ellas	them

When to Use Prepositional Pronouns

Consider the following examples:

1. *Cómprale un regalo de cumpleaños.*   Buy **him** a birthday present.
2. *Vamos al teatro sin él.*   We're going to the theater without **him**.

Notice that in the first example, *him* is translated as **le**, whereas in the second, *him* is translated as **él**. What exactly is the deal with that?! Why isn't it the same word in Spanish, as it is in English? In Spanish, the different pronouns distinguish the different functions of the word within the sentence.

In the first example, *him* is the indirect object of the verb *to buy* (buy the gift for whom? For him—*him* receives the direct object), so we use the indirect object pronoun **le**. In the second example, however, *him* is the object of the preposition *without*, so we use the prepositional pronoun **él**. Here are some more examples that involve prepositional pronouns. Notice that they all have explicitly stated prepositions.

*Las flores son **para ti**.*   The flowers are **for** you.

*Estamos enojados **con él**.*   We are angry **with** him.

*Quieren ir de vacaciones **sin Uds**.*   They want to go on vacation **without** you.

In two special cases, when the preposition is **con** and the object of the preposition is **mí** or **ti**, the preposition and the pronoun are combined to form **conmigo** *(with me)* and **contigo** *(with you)*.

*¿Quieres ir al concierto **conmigo**?*   Do you want to go to the concert **with me**?

*No, no puedo ir **contigo**.*   No, I can't go **with you**.

When the subject is **él, ella, ellos, ellas, Ud.,** or **Uds.,** and the object of the preposition is the **same** as the subject, the prepositional pronoun is **sí** and is usually accompanied by **mismo/a** or **mismos/as.**

*Alejandro es muy egoísta. Siempre habla de **sí mismo**.*

Alejandro is very egotistical. He always talks about **himself**.

*Ellos compran ropa para **sí mismos** cuando van de compras.*

They buy clothes for **themselves** when they go shopping.

POSSESSIVE ADJECTIVES AND PRONOUNS

Possessive adjectives and pronouns are used to indicate ownership. When you want to let someone know what's yours, use the following pronouns or adjectives:

Stressed Possessive Adjectives

mío/mía	mine	**nuestro/nuestra**	ours
tuyo/tuya	yours (*tú* form)	**vuestro/vuestra**	yours (*vosotros* form)
suyo/suya	his/hers/yours (*Ud.* form)	**suyo/suya**	theirs/yours (*Uds.* form)

Unstressed Possessive Adjectives

mi	my	**nuestro/nuestra**	our
tu	your (*tú* form)	**vuestro/vuestra**	yours (*vosotros* form)
su	his/hers/your (*Ud.* form)	**su**	their/your (*Uds.* form)

When to Use Possessive Adjectives

The first question is, "When do you use an unstressed adjective, and when do you use a stressed adjective?" Check out these examples, and then we'll see what the rule is:

*Esta es **mi** casa.*
This is **my** house.

*Esta casa es **mía**.*
This house is **mine**.

*Aquí está **tu** billetera.*
Here is **your** wallet.

*Esta billetera es **tuya**.*
This wallet is **yours**.

The difference between stressed and unstressed possessive adjectives is emphasis as opposed to meaning. Saying *This is my house* puts emphasis on the house, while saying *This house is mine* takes the focus off the house and stresses the identity of its owner—me. To avoid getting confused, just remember that unstressed is the Spanish equivalent of *my* and stressed is the Spanish equivalent of *mine*.

In terms of structure, there is an important difference between the two types of adjectives, but it's easy to remember: A stressed adjective comes after the verb, but an unstressed adjective comes before the noun. Notice that neither type agrees with the possessor; they agree with the possessed thing.

If it's not clear to you why these are adjectives when they look so much like pronouns, consider their function. When you say *my house*, the noun *house* is being described by *my*. Any word that describes a noun is an adjective, even if that word looks a lot like a pronoun. The key is how it's being used in the sentence.

Possessive Pronouns

These look like stressed possessive adjectives, but they mean something different. Possessive pronouns *replace* nouns; they don't *describe* them.

When to Use Possessive Pronouns

This type of pronoun is formed by combining the article of the noun that's being replaced with the appropriate stressed possessive adjective. Just like stressed possessive adjectives, possessive pronouns must agree in gender and number with the nouns they replace.

Mi bicicleta es azul.	*La mía es azul.*
My bicycle is blue.	**Mine** is blue.

Notice how the pronoun not only shows possession but also replaces the noun. Here are some more examples.

Mis zapatos son caros.	*Los míos son caros.*
My shoes are expensive.	**Mine** are expensive.
Tu automóvil es rápido.	*El tuyo es rápido.*
Your car is fast.	**Yours** is fast.
No me gustaron los discos **que ellos trajeron**.	*No me gustaron* **los suyos**.
I didn't like the records **they brought**.	I didn't like **theirs**.

Reflexive Pronouns

Remember those reflexive verbs you saw in the vocabulary review (like **ponerse** and **hacerse**)? Those all have a common characteristic: They indicate that the action is being done to or for oneself. When one of those verbs is conjugated, the reflexive pronoun (which is always **se** in the infinitive) changes according to the subject.

Reflexives
Many reflexive verbs can be used non-reflexively. Ask yourself—is the person doing the action the one who is receiving it? If so, the verb is reflexive. If not, the verb is normal (or transitive).

me	myself	nos	ourselves
te	your (*tú* form)	os	yours (*vosotros* form)
se	himself/herself/yourself (*Ud.* form)	se	themselves/yourselves (*Uds.* form)

A reflexive pronoun is used when the subject and indirect object of the sentence are the same. This may sound kind of strange, but after you see some examples it should make more sense.

> *Alicia se pone el maquillaje.*
> Alicia puts on makeup.

> What does she put on? **Makeup**—direct object.
> Who "receives" the makeup? **Alicia**—she's also the subject.

The action is thus *reflected* back on itself: Alicia does the action and then receives it. No outside influences are involved.

Another meaning for reflexive verbs is literally that the person does something directly to or for him/herself.

> *Rosa se cortó con el cuchillo.*
> Rosa **cut herself** with the knife.

> *Roberto tiene que comprarse una libreta nueva.*
> Roberto has to **buy himself** a new notebook.

The Pronoun *Que*

The Pronoun *Que*
Keep in mind that what follows que is generally an expression that further describes the noun just before it.

The pronoun **que** can mean *who*, *that*, or *which*, depending on the context of the sentence. In other words, it can take the place of a person or a thing. Fortunately, it isn't too tough to tell which meaning is correct.

> *¿Cómo se llama la maestra que tuvimos ayer?*
> What's the name of the teacher **whom** we had yesterday?

> *Ese es el equipo que más me gusta.*
> That's the team **that** I like the most.

*¿Cuál es la revista **que** compraste ayer?*
Which is the magazine **that** you bought yesterday?

In the first example, **que** means *whom,* because you are talking about a person. In the other examples, **que** refers to things, so it means *that* or *which.*

When to Use *Que*

Although in English we sometimes leave out the pronouns *who, that,* and *which* (for example, *the food [that] I ate*), in Spanish you have to use **que**. **Que** always follows the noun (as in the previous examples) because it begins a clause that further describes the noun.

When referring to people, **quien** (or **quienes**) replaces **que** if the pronoun follows a preposition.

*El maestro sin **quien** yo no pudiera haber aprendido español está aquí hoy.*
The teacher without **whom** I couldn't have learned Spanish is here today.

*Los tipos con **quienes** juego a la pelota son jugadores magníficos.*
The guys with **whom** I play ball are magnificent players.

The Pronoun *Cuál*

Cuál (meaning *which* or *what*) is used when a choice is involved. It's used in place of **que** before the verb **ser**, and it has only two forms: singular (**cuál**) and plural (**cuáles**). Both **cuál** and the verb **ser** must agree in number with the thing(s) being asked about.

*¿**Cuál** es tu ciudad favorita?*   **What** is your favorite city?
*¿**Cuáles** son nuestros regalos?*   **Which** presents are ours?

Demonstrative Pronouns and Adjectives

First, learn the construction and meaning.

este/esta	this (one)	estos/estas	these
ese/esa	that (one)	esos/esas	those
aquel/aquella	that (one over there)	aquellos/aquellas	those (over there)

Demonstrative Adjectives
This and *these* in Spanish have T's (este/esta and estos/estas).

Adjective or Pronoun—Which Is It?

If the demonstrative word *comes before* a noun, then it is an adjective.

Este plato de arroz con pollo es mío.	**This** plate of chicken with rice is mine.
Ese edificio es de mi hermano.	**That** building is my brother's.

If the demonstrative word *takes the place of* a noun, then it's a pronoun.

*Dije que **este** es mío.*	I said that **this one** is mine.
*Sabemos que **ese** es de mi hermano.*	We know **that one** is my brother's.

When used as adjectives, these words mean *this*, *that*, and so on. When used as pronouns, they mean *this one*, *that one*, and so on. Don't worry about the use of **ese** versus **aquel**. No question on this exam will ask you to pick between the two.

TIPS FOR PRONOUN QUESTIONS

- The types of pronouns that you need to know are subject, object (direct and indirect), possessive, prepositional (which you'll see again later), reflexive, demonstrative, and a couple of odds and ends like **que** and **cuál**. We're not guaranteeing that only these types will appear, but, if you know these inside and out, you should feel confident that you'll be able to tackle most (if not all) of the pronoun questions.
- Don't just memorize what the different pronouns look like! Recognizing them is important, but it's just as important that you understand how and when to use them.
- Don't forget about POE. The test writers may try to trip you up on simple things (like the gender of a pronoun) that are easy to overlook if you're not on your toes. Before you start thinking about grammar on a pronoun question, eliminate answers that are wrong based on flagrant stuff like gender, singular versus plural, and so on.
- If all else fails, your ear can sometimes be your guide. In learning Spanish, you probably spoke and heard the language on a pretty regular basis, and so you have a clue as to what correct Spanish sounds like. You don't want to use your ear if you can eliminate answers based on the rules of grammar, but if you've exhausted the rules and you're down to two answers, one of which sounds much better than the other, guess the nice-sounding one. The fact is that many grammatical rules were born out of a desire to make the language sound good.
- Last (but not least), don't forget to pace yourself wisely and use the Three-Pass System. Look for questions that test the pronouns with which you're most comfortable, and skip the tough ones. If you're stumped by a question, leave it for the third pass, eliminate what you can, and guess, but never spend too much time on a question that tests something you don't really know.

Helpful Hints
When it comes to pronouns, understanding how and when to use them is key. We also encourage you to use POE and the Three-Pass System. And remember: pace yourself!

VERBS

You probably learned what felt like a zillion different verbs and tenses in Spanish class. For the purposes of this section, you only need to know a few of the tenses you learned. What's even better is that you don't need to know how to conjugate verbs in the different tenses, nor do you need to know the names for the different tenses. You do need to know how to recognize them, however. For example, you don't need to know how or why the conditional is used; all that you need to know is what it looks like when a verb is in the conditional, and when the conditional should be used.

You should focus on recognizing clues in the sentences that suggest certain tenses, and then finding answers in the appropriate tenses. Remember, even if you don't know which answer is in the tense that corresponds with the sentence, you can still eliminate answers that definitely aren't in that tense. Use POE! A brief review of the tenses that show up in the test is probably a good place to begin, so let's get right to it.

The Present Tense (or the Present Indicative)

The present tense is the easiest, and probably the first tense you ever learned. It is used when the action is happening in the present, as in the following:

Yo **hablo** con mis amigos todos los días.
I **speak** with my friends every day.

Because the present is the most basic, and probably the easiest tense, it rarely shows up as the right answer to a question. So why go over it? Because it sometimes does show up as a right answer, and it often shows up as a wrong answer. You need to know how to recognize it to eliminate it if it's incorrect. Take a quick glance at the present tense of the following verbs just to refresh your memory.

	trabajar	vender	escribir
yo	trabajo	vendo	escribo
tú (fam.)	trabajas	vendes	escribes
él/ella/Ud.	trabaja	vende	escribe
nosotros/nosotras	trabajamos	vendemos	escribimos
vosotros/vosotras (fam.)	trabajáis	vendéis	escribís
ellos/ellas/Uds.	trabajan	venden	escriben

Remember
Usted (Ud.) and Ustedes (Uds.) may have the same verb forms as él/ella and ellos/ellas, but they mean the same things as tú and vosotros, respectively.

Stem-Changing Verbs

Not all verbs are created equal. When you conjugate some verbs, the stems change in the first-, second-, and third-person singular and in the third-person plural. These verbs fall into three main categories: verbs that change -e to -ie, -o to -ue, and -e to -i.

	cerrar (e : ie)	volver (o : ue)	pedir (e : i)
yo	cierro	vuelvo	pido
tú (fam.)	cierras	vuelves	pides
él/ella/Ud.	cierra	vuelve	pide
nosotros/nosotras	cerramos	volvemos	pedimos
vosotros/vosotras (fam.)	cerrais	volveis	pedis
ellos/ellas/Uds.	cierran	vuelven	piden

Other verbs that follow this pattern include:

(e : ie)	(o : ue)	(e : i)
comenzar	almorzar	conseguir
empezar	costar	decir
entender	dormir	repetir
perder	poder	seguir
preferir	recordar	servir
querer	volar	

The Past Tense (AKA the Preterite)

The past tense is used to describe an action that had a *definite beginning and ending in the past* (as opposed to an action that may be ongoing), as in the following example:

> *Ayer yo hablé con mis amigos.*
> Yesterday I **spoke** with my friends. (The action began and ended.)

There are a bunch of different tenses that are past tenses that describe actions that took place at various points in the past. There are different tenses for saying *I spoke, I was speaking, I have spoken,* and so on. Let's start by reviewing the most basic of these, the plain past tense.

	trabajar	vender	escribir
yo	trabajé	vendí	escribí
tú (fam.)	trabajaste	vendiste	escribiste
él/ella/Ud.	trabajó	vendió	escribió
nosotros/nosotras	trabajamos	vendimos	escribimos
vosotros/vosotras (fam.)	trabajasteis	vendisteis	escribisteis
ellos/ellas/Uds.	trabajaron	vendieron	escribieron

The easiest forms to spot are the first- and third-person singular (**yo** and **él/ella/Ud.** forms) because of the accents.

The Imperfect

The imperfect is another past tense, used to describe actions that occurred continuously in the past and exhibited no definitive end at that time. This is different from the preterite, which describes one-time actions that began and ended at the moment in the past that is being described. Look at the two together, and the difference between them will become clear.

> *Ayer **hablé** con mis amigos y entonces me fui.*
> Yesterday **I spoke** with my friends and then left.
> (The act of speaking obviously ended, because I left afterward.)

> *Yo **hablaba** con mis amigos mientras caminábamos.*
> **I spoke** with my friends while we walked.
> (The act of speaking was **in progress** at that moment, along with walking.)

The imperfect is also used to describe conditions or circumstances in the past that are obviously ongoing occurrences.

> *Era una noche oscura y tormentosa.*
> **It was** a dark and stormy night.

> *Cuando **tenía** diez años...*
> When **I was** ten years old...

In the first example, it didn't just start or just stop being a stormy night, did it? Was the dark and stormy night already a past event at that point? No. The dark and stormy night was **in progress** at that moment, so the imperfect is used, not the preterite.

Preterite vs. Imperfect
Think of the preterite as a self-contained unit of time (*She finished her homework*). The imperfect, in contrast, refers to something in the past that doesn't have a clear beginning or end (*She was doing her homework when the doorbell rang*).

In the second example, did I start or stop being ten years old at that point? Neither. Was being ten already a past event at the moment I am describing? No. I was simply in the process of being ten years old at that moment in the past, so the imperfect is the more precise tense to use.

Make sense? Good; now check out the formation:

	trabajar	vender	escribir
yo	trabajaba	vendía	escribía
tú (fam.)	trabajabas	vendías	escribías
él/ella/Ud.	trabajaba	vendía	escribía
nosotros/nosotras	trabajábamos	vendíamos	escribíamos
vosotros/vosotras (fam.)	trabajabais	vendíais	escribíais
ellos/ellas/Uds.	trabajaban	vendían	escribían

Remember:
Context clues that denote a use of the imperfect tense include siempre, normalmente, cada año, usualmente, todos los años, de niño/a, and so on. Look for clues that indicate a habitual action.

Although the imperfect tense is similar to the other past tenses you've seen (such as the preterite and the present perfect) because it speaks of past actions, it looks quite different. That's the key, because half of your job is just to know what the different tenses look like. The toughest part will be distinguishing the preterite from the imperfect.

The Future Tense

The future tense is used to describe things that will *definitely* happen in the future. The reason we stress "definitely" is because there is a different verbal mode (the subjunctive) used to describe things that *may* happen in the future. In Spanish, just as in English, there is a difference between being certain *(I will go)* and being uncertain *(I might go),* and different forms are used for the different degrees of certainty. You'll see the fancier stuff later. First take a look at the regular future tense.

> *Mañana yo **hablaré** con mis amigos.*
> Tomorrow I **will speak** with my friends.

Notice that what takes two words to say in English *(will speak)* takes only one word to say in Spanish (**hablaré**). The future is a nice, simple tense (no auxiliary verb, only one word) that is easy to spot thanks to the accents and the structure. The future is formed by tacking on the appropriate ending to the infinitive of the verb *without dropping the -ar, -er, or -ir.*

	trabajar	vender	escribir
yo	trabajaré	venderé	escribiré
tú (fam.)	trabajarás	venderás	escribirás
él/ella/Ud.	trabajará	venderá	escribirá
nosotros/nosotras	trabajaremos	venderemos	escribiremos
vosotros/vosotras (fam.)	trabajaréis	venderéis	escribiréis
ellos/ellas/Uds.	trabajarán	venderán	escribirán

Back to the Future: The Conditional

Remember, when you want to describe actions that are *definitely* going to happen in the future, use the future tense. When you want to describe actions that *might* happen in the future, use the conditional tense.

The conditional describes what could, would, or might happen in the future.

> Me **gustaría** hablar con mis amigos todos los días.
> I **would like** to talk to my friends every day.

> Si tuviera más tiempo, **podría** hablar con ellos el día entero.
> If I had more time, I **could** speak with them all day long.

> Si gastara cinco pesos, solamente me **quedarían** tres.
> If I spent (were to spend) five dollars, I **would have** only three left.

It can also be used to make a request in a more polite way.

> ¿**Puedes** prestar atención?   ¿**Podrías** prestar atención?
> **Can you** pay attention?   **Could you** pay attention?

The conditional is formed by taking the future stem of the verb (which is the infinitive) and adding the conditional ending.

	trabajar	vender	escribir
yo	trabajaría	vendería	escribiría
tú (fam.)	trabajarías	venderías	escribirías
él/ella/Ud.	trabajaría	vendería	escribiría
nosotros/nosotras	trabajaríamos	venderíamos	escribiríamos
vosotros/vosotras (fam.)	trabajaríais	venderíais	escribiríais
ellos/ellas/Uds.	trabajarían	venderían	escribirían

To avoid confusing the conditional with the future, concentrate on the conditional endings. The big difference is the accented **í**, which is in the conditional, but not in the future.

Future	Conditional
trabajaré	trabajaría
venderán	venderían
escribiremos	escribiríamos

The Present Perfect
This is where it gets a little weird: If something happens in the very recent past, we can also use the present perfect to show its proximity to the present. We hardly ever do this in American English.

The Present Perfect

The present perfect is used to refer to an action that began in the past and is continuing into the present (and possibly beyond). It is also used to describe actions that were completed very close to the present. Compare these sentences.

1. *Ayer **hablé** con mis amigos.*
   Yesterday I **spoke** with my friends.

   ***Decidiste** no ir al cine.*
   You decided not to go to the movies.

2. *He **hablado** mucho con mis amigos recientemente.*
   I **have spoken** a lot with my friends lately.

   ***Has decidido** hacerte abogado.*
   You have decided (recently) to become a lawyer.

The first examples are in the plain past tense: You started and finished talking with your friends yesterday, and you completed the process of deciding not to go to the movies. In the second examples, the use of the present perfect tense moves the action to the very recent past, instead of leaving it in the more distant past. The present perfect, then, is essentially a more precise verb form of the past, used when the speaker wants to indicate that an action happened very recently in the past.

Spotting the perfect tenses is rather easy. This is a compound tense, meaning that it is formed by combining two verbs: a tense of the auxiliary (or helping) verb **haber** (present, imperfect, future, conditional) and the past participle of the main verb.

	trabajar	vender	escribir
yo	he trabajado	he vendido	he escrito
tú (fam.)	has trabajado	has vendido	has escrito
él/ella/Ud.	ha trabajado	ha vendido	ha escrito
nosotros/nosotras	hemos trabajado	hemos vendido	hemos escrito
vosotros/vosotras (fam.)	habéis trabajado	habéis vendido	habéis escrito
ellos/ellas/Uds.	han trabajado	han vendido	han escrito

Most past participles are formed by dropping the last two letters from the infinitive and adding **-ido** (for **-er** and **-ir** verbs) or **-ado** (for **-ar** verbs). **Escribir** has an irregular past participle, as do some other verbs, but don't worry about it. This is no problem because the irregulars still look and sound like the regulars, and with respect to this tense, you still know it's the present perfect because of **haber**.

The Subjunctive

Don't give up now! Just two more verb modes (not tenses—the subjunctive is a different *manner* of speaking) and you'll be done with all this verb business (give or take a couple of special topics).

The Present Subjunctive

The present subjunctive is used in sentences that have *two distinct subjects* in *two different clauses*, generally (on this test, at least) in four situations.

1. When a *desire* or *wish* is involved

   *Quiero que **comas** los vegetales.*
   I want you **to eat** the vegetables.

   *Deseamos que Uds. nos **sigan**.*
   We want you (pl.) **to follow** us.

2. When *emotion* is involved

   *Me alegro que **haga** buen tiempo hoy.*
   I am happy that the weather **is** nice today.

   *Te enoja que tu novio nunca te **escuche**.*
   It makes you angry that your boyfriend never **listens** to you.

3. When *doubt* is involved

   *Ellos no creen que **digamos** la verdad.*
   They don't believe that **we are telling** the truth.

   *Jorge duda que su equipo **vaya** a ganar el campeonato.*
   Jorge doubts that his team **is going** to win the championship.

A Quick Note
If the subject is expressing a personal desire, then the infinitive is used. For example, **Quiero** *ser* médico. *I want to be a doctor.*

4. When an *impersonal, subjective commentary* is made

*Es ridículo que yo no **pueda** encontrar mis llaves.*
It's ridiculous that I **can't** find my keys.

*Es importante que los estudiantes **estudien** mucho.*
It's important that students **study** a lot.

The subjunctive is formed by taking the **yo** form of the present tense, dropping the -**o**, and adding the appropriate ending.

	trabajar	vender	escribir
yo	trabaje	venda	escriba
tú (fam.)	trabajes	vendas	escribas
él/ella/Ud.	trabaje	venda	escriba
nosotros/nosotras	trabajemos	vendamos	escribamos
vosotros/vosotras (fam.)	trabajéis	vendáis	escribáis
ellos/ellas/Uds.	trabajen	vendan	escriban

The present subjunctive is easy to spot because certain key phrases tell you that a wish or desire, emotion, doubt, or an impersonal commentary is being made.

Commands

Commands also use the present subjunctive form because they are an obvious attempt to tell someone what to do. The one exception is the **tú** form of affirmative commands, which uses the same ending as the present indicative of **él/ella/Ud.** Let's look at the differences.

Ud.	tú
¡Trabaje con su hijo! Work with your son!	*¡Trabaja con tu padre!* Work with your father!
¡Escriba la carta! Write the letter!	*¡Escribe la carta!* Write the letter!
¡No trabaje con su hijo! Don't work with your son!	*¡No trabajes con tu padre!* Don't work with your dad!
¡No escriba la carta! Don't write the letter!	*¡No escribas la carta!* Don't write the letter!

The Imperfect Subjunctive

Here we are, at the final verb form you'll need to know for the Spanish Subject Test! This version of the subjunctive is used with the same expressions as the present subjunctive (wish or desire, emotion, doubt, impersonal commentaries), but it's used in the *past tense.*

> *Quería que **comieras** los vegetales.*
> I wanted you **to eat** the vegetables.

> *Me alegré que **hiciera** buen tiempo ayer.*
> I was happy that the weather **was** nice yesterday.

> *No creían que **dijéramos** la verdad.*
> They didn't believe that **we told** the truth.

> *Era ridículo que yo **no pudiera** encontrar mis llaves.*
> It was ridiculous that **I couldn't** find my keys.

One very important thing to notice in the previous examples is that because the *expression* is in the past, you use the imperfect subjunctive. If you're looking at a sentence that you know takes the subjunctive, but you're not sure whether it's present or imperfect, focus on the expression. If the expression is in the present, use the present subjunctive. If the expression is in the past, use the imperfect subjunctive.

The imperfect subjunctive is also always used after the expression **como si**, which means *as if.* This expression is used to describe hypothetical situations:

> *El habla como si lo **supiera** todo.*
> He speaks as if **he knew** it all.

> *Gastamos dinero como si **fuéramos** millonarios.*
> We spend money as if **we were** millionaires.

The imperfect subjunctive is formed by taking the **ellos/ellas/Uds.** form of the preterite (which you already know, right?), removing the **-on,** and adding the correct ending.

	trabajar	vender	escribir
yo	trabajara	vendiera	escribiera
tú (fam.)	trabajaras	vendieras	escribieras
él/ella/Uds.	trabajara	vendiera	escribiera
nosotros/nosotras	trabajáramos	vendiéramos	escribiéramos
vosotros/vosotras (fam.)	trabajarais	vendierais	escribierais
ellos/ellas/Uds.	trabajaran	vendieran	escribieran

Verbs that are in the imperfect subjunctive shouldn't be too tough to spot when they show up in the answer choices. The imperfect subjunctive has completely different endings than the preterite. It's not a compound tense, so you won't confuse it with the present perfect. The stems are different from the present subjunctive, so distinguishing between those two shouldn't be a problem.

Special Topics

Irregular Verbs

Good news: you've made it through the major verb conjugations. Not-so-good-news: there are exceptions. Some verbs don't follow a set pattern, and, well, you just have to be able to recognize them. Here are some of the most common ones, in all their irregular glory. Please note that the six columns are for the verb conjugations in the **yo, tú, él/ella/Ud., nosotros/nosotras, vosotros/vosotras,** and **ellos/ellas/Uds.** forms, respectively.

dar (to give)						
present:	doy	das	da	damos	dais	dan
preterite:	di	diste	dio	dimos	disteis	dieron
imperfect:	daba	dabas	daba	dábamos	dabais	daban
future:	daré	darás	dará	daremos	daréis	darán
conditional:	daría	darías	daría	daríamos	daríais	darían
present subjunctive:	dé	des	dé	demos	deis	den
imperfect subjunctive:	diera	dieras	diera	diéramos	dierais	dieran

decir (to say, to tell)						
present:	digo	dices	dice	decimos	decís	dicen
preterite:	dije	dijiste	dijo	dijimos	dijisteis	dijeron
imperfect:	decía	decías	decía	decíamos	decíais	decían
future:	diré	dirás	dirá	diremos	diréis	dirán
conditional:	diría	dirías	diría	diríamos	diríais	dirían
present subjunctive:	diga	digas	diga	digamos	digáis	digan
imperfect subjunctive:	dijera	dijeras	dijera	dijéramos	dijerais	dijeran

estar (to be)

present:	estoy	estás	está	estamos	estáis	están
preterite:	estuve	estuviste	estuvo	estuvimos	estuvisteis	estuvieron
imperfect:	estaba	estabas	estaba	estábamos	estabais	estaban
future:	estaré	estarás	estará	estaremos	estaréis	estarán
conditional:	estaría	estarías	estaría	estaríamos	estaríais	estarían
present subjunctive:	esté	estés	esté	estemos	estéis	estén
imperfect subjunctive:	estuviera	estuvieras	estuviera	estuviéramos	estuvierais	estuvieran

haber (to have)

present:	he	has	ha	hemos	habéis	han
preterite:	hube	hubiste	hubo	hubimos	hubisteis	hubieron
imperfect:	había	habías	había	habíamos	habíais	habían
future:	habré	habrás	habrá	habremos	habréis	habrán
conditional:	habría	habrías	habría	habríamos	habríais	habrían
present subjunctive:	haya	hayas	haya	hayamos	hayáis	hayan
imperfect subjunctive:	hubiera	hubieras	hubiera	hubiéramos	hubierais	hubieran

hacer (to make, to do)

present:	hago	haces	hace	hacemos	hacéis	hacen
preterite:	hice	hiciste	hizo	hicimos	hicisteis	hicieron
imperfect:	hacía	hacías	hacía	hacíamos	hacíais	hacían
future:	haré	harás	hará	haremos	haréis	harán
conditional:	haría	harías	haría	haríamos	haríais	harían
present subjunctive:	haga	hagas	haga	hagamos	hagáis	hagan
imperfect subjunctive:	hiciera	hicieras	hiciera	hiciéramos	hicierais	hicieran

ir (to go)

present:	voy	vas	va	vamos	vais	van
preterite:	fui	fuiste	fue	fuimos	fuisteis	fueron
imperfect:	iba	ibas	iba	íbamos	ibais	iban
future:	iré	irás	irá	iremos	iréis	irán
conditional:	iría	irías	iría	iríamos	iríais	irían
present subjunctive:	vaya	vayas	vaya	vayamos	vayáis	vayan
imperfect subjunctive:	fuera	fueras	fuera	fuéramos	fuerais	fueran

poder (to be able)

present:	puedo	puedes	puede	podemos	podéis	pueden
preterite:	pude	pudiste	pudo	pudimos	pudisteis	pudieron
imperfect:	podía	podías	podía	podíamos	podíais	podían
future:	podré	podrás	podrá	podremos	podréis	podrán
conditional:	podría	podrías	podría	podríamos	podríais	podrían
present subjunctive:	pueda	puedas	pueda	podamos	podáis	puedan
imperfect subjunctive:	pudiera	pudieras	pudiera	pudiéramos	pudierais	pudieran

poner (to put, to place)

present:	pongo	pones	pone	ponemos	ponéis	ponen
preterite:	puse	pusiste	puso	pusimos	pusisteis	pusieron
imperfect:	ponía	ponías	ponía	poníamos	poníais	ponían
future:	pondré	pondrás	pondrá	pondremos	pondréis	pondrán
conditional:	pondría	pondrías	pondría	pondríamos	pondríais	pondrían
present subjunctive:	ponga	pongas	ponga	pongamos	pongáis	pongan
imperfect subjunctive:	pusiera	pusieras	pusiera	pusiéramos	pusierais	pusieran

querer (to want, to wish, to love)

present:	quiero	quieres	quiere	queremos	queréis	quieren
preterite:	quise	quisiste	quiso	quisimos	quisisteis	quisieron
imperfect:	quería	querías	quería	queríamos	queríais	querían
future:	querré	querrás	querrá	querremos	querréis	querrán
conditional:	querría	querrías	querría	querríamos	querríais	querrían
present subjunctive:	quiera	quieras	quiera	queramos	queráis	quieran
imperfect subjunctive:	quisiera	quisieras	quisiera	quisiéramos	quisierais	quisieran

saber (to know)

present:	sé	sabes	sabe	sabemos	sabéis	saben
preterite:	supe	supiste	supo	supimos	supisteis	supieron
imperfect:	sabía	sabías	sabía	sabíamos	sabíais	sabían
future:	sabré	sabrás	sabrá	sabremos	sabréis	sabrán
conditional:	sabría	sabrías	sabría	sabríamos	sabríais	sabrían
present subjunctive:	sepa	sepas	sepa	sepamos	sepáis	sepan
imperfect subjunctive:	supiera	supieras	supiera	supiéramos	supierais	supieran

salir (to leave)

present:	salgo	sales	sale	salimos	salís	salen
preterite:	salí	saliste	salió	salimos	salisteis	salieron
imperfect:	salía	salías	salía	salíamos	salíais	salían
future:	saldré	saldrás	saldrá	saldremos	saldréis	saldrán
conditional:	saldría	saldrías	saldría	saldríamos	saldríais	saldrían
present subjunctive:	salga	salgas	salga	salgamos	salgáis	salgan
imperfect subjunctive:	saliera	salieras	saliera	saliéramos	salierais	salieran

ser (to be)

present:	soy	eres	es	somos	sois	son
preterite:	fui	fuiste	fue	fuimos	fuisteis	fueron
imperfect:	era	eras	era	éramos	erais	eran
future:	seré	serás	será	seremos	seréis	serán
conditional:	sería	serías	sería	seríamos	seríais	serían
present subjunctive:	sea	seas	sea	seamos	seáis	sean
imperfect subjunctive:	fuera	fueras	fuera	fuéramos	fuerais	fueran

tener (to have)						
present:	tengo	tienes	tiene	tenemos	tenéis	tienen
preterite:	tuve	tuviste	tuvo	tuvimos	tuvisteis	tuvieron
imperfect:	tenía	tenías	tenía	teníamos	teníais	tenían
future:	tendré	tendrás	tendrá	tendremos	tendréis	tendrán
conditional:	tendría	tendrías	tendría	tendríamos	tendríais	tendrían
present subjunctive:	tenga	tengas	tenga	tengamos	tengáis	tengan
imperfect subjunctive:	tuviera	tuvieras	tuviera	tuviéramos	tuvierais	tuvieran

ver (to see)						
present:	veo	ves	ve	vemos	veis	ven
preterite:	vi	viste	vio	vimos	visteis	vieron
imperfect:	veía	veías	veía	veíamos	veíais	veían
future:	veré	verás	verá	veremos	veréis	verán
conditional:	vería	verías	vería	veríamos	veríais	verían
present subjunctive:	vea	veas	vea	veamos	veáis	vean
imperfect subjunctive:	viera	vieras	viera	viéramos	vierais	vieran

venir (to come)						
present:	vengo	vienes	viene	venimos	venís	vienen
preterite:	vine	viniste	vino	vinimos	vinisteis	vinieron
imperfect:	venía	venías	venía	veníamos	veníais	venían
future:	vendré	vendrás	vendrá	vendremos	vendréis	vendrán
conditional:	vendría	vendrías	vendría	vendríamos	vendríais	vendrían
present subjunctive:	venga	vengas	venga	vengamos	vengáis	vengan
imperfect subjunctive:	viniera	vinieras	viniera	viniéramos	vinierais	vinieran

Ser vs. *Estar*

The verbs **ser** and **estar** both mean *to be* when translated into English. You might wonder, "Why is it necessary to have two verbs that mean exactly the same thing?" Good question. The answer is that in Spanish, unlike in English, there is a distinction between temporary states of being (for example, *I am hungry*) and fixed, or permanent states of being (for example, *I am Cuban*). Although this difference seems pretty simple and easy to follow, there are some cases when it isn't so clear. Consider the following examples:

> *El señor González _____ mi doctor.*
> *Cynthia _____ mi novia.*

Would you use **ser** or **estar** in these two sentences? After all, Cynthia may or may not be your girlfriend forever, and the same goes for Mr. González's status as your doctor. You might get rid of both of them tomorrow (or one of them might get rid of you). So which verb do you use?

In both cases, the answer is **ser** because in both cases there is no *foreseeable* end to the relationships described. In other words, even though they may change, nothing in either sentence gives any reason to think they will. So whether you and Cynthia go on to marry or she dumps you tomorrow, you would be correct if you used **ser**. When in doubt, ask yourself, "Does this action/condition have a definite end in the near or immediate future?" If so, use **estar**. Otherwise, use **ser**.

Ser vs. *Estar* Drill

Fill in the blanks with the correct form of **ser** or **estar**. Answers and explanations can be found in Part IV.

1. Pablo _____ muy cansado.
2. El automóvil _____ descompuesto.
3. No puedo salir de casa esta noche porque _____ castigado.
4. Mi hermano _____ muy gracioso.
5. Mis profesores _____ demasiado serios.
6. Ayer salí sin abrigo, por eso hoy _____ enfermo.
7. Los tacos que mi madre cocina _____ ricos.
8. ¡No podemos empezar! Todavía no _____ listos.
9. _____ muy enojado con el tipo que me insultó.

Don't assume that certain adjectives (like **enfermo**, for example) necessarily take **estar**. If you're saying someone is sick as in *ill,* then **estar** is appropriate. If you're saying that someone is sick, as in, *a sickly person,* then **ser** is correct.

Unfortunately, usage is not the only tough thing about these two verbs. They are both irregular, and they come up all over this exam. Spend a little time reviewing the conjugations of **ser** and **estar** before you move on.

estar	
present:	estoy, estás, está, estamos, estáis, están
preterite:	estuve, estuviste, estuvo, estuvimos, estuvisteis, estuvieron
present subjunctive:	esté, estés, esté, estemos, estéis, estén
imperfect subjunctive:	estuviera, estuvieras, estuviera, estuviéramos, estuvierais, estuvieran

The other tenses of **estar** follow the regular patterns for **-ar** verbs.

ser	
present:	soy, eres, es, somos, sois, son
imperfect:	era, eras, era, éramos, erais, eran
preterite:	fui, fuiste, fue, fuimos, fuisteis, fueron
present subjunctive:	sea, seas, sea, seamos, seáis, sean
imperfect subjunctive:	fuera, fueras, fuera, fuéramos, fuerais, fueran

The other tenses of **ser** follow the regular patterns for **-er** verbs.

Conocer vs. Saber

We hate to do this to you again, but there is another pair of verbs that have the same English translation but are used differently in Spanish. However, don't worry; these two have (for the most part) regular conjugations, and knowing when to use them is really very straightforward.

The words **conocer** and **saber** both mean *to know*. In Spanish, knowing a person or a thing (basically, a noun) is different from knowing a piece of information. Compare the uses of **conocer** and **saber** in these sentences.

¿Sabes cuánto cuesta la camisa?
Do you know how much the shirt costs?

¿Conoces a mi primo?
Do you know my cousin?

Sabemos que Pelé era un gran futbolista.
We know that Pelé was a great soccer player.

Conocemos a Pelé.
We know Pelé.

When what's known is a person, place, or thing, use **conocer**. It's like the English, *to be acquainted with*. When what's known is a fact, use **saber**. The same basic rule holds for questions.

> *¿Saben a qué hora llega el presidente?*
> **Do you know** at what time the president arrives?

> *¿Conocen al presidente?*
> **Do you know** the president?

Now that you know how they're used, take a look at their conjugations.

conocer	
present:	conozco, conoces, conoce, conocemos, conocéis, conocen
present subjunctive:	conozca, conozcas, conozca, conozcamos, conozcáis, conozcan

The other tenses of **conocer** follow the regular **-er** pattern.

saber	
present:	sé, sabes, sabe, sabemos, sabéis, saben
preterite:	supe, supiste, supo, supimos, supisteis, supieron
future:	sabré, sabrás, sabrá, sabremos, sabréis, sabrán
conditional:	sabría, sabrías, sabría, sabríamos, sabríais, sabrían
present subjunctive:	sepa, sepas, sepa, sepamos, sepáis, sepan
imperfect subjunctive:	supiera, supieras, supiera, supiéramos, supierais, supieran

The other tense of **saber** (the conditional) follows the regular **-er** pattern.

Conocer vs. *Saber* Drill

Fill in the blanks with the correct forms of **conocer** or **saber**. Answers and explanations can be found in Part IV.

1. ¡Él _____ cocinar muy bien!
2. ¿ _____ el libro que ganó el premio? (tú)
3. Las mujeres _____ bailar como si fueran profesionales.
4. ¿Es verdad que _____ a Oprah? (ustedes)
5. Es importante _____ nadar.
6. No _____ cómo voy a ganar la carrera.
7. ¿Cómo puede ser que tú no _____ la casa donde viviste?
8. Los dos abogados no se _____ el uno al otro porque nunca han trabajado juntos.
9. _____ que vamos a divertirnos en el circo esta noche. (yo)

TIPS FOR VERB QUESTIONS

- The tenses you need to know are the present, past, future, conditional, imperfect, and present perfect. You also need to know the subjunctive mode (both present and imperfect) and commands. In terms of memorizing and reviewing them, we think the best approach is to lump them together in the following way:

Present Tenses	Past Tenses	Future Tenses	Subjunctive Mode/ Commands
Present	Preterite	Future	Present
	Imperfect	Conditional	Imperfect
	Present Perfect		Commands

By thinking in terms of these groupings, you'll find that eliminating answer choices is a snap once you've determined the tense of the sentence. That is your first step on a question that tests your knowledge of verb tenses: Determine the tense of the sentence (or at least whether it's a past, present, or future tense), and eliminate.

Verb Clues

Often, superficial characteristics like accent marks indicate what tense a verb is in. Clues like these can guide you to the right answer.

- When memorizing the uses of the different tenses, focus on clues that point to one tense or another.
- There are certain expressions (wish or desire, emotion, doubt, and impersonal commentaries) that tell you to use the subjunctive, and whether the expression is in the present or the past tells you which subjunctive form to use.
- To distinguish between future and conditional, focus on the certainty of the event's occurrence.
- The three past tenses are differentiated by the end (or lack of an end) of the action and when that end occurred (if it occurred).
  - o If the action had a clear beginning and ending in the past, use the regular **past tense**.
  - o If the action was a continuous action in the past, use the **imperfect tense**.
  - o If the action began in the past and is continuing into the present, or ended very close to the present, use the **present perfect tense**.
- Recognizing the different tenses shouldn't be too tough if you focus on superficial characteristics.
- The only compound tenses you're likely to see are the perfect tenses.
- Certain tenses have accents; others do not.
- As far as pacing goes, apply the same principles that we outlined for pronoun questions: Spend time on the easy questions and use POE and guess on the tougher ones. Keep in mind that, although the simple tenses (present, past, and future) do appear, they are seldom the correct answers. Why? Because they're the first tenses you learned, they're the easiest to use, and the test writers know that you'll guess them if you're stuck on a question. They don't want you to guess successfully, so they frequently use these basic tenses as trap answers. Careful now, we didn't say that the basic tenses were never right.

PREPOSITIONS

Prepositions are those little words that show the relationship between two other words. In English, they include words like *to*, *from*, *at*, *for*, and *about*. In Spanish, they include words such as **a**, **de**, and **sobre**.

Part of what you need to know about prepositions is what the different ones mean. That's the easy part. The other thing you need to know is how and when to use them. You need to know which verbs and expressions take prepositions and which prepositions they take. This isn't too difficult to learn either, but it can be tricky.

The good news is that only a very small number of prepositions appears on the test, so you can limit your study to those instead of trying to master every preposition in existence. Yes, it is much like doing vocabulary work, but once again, you probably already know many of these expressions, so it shouldn't be too terrible.

Remember in the beginning of this chapter, when you learned that some of the sentence completion part of the exam would focus on grammar instead of meaning, and that because of this, answer choices on a given question would mean roughly the same thing? Well, we lied (sort of), but that's actually a good thing. What we're getting at is that, with preposition questions (unlike verb and pronoun questions), the answers sometimes do have different meanings, and this makes POE a lot easier.

Common Prepositions and Their Uses
a: to; at

> ¿*Vamos a la obra de teatro esta noche?*   *Llegamos a las cinco.*
> Are we going to the play tonight?   We arrive at 5:00.

de: of; from

> *Son las gafas de mi hermano.*   *Soy de Argentina.*
> Those are my brother's glasses.   I am from Argentina.
> (Literally, *the glasses of my brother.*)

con: with

> *Me gusta mucho el arroz con pollo.*
> I like chicken with rice a lot.

sobre: on; about; over

> *La chaqueta está sobre la mesa.*
> The jacket is on the table.

> *La conferencia es sobre la prevención del SIDA.*
> The conference is about AIDS prevention.

Prepositions
Prepositions are often idiomatic, which means there are no rules for their use—they just sort of sound right. It's the same reasoning behind our use of prepositions in English.

Los Yankees triunfaron sobre los Padres en la serie mundial.
The Yankees triumphed over the Padres in the World Series.

antes de: before

Antes de salir quiero ponerme un sombrero.
Before leaving I want to put on a hat.

después de: after

Después de la cena me gusta caminar un poco.
After dinner I like to walk a little.

en: in

Regresan en una hora.
They'll be back in an hour.

Alguien está en el baño.
Someone is in the bathroom.

entre: between

La carnicería está entre la pescadería y el cine.
The butcher shop is between the fish store and the movie theater.

La conferencia duró entre dos y tres horas.
The conference lasted between two and three hours.

durante: during

Durante el verano me gusta nadar todos los días.
During the summer I like to swim every day.

desde: since; from

He tomado vitaminas desde mi juventud.
I've been taking vitamins since my childhood.

Se pueden ver las montañas desde aquí.
The mountains can be seen from here.

Para vs. *Por*

The prepositions **para** and **por** both mean *for* (as well as other things, depending on context), but they are used for different situations, and so they tend to cause a bit of confusion.

There are some pretty clear-cut rules as to when you use **para** and when you use **por,** which is fortunate because they both tend to sound fine even when they're being used incorrectly. Try to avoid using your ear when choosing between these two.

When to Use *Para*

The following are examples of the most common situations in which **para** is used. Instead of memorizing some stuffy rule, we suggest that you get a feel for what types of situations imply the use of **para**, so that when you see those situations come up on your test, you'll recognize them.

The preposition **para** expresses the idea of *destination*, but in a very broad sense.

Destination in time

> *El helado es **para** mañana.*
> The ice cream is for tomorrow. (Tomorrow is the ice cream's destination.)

Destination in space

> *Me voy **para** el mercado.*
> I'm leaving for the market. (The market is my destination.)

Destination of purpose

> *Compraste un regalo **para** Luis.*
> You bought a gift for Luis. (Luis is the destination of your purchase.)

> *Estudiamos **para** sacar buenas notas.*
> We study to get good grades. (Good grades are the destination of our studies.)

Destination of work

> *Trabajo **para** IBM.*
> I work for IBM. (IBM is the destination of my work.)

When to Use *Para*
Para is almost always used to indicate some sort of destination—time, space, a person, an event, a resulting action (an effect)—so be on the lookout for this type of meaning in the sentence.

The following two uses of *para* do not indicate a sense of destination:

To express opinion

> *Para mí, el lunes es el día más largo de la semana.*
> For me, Monday is the longest day of the week.

To qualify or offer a point of reference

> *Para ser un niño joven, tiene muchísimo talento.*
> For a young boy, he has a lot of talent.

When to Use *Por*

Chances are, if you're not discussing destination in any way, shape, or form, or the other two uses of **para**, then you need to use **por**. If this general rule isn't enough for you, though, study the following possibilities and you should have all the bases covered.

To express a period of time

> *Trabajé con mi amigo por quince años.*
> I worked with my friend for 15 years.

To express how you got somewhere (by)

> *Fuimos a Italia por barco.*
> We went to Italy by boat.

> *Pasamos por esa tienda ayer cuando salimos del pueblo.*
> We passed by that store yesterday when we left the town.

To describe a trade (in exchange for)

> *Te cambiaré mi automóvil por el tuyo este fin de semana.*
> I'll trade you my car for yours this weekend.

To lay blame or identify cause (by)

> *Todos los barcos fueron destruidos por la tormenta.*
> All the boats were destroyed by the storm.

To identify gain or motive (for; as a substitute for)

> *Ella hace todo lo posible por su hermana.*
> She does everything possible for her sister.

> *Cuando Arsenio está enfermo, su madre trabaja por él.*
> When Arsenio is ill, his mother works (as a substitute) for him.

Ir a and *Acabar de*

Ir a is used to describe what the future will bring, or, in other words, what is going to happen. The expression is formed by combining the appropriate form of **ir** in the present tense (subject and verb must agree) with the preposition **a**.

*Mañana **vamos a** comprar el árbol de Navidad.*
Tomorrow we are going to buy the Christmas tree.

*¿**Vas a** ir a la escuela aun si te sientes mal?*
You're going to go to school even if you feel ill?

Acabar de is the Spanish equivalent of *to have just,* and is used to talk about what has just happened. It is formed just like **ir a**, with the appropriate form of **acabar** in the present tense followed by **de**.

***Acabo de** terminar de cocinar el pavo.*
I have just finished cooking the turkey.

*Ellos **acaban de** regresar del mercado.*
They have just returned from the supermarket.

Other Prepositions to Remember

Following is a list of other prepositions and prepositional phrases you should know. Notice that many of these are merely adverbs with a **de** tacked on to the end to make them prepositions.

a la derecha de	to the right of
a la izquierda de	to the left of
al lado de	next to
alrededor de	around, surrounding
cerca de	near
debajo de	underneath
delante de	in front of
dentro de	inside of
detrás de	behind
en medio de	in the middle of
encima de	above, on top of
enfrente de	in front of
frente a	in front of
fuera de	outside of
hacia	toward
hasta	until
lejos de	far from
tras	behind

First Pass
Easy vocabulary; present, past, and future tenses; simple prepositions that you've already memorized

Second Pass
Not so obvious vocabulary; subjunctive and conditional tenses; harder prepositions

Third Pass
More obscure vocabulary and grammar; the imperfect subjunctive tense

Whew! That was a long chapter. Don't forget to give your brain a study break: grab a snack, take a walk, watch goat videos, etc.

TIPS FOR PREPOSITION QUESTIONS

- Much of your work with prepositions boils down to memorization: which expressions and verbs go with which prepositions, and so on. Keep in mind that preposition questions account for less than 15 percent of the questions on the sentence completion section of your exam, so don't drive yourself nuts trying to memorize every single one you've ever seen.

- You should concentrate on the boldface examples at the beginning of the preposition section because those are the most common. Once you're comfortable with them, the subsequent list should be a snap because many of those expressions are merely adverbs with **a** or **de** after them.

- Some verbs take prepositions all the time, some never do, and others sometimes do. This isn't as confusing as it may sound, though, because prepositions (or lack thereof) change the meanings of verbs. Consider the following:

  Voy a tratar ------- despertarme más temprano.

  (A) a
  (B) de
  (C) con
  (D) sin

  Which one of these goes with **tratar**? Well actually, each of them does, depending on what you are trying to say. In this case you want to say *try to,* so **de** is the appropriate preposition. **Tratar con** means *to deal with,* and **tratar sin** means *to try/treat without,* while **tratar a** doesn't mean anything unless a person is mentioned afterward, in which case it means *to treat.* None of them makes sense in this sentence. The moral of the story is to not try to memorize which verbs go with which prepositions; instead, concentrate on meaning.

- Just like you did with the vocabulary list, scan the prepositional phrase list and check off the expressions with which you are comfortable and which you are certain you'll remember on the day of the exam. You may want to review them briefly as you approach the date of the test, but for now focus your efforts on the ones with which you have trouble.

Drill 1: Pronouns

Answers and explanations can be found in Part IV.

1. Si él puede hacerlo solo, yo no ------- tengo que ayudar.

   (A) la
   (B) lo
   (C) le
   (D) los

2. Pedimos asientos cerca de una ventana, pero ------- dieron estos.

   (A) nos
   (B) les
   (C) nuestros
   (D) me

3. Cuando sus estudiantes se portan mal, la profesora ------- castiga.

   (A) las
   (B) los
   (C) les
   (D) le

4. ¿Son ------- aquellos guantes que están sobre la butaca?

   (A) mío
   (B) mía
   (C) míos
   (D) mías

5. Para tu cumpleaños ------- daré un caballo nuevo.

   (A) le
   (B) te
   (C) a ti
   (D) me

6. ¿ ------- es tu cantante favorito?

   (A) Quién
   (B) Cuál
   (C) Quiénes
   (D) Qué

7. ¿ ------- prefieres? ¿El azul o el rojo?

   (A) Qué
   (B) Cuál
   (C) Cuáles
   (D) Ese

Drill 2: Verbs

Answers and explanations can be found in Part IV.

1. Cuando tenga dinero, te ------- un automóvil de lujo.

    (A) compraré
    (B) compré
    (C) compraría
    (D) compraste

2. Quiero que ------- la tarea antes de acostarte.

    (A) hiciste
    (B) hace
    (C) haga
    (D) hagas

3. Yo no ------- a la mama de mi amiga.

    (A) conoció
    (B) conoces
    (C) conozco
    (D) conozcas

4. Si tuvieran tiempo, ------- pasar el tiempo relajándose.

    (A) quieren
    (B) querían
    (C) quieran
    (D) querrían

5. ¿ ------- tú el numero de teléfono de la estación de trenes?

    (A) Sabes
    (B) Sabré
    (C) Sabrán
    (D) Sé

6. Carlos ------- mucho tiempo estudiando la biología últimamente.

    (A) pasó
    (B) pasaría
    (C) pasaba
    (D) ha pasado

Drill 3: Prepositions

Answers and explanations can be found in Part IV.

1. Quiero llegar a la fiesta antes ------- María.

   (A) de
   (B) de que
   (C) a
   (D) sin

2. La cafetería esta ------- la biblioteca.

   (A) alrededor de
   (B) en frente de
   (C) por abajo de
   (D) sobre

3. Mi escuela esta ------- la estación de autobús.

   (A) lejos de
   (B) por
   (C) dentro de
   (D) encima de

4. ------- un poco de suerte, ¡no va a llover el día del casamiento!

   (A) A mas de
   (B) Por
   (C) Para
   (D) Con

5. La próxima semana ellos van ------- tocar aquí.

   (A) a
   (B) de
   (C) con
   (D) por

6. No me gusta ver las películas de horror ------- la noche.

   (A) tras de
   (B) sobre
   (C) en
   (D) durante

7. Me voy en excursión a Italia ------- poder aprender el italiano mas rápido.

   (A) por
   (B) en
   (C) para
   (D) a

Summary

o Pronouns are commonly tested on the exam. You should be familiar with the various types (subject, direct object, indirect object, possessive, prepositional, reflexive, demonstrative) and know how and when to use them.

o There are a number of verb tenses and modes you should know (though you don't have to know all of them). The ones with which you should be familiar are present, past (preterite, imperfect, and present perfect), future, conditional, subjunctive (present and imperfect), and command.

o Prepositions are also tested, though to a lesser extent than pronouns and verbs. You simply have to know certain expressions and the prepositions they use.

o You can do a lot of POE based on grammar. Use the grammar rules that apply to the context of the sentence to eliminate choices that aren't possible. You don't need to understand all of the words in the sentence to do this effectively.

Chapter 5
Paragraph
Completion

Paragraph completion is the second section of the SAT Subject Test in Spanish. The section is designed to test vocabulary and grammar within the context of an entire paragraph. In this chapter, we focus on strategies for effectively handling this question type.

PARAGRAPH COMPLETION BASICS

In this chapter we take a look at the paragraph completion questions that appear in Part B of the Spanish Subject Test and Part B of the reading section of the Spanish with Listening Subject Test. To simplify things, we simply refer to this section of each respective exam as Part B.

If you've made it this far, you've completed the review of all the grammar and vocabulary that's likely to appear on your Spanish Subject Test. We won't be presenting any more new material (although it would probably be wise to continue reviewing anything that gave you trouble up to now). Just as you did in the last chapter, the first thing you should do is memorize the directions.

Part B

Directions: In each of the following passages, there are numbered blanks indicating that words or phrases have been omitted. For each numbered blank, four completions are provided. First read through the entire paragraph. Then, for each numbered blank, choose the completion that is most appropriate given the context of the entire paragraph and fill in the corresponding oval on the answer sheet.

Part B is a lot like sentence completions (Part A). You're given two to four (most likely three) brief paragraphs (roughly five to seven sentences each) with several words or phrases replaced by blanks. Your job is to fill in the blanks with the answers that are appropriate based on either meaning or grammar. How do you know whether it's a "meaning" blank or a "grammar" blank? If it's a grammar blank the answers all have the same (or very similar) meanings and you have to choose based on form or verb tense. Sound familiar? It should, because it's the same as in Part A. The meaning blank answers have different meanings, only one of which makes sense in the context of the passage. These questions are just like those in Part A.

So What's the Difference Between Parts A and B?

In Part A, if a sentence makes no sense you just skip it and go on to the next one—no sweat. In Part B, missing a sentence is a little more important, because it can make understanding the overall passage difficult. You don't need to get every single word, but getting at least the main idea of each of the sentences is definitely helpful.

As we mentioned earlier, you've already covered the material necessary to answer the questions in Part B. The vocabulary is all you need for the meaning questions, and the grammar (especially verb tenses) is all you need for the grammar questions. This does not mean you're ready to do drills! First, you need to learn the best way to approach the section.

PACING

Because the passages in Part B have different degrees of difficulty but are in no particular order, you first have to decide on the order in which to attack these questions. As in Part A, you want to start with the easiest questions and finish up with the toughest ones. In Part B this decision will be more involved and more important because if you choose a really tough passage first, you will probably waste time and throw off your pacing for the remainder of the section. We're not trying to make it sound like life or death. We're just saying that by taking on these passages in a certain order, you can make the section easier for yourself. You're eventually going to do all three, but you're going to do them in the order that you like.

Your decision should be based on a brief skim of the first couple of sentences of the passage. If these sentences make sense, and the writing style strikes you as being pretty clear, go for it. If you have any doubt as to whether the passage is going to be easy, go on and see what the next one looks like. Your goal is to find the easiest one and to do it first.

Don't base your decision on subject matter. The fact that a passage pertains to something you know about or find interesting doesn't mean much if you can't understand every third word. You're not going to be asked about content (that comes later in the reading comprehension section); you'll only be asked to fill in blanks. You don't need to retain the information in the passage, but you need to understand the tense that it's in and the meanings of individual sentences. In other words, topic doesn't count for much. Base your decision on writing style and vocabulary.

Do What Works for You
Answer Part B questions in the order that you like, not the order that the test writers like!

USING THE THREE-PASS SYSTEM

Once you've decided which passage you're doing first, what next? Answer the questions in the order that's best for you. Keep in mind that you will want to do all three passes within one passage *before* you move on to the next one.

First Pass

Read through the questions in part B in order to gain context of the passage, but also remember to find the easiest questions on a first pass. Starting at the beginning will give you some sense of the passage's structure, which will probably make you more comfortable with it overall. However, on your first pass through the passage you should skip any question that looks like it *might* be tricky. Attempt only the very easiest questions on this pass. Focus on the ones for which you know the answer without using POE or anything but your knowledge of grammar or vocabulary.

Three Is the Magic Number
Before you move on to the next passage, do all THREE passes.

Second Pass

On the second pass start using POE to eliminate and guess. Go back to the questions you left blank on the first pass and see whether there are any answers that can be eliminated. Look to cancel wrong answers. You'll find (just as you did on Part A) that some of the wrong answers are pretty obviously wrong, and in some cases you'll be able to eliminate all but one—the right one.

Don't be intimidated if the sentence that contains a certain blank is difficult. You can determine what tense a verb is even if you don't understand the verb's meaning! The same goes for pronouns and prepositions. If you are pretty sure that the noun being replaced is feminine, then eliminate the masculine pronouns. You have to be aggressive if you want to take advantage of POE.

As far as *meaning* blanks are concerned, use the same technique you learned for second-pass questions on Part A. Piece together any words in the sentence that you know to try to get some sense of the context. See whether any of the answers are completely wacky based on that context. This is where a general knowledge of the passage can be helpful to you as well. Any sentence in the passage, even if you don't understand it, has to make sense within the topic and intention of the overall passage. In other words, there won't be a sentence about the history of the toothpick in a passage about military strategies. Answer choices that seem to stray off the subject of the overall passage are probably wrong.

Third Pass

As before, spend very little time, eliminate what you can based on whatever clues the sentence or passage has to offer, use your ear if necessary, and guess. The same rule about not guessing holds here as well. If you can't eliminate any of the answers, then it's fine to leave a question blank.

It's very easy to fall into a mindset that says you're not done with a passage until every single question is answered, but this is a dangerous mindset. Just because a passage is easy overall doesn't mean every single question in that passage is a gift.

Don't waste your time: If you've answered all the questions that you can and there are still one or two blanks, move on to the next passage. You may never have to, but you should be prepared to skip some questions.

Let's apply some of what we've learned so far to maximize your performance.

Drill 1: Paragraph Completion

Answers and explanations can be found in Part IV.

Part B

Directions: In each of the following passages, there are numbered blanks indicating that words or phrases have been omitted. For each numbered blank, four completions are provided. First, read through the entire paragraph. Then, for each numbered blank, choose the completion that is most appropriate given the context of the entire paragraph and fill in the corresponding oval on the answer sheet.

Emma dejó caer el papel. Su primera (1) fue de malestar en el vientre y en las rodillas; luego, de ciega culpa, de irrealidad, de frío, de (2) ; luego, quiso ya (3) en el día siguiente. Acto seguido comprendió que ese deseo era inútil porque (4) muerte de su padre era lo único que (5) en el mundo, y (6) sucediendo sin fin. Recogió el papel y se fue a su cuarto. Furtivamente lo (7) en un cajón, como si de algún modo ya (8) los hechos ulteriores.

1. (A) tiempo
   (B) vista
   (C) puesto
   (D) impresión

2. (A) juventud
   (B) temor
   (C) alegría
   (D) hambre

3. (A) estar
   (B) ser
   (C) estaré
   (D) ir

4. (A) lo
   (B) el
   (C) la
   (D) las

5. (A) entraba
   (B) crecía
   (C) había terminado
   (D) había sucedido

6. (A) seguiría
   (B) pararía
   (C) cambiaría
   (D) sentiría

7. (A) sacó
   (B) guardó
   (C) encontró
   (D) quitó

8. (A) sabe
   (B) sabía
   (C) supiera
   (D) sabría

Drill 2: Paragraph Completion

Answers and explanations can be found in Part IV.

Part B

Directions: In each of the following passages, there are numbered blanks indicating that words or phrases have been omitted. For each numbered blank, four completions are provided. First read through the entire paragraph. Then, for each numbered blank, choose the completion that is most appropriate given the context of the entire paragraph and fill in the corresponding oval on the answer sheet.

Después __(1)__ haber mandado dos expediciones a explorar la costa de México, el gobernador de Cuba __(2)__ otra expedición bajo el mando de Hernán Cortés en 1519. En las tres expediciones __(3)__ parte un soldado que se __(4)__ Bernal Díaz del Castillo. __(5)__ soldado, cuando ya era casi un viejo y __(6)__ retirado en Guatemala, __(7)__ sus recuerdos de las guerras mexicanas, que forman la mejor narración __(8)__ la conquista de México y que se titula "Historia verdadera de la conquista de la Nueva España."

La expedición de Cortés constaba de once navíos que __(9)__ poco más de seiscientos hombres y dieciséis __(10)__ . Cuando Cortés estaba listo __(11)__ salir, el gobernador trató de quitarle el mando, pero él decidió hacerse a la mar.

1. (A) que
   (B) de
   (C) a
   (D) por

2. (A) puso fin a
   (B) ensayó
   (C) preguntó
   (D) organizó

3. (A) hizo
   (B) dio
   (C) dejó
   (D) tomó

4. (A) llamó
   (B) llama
   (C) llamaba
   (D) había llamado

5. (A) Este
   (B) Esa
   (C) Un
   (D) La

6. (A) paraba
   (B) pensaba
   (C) oía
   (D) vivía

7. (A) escribió
   (B) corrió
   (C) perdió
   (D) pidió

8. (A) encima de
   (B) junto a
   (C) sobre
   (D) en vez de

9. (A) llevaba
    (B) llevaron
    (C) llevaban
    (D) llevan

10. (A) automóviles
    (B) aviones
    (C) caballos
    (D) guantes

11. (A) por
    (B) para
    (C) en
    (D) de

Drill 3: Paragraph Completion

Answers and explanations can be found in Part IV.

Part B

Directions: In each of the following passages, there are numbered blanks indicating that words or phrases have been omitted. For each numbered blank, four completions are provided. First read through the entire paragraph. Then, for each numbered blank, choose the completion that is most appropriate given the context of the entire paragraph and fill in the corresponding oval on the answer sheet.

Pero hoy, en esta mañana fría, en que tenemos más prisa que nunca, la niña y yo (1) de largo delante de la fila tentadora de autos parados. Por (2) vez en la vida vamos al colegio...Al colegio, le digo, no (3) ir en taxi. Hay que correr un poco por las calles, hay que tomar el metro, hay que (4) luego, a un sitio determinado, para un autobús...Es que yo he escogido un colegio muy (5) para mi niña, esa es la verdad; un colegio que (6) mucho, pero está muy lejos...Sin embargo, yo no estoy impaciente hoy, ni (7) , y la niña lo sabe. Es ella ahora la que inicia una caricia tímida con su manita (8) la mía; y por primera vez me doy cuenta de que su mano de cuatro años es (9) mi mano grande: tan decidida, tan suave, tan nerviosa como la mía.

1. (A) pasamos
   (B) entramos
   (C) dábamos
   (D) pagamos

2. (A) ninguna
   (B) primera
   (C) siempre
   (D) costumbre

3. (A) se engaña
   (B) conocemos
   (C) se puede
   (D) sobran

4. (A) dormir
   (B) tocar
   (C) jugar
   (D) caminar

5. (A) cerrado
   (B) lejano
   (C) oscuro
   (D) difícil

6. (A) me gusta
   (B) odio
   (C) no conozco
   (D) dudamos

7. (A) vieja
   (B) alta
   (C) cansada
   (D) fresca

8. (A) dentro de
   (B) fuera de
   (C) cerca de
   (D) sin

9. (A) diferente a
   (B) igual a
   (C) cerca de
   (D) encima de

Summary

o The paragraph completion section is a combination of the two that preceded it: no new information, just a different format. You should be warmed up and confident going in.

o The majority of the blanks test you on meaning. If the answer to a meaning question isn't immediately apparent, leave it for the second pass. When you come back to it, try to determine the context of the sentence and use POE.

o Determine the best order for you to attack the passages—this could make the difference between smooth sailing and a really big headache, so don't rush your decision.

o Use the Three-Pass System: Do easy questions first, do tougher questions second, eliminate what you can, and guess on whatever's left.

o Don't feel as if you have to answer every single question on a given passage. Sometimes your best move is to go on to the next passage.

Chapter 6
Reading
Comprehension

Reading comprehension questions on the SAT Subject Test in Spanish are designed to evaluate your ability to read and interpret information from a piece of text. In this chapter, we focus on strategies for how most effectively to approach this section.

THE LAST SECTION: READING COMPREHENSION

Welcome to Part C. Reading comprehension is the last section of the exam, as well as the section that many consider the most difficult. Even so, there are two good reasons you shouldn't worry.

1. You can afford to leave some (or most) of the reading comprehension questions blank and still come away with a great score.
2. By carefully choosing the right question(s) to leave blank, you can make the reading comprehension section much easier.

As usual, the first step is to get acquainted with the directions.

Part C

Directions: Read the following texts carefully for comprehension. Each passage is followed by a number of questions or incomplete statements. Select the answer or completion that is best according to the text and fill in the corresponding oval on the answer sheet.

This section contains approximately 28 questions on the Spanish Subject Test and approximately 17 questions on the Spanish with Listening Subject Test. On each test you will have between four and nine passages or pictures (ads, announcements, menus, and so on) that contain between one and six questions each. The longer passages are usually followed by more questions. We'll get into how to choose which passages to do later, but for now realize that the length of the passage tells you nothing about its difficulty, so don't assume that the long passages are the hardest ones.

Remember...
The length of a passage tells you NOTHING about its level of difficulty!

One of the nicest things about Reading Comprehension is that you may not need to do very much of it to get your desired score. In terms of the big picture, you should *not* rush through Parts A and B to get to Part C. In fact, because the other two parts lend themselves to POE and educated guessing, you should do the opposite. Take your time on the questions that are the most "technique-able" (Parts A and B), and if this means leaving some of the reading questions blank, that's just fine. It's not that this section is impossible, but rather that it lends itself less to shortcuts and techniques.

HOW TO CRACK THIS SECTION

The first and most important step in beating the reading comprehension section is choosing which passages to do and which to skip. Luckily, you've already had an introduction to this type of decision in Part B of the exam. The idea is very similar: If the writing style is familiar (that is, you can understand it without a major struggle) and there isn't too much tough vocabulary, then you're probably looking at a passage that you should do. This doesn't mean that you must know every single word in the passage. In fact, most passages will have some words (if only one or two) that you don't know. If you can understand the gist of the overall passage, then you can answer the questions that follow.

Basic Approach for Reading Comprehension Questions

- Preview the questions to see what you're going to be asked.
- Read the passage for the big picture.
- Read a question.
- Go back to the passage to find your answer.
- Use Process of Elimination.

How to Read the Spanish Passages

Over the years, you've probably developed a reading style that includes a pace at which you're comfortable, a certain level of attention to detail, and so on. When you know that someone is going to ask you questions about what you've read, you usually change your reading style to match the situation. You read much more slowly, and you pay much more attention to detail than you would if you were reading, say, an article in a newspaper. The reason for this is simple: You assume that by reading more slowly and carefully you will better understand what you've read. Makes sense, right? Unfortunately, even though it seems logical, this approach can be disastrous when it comes to the reading comprehension section of the SAT Subject Test in Spanish.

What usually happens when you try to read ultra-slowly and virtually memorize the passage is that you finish reading with no sense of what the overall passage is about. You may have picked up a few details, but who knows whether those particular details will be asked? What eventually happens is that on each question (or at least on most questions) you end up going back to the passage and rereading what you just read a minute ago. This approach is time consuming and can be very frustrating. There is a better way.

Looking back at the passage to find the answer to a question is a very good idea. The problem is the initial time wasted in trying to memorize the passage in one reading. If you're going to refer to the passage anyway, then what's the point? It doesn't make sense to read the passage slowly and carefully twice, especially if one of those two readings doesn't help you answer questions.

Reading Comprehension or Treasure Hunt?

We know that the instructions to the section ask you to read for comprehension, but we also know that those same instructions are written by the people who wrote the rest of the exam. Is this section really about reading for comprehension, or is it about answering a few silly questions? Not surprisingly, it's about answering a few silly questions. Treat the reading comprehension section like a treasure hunt; the answers to the individual questions are hidden somewhere in the passage, and your job is to find them. Here's the best way to approach that task.

Get the Big Picture

Think Big
Don't get hung up on individual words. If you don't know what a word means, try to see whether you can still get the gist of the sentence. You can spend a lot of time trying to decipher words you may not even need to know.

You've already seen that it's a waste of time to try to memorize the passage in one reading. Instead of trying to memorize the entire thing, your first reading should be dedicated to finding the *topic* and the *structure* of the passage. This means that if you finish your initial read and you know what the overall passage is about, as well as the main point of each paragraph, you've read the passage properly. Don't worry about facts or details (such as names, dates, places, titles, and the like). Focus on what the whole passage is about and, in a very general sense, what each paragraph is about. A good way to test whether you've done this well is to try to summarize the passage in a few words (no more than five or six) in English, and summarize the content of each paragraph in even fewer words. If you can do both of these things, you've definitely got a handle on the big picture, and that's going to be a big help in answering the questions.

There's no way we can tell you how long this initial reading should take, simply because everyone reads at a different pace. We can tell you that if you're stopping to try to decipher the meaning of every unknown word you come across, or if you're reading the same difficult sentence again and again, you've missed the boat. Focus on ideas, not on specific words or facts.

> The point of reading this way is not to enable you to answer *all* the questions without looking back (we wish it were that easy too). The point is to give you a sense of where things are, so that when a question asks about a particular fact or detail, even if you don't know the answer, you *will* know where to look to find it.

Sample Passage

Let's take a look at a sample passage. Read through it with the aim of getting the general idea and don't get caught up with unfamiliar vocabulary. Jot down just a few words summing up each paragraph and a few words summing up the entire passage.

Mark It Up
While you're reading for the big picture, you may notice a word or phrase that stands out. Flag it. It may help when searching for the answer to a question.

España, con una superficie aproximada de dos veces la del estado de Wyoming y una población de una vez y media la de California, está situada en el suroeste de Europa, separada de Francia por las montañas de los Pirineos y de África por el estrecho de Gibraltar. Su territorio está formado por la Península Ibérica, excepto Portugal, y los archipiélagos de las Islas Baleares, en el Mar Mediterráneo, y de las Islas Canarias, en el Océano Atlántico. Además, ejerce su soberanía en dos ciudades de la costa de Marruecos, Ceuta y Melilla, y no la ejerce en un peñón, en su propia costa, el Peñón de Gibraltar, que es una posesión inglesa.

El español, aunque tiene muy poco que ver en muchos aspectos con los habitantes del norte y centro de Europa, es europeo y latino, por su historia y por su cultura. A pesar de todo, algunos dicen que "África empieza en los Pirineos," y esto se debe a la influencia que tuvieron los casi ocho siglos de dominación árabe.

Para mucha gente, los españoles son personas pequeñas, morenas, que pasan la vida cantando y bailando flamenco, muy aficionadas a las corridas de toros, que les gusta mucho perder el tiempo hablando de todo en las tertulias y en la sobremesa y que cuando están contentas, que es muy frecuente, dicen "olé." Esta idea es tan falsa como la que en España mucha gente también tiene de los estadounidenses. El estadounidense típico, para ellos, es el *cowboy*, el gangster o el artista de Hollywood. Sin embargo hay españoles en los Estados Unidos que han visto, oído, cantado y bailado más flamenco aquí que en España, lo mismo que la mayoría de los estadounidenses no tienen nada que ver ni con un *cowboy*, ni con un gangster ni con Hollywood.

Here are some possible summaries.

Paragraph 1: "borders of Spain" or "Spain's territory"
Paragraph 2: "Spain's not like much of Europe"
Paragraph 3: "there are misconceptions about Spanish people"

So what's the passage about? Spain and Spanish people.

Do you see how brief and simple we're being? And there is certainly some tricky vocabulary at the end of the first paragraph—**ejerce, soberanía, peñón**—but you don't need to know what all the words mean to understand the big picture.

Use POE
Wrong answers to reading comprehension questions are often lousy. Be sure to use POE to eliminate those bogus answers.

Using Process of Elimination

One of the biggest problems students have with this section is that they don't like any of the answer choices to some questions. It's as if on some questions the test writers forgot to include the correct answer in the choices. The key to using Process of Elimination on Part C is that, when you're stuck, you should forget about finding the right answer and concentrate on finding wrong answers. If you read all four choices and none of them looks good to you, don't panic. A couple of them probably look pretty bad to you, and those are just as helpful as the choices that look good. Eliminate the ones you know are wrong, and choose from whatever is left.

We know this is a bitter pill to swallow, but the fact is that sometimes you'll end up choosing an answer that you don't like or even understand. That's fine, though, because if you're sure three of the choices are incorrect, then you must have confidence that the last one is the right one. Too often students shy away from answer choices they don't understand or don't like. Unfortunately, this section has little to do with what you like or understand. You're looking for the answer that will earn you a point, not the one with which you agree.

Yes!
You can skip entire passages! After all, if you don't understand the passage, it's unlikely that you'll answer most of the questions correctly. Do the easy passages first and skip the one that's most difficult for you.

TYPES OF PASSAGES AND QUESTIONS

In the reading comprehension section you will primarily encounter passages based on fictional events or characters, history, or current events. However, you may also come across ads, announcements, or menus. Although subject matter has nothing to do with the difficulty of a passage, you may find that a certain passage, because it's about a familiar topic, has vocabulary that you understand. Don't take this on faith. Read a few sentences to make sure.

Although there are some general questions (main idea, or what the passage is about), most of the questions ask you about more specific things that come from a particular place in the passage. You should deal with these two types of questions separately.

There will be times when the correct answer is so obvious that it practically jumps off the page at you. Some of the time, however, it won't be quite that easy. If you know how to work through the answer choices efficiently, and understand how they might try to stump you, even the most difficult questions can be mastered.

General Questions

Once you've finished your first reading, you should go right to the questions to see whether there are any general ones. Why? Because if you know the topic and structure of the passage, you can answer any general question without having to scrutinize every detail of the passage. The general questions (when they appear) ask you for general ideas. Here are some examples of general questions.

¿De qué se trata este artículo?
What is this passage about?

¿Quién narra este pasaje?
Who narrates this passage?

Very few of these appear on a given reading section, but when they do appear they are very easy. You may want to do the general questions first if you choose a passage that contains any.

Trap Answers

On *general questions,* the main thing to be on the lookout for is an answer that is too specific. Unlike the answer to a specific question, the answer to a general question can't be located in one particular place in the passage. This makes sense because the answer to a general question should encompass the contents of the entire passage.

The test writers try to trip you up by providing answers that come from one part of the passage or another, but are not general enough to be correct. These answers tend to be very tempting because they are in the passage that you just finished reading and you recognize them. If the answer to a general question is about a specific part of the passage, it's probably a trap.

Try to answer this general question about the passage you just read.

General Question Traps
Be wary of answers that are too specific when you're tackling general questions.

---

1. El pasaje se trata de

   (A) la geografía de España y los españoles
   (B) los vaqueros estadounidenses
   (C) la influencia de la dominación árabe en España
   (D) la manera en cual los españoles verdaderamente viven

Here's How to Crack It

Since this is a question about the entire passage, our correct answer should sum up all three paragraphs. Any choice that refers to just one part of the passage, even if accurate, cannot be the correct answer.

Choice (A), which translates to *the geography of Spain and the Spaniards,* seems to be right on the money. Notice that each of the other choices—(B) *American cowboys,* (C) *the influence of Arab domination in Spain,* and (D) *the way in which Spaniards truly live*—refers to only a small part of the passage. Therefore, (A) is the answer.

———————○———————

Specific Questions

The vast majority of reading comprehension questions require you to refer to the passage to find the answer. This is why it's so important to get a sense of structure before you attempt to answer them. Otherwise you waste lots of time looking for the part of the passage from which the question came. The approach to these questions is simple.

On *specific questions*, the most important thing to remember is that the correct answer must come from the passage. We know this seems obvious, but one of the test writers' favorite tricks on these questions is to provide answers that are reasonable and logical and gel with the contents of the passage, but are not *in* the passage. For this reason it's important that you stick to what you read when you refer to the passage. Don't think in terms of what the author might think or what you think. What's on the page in black and white is all you should go by to answer these questions.

Basic Approach for Specific Questions

- Read the question.
- Locate the source of the question by using guide words (we'll discuss guide words soon).
- Carefully read the section of the passage from where the question came.
- Go to the answers and find the one that matches what you just read.
- When you don't understand what you just read, use POE to eliminate wrong answers.

Correct answers to specific questions won't be exact quotes from the passage, but they'll be pretty darn close. They'll have the same exact meaning as the corresponding words in the passage, with maybe a couple of the words moved around or changed so that it looks a little different. In other words, the right answers are *close* paraphrases of the passage.

How Do You Know Where to Look?

Any specific question will have a word or words that tell you what the question is about. We call these *guide words* because they guide you to the place in the passage where the question originated. If you can determine the subject of the question, you should be able to tell (at least roughly) from where it came. Now all that's left is for you to read the source of the question carefully, and match it up with one of your answer choices.

Here is the passage we saw on page 151. Take a crack at some specific questions.

España, con una superficie aproximada de dos veces la del estado de Wyoming y una población de una vez y media la de California, está situada en el suroeste de Europa, separada de Francia por las montañas de los Pirineos y de África por el estrecho de Gibraltar. Su territorio está formado por la Península Ibérica, excepto Portugal, y los archipiélagos de las Islas Baleares, en el Mar Mediterráneo, y de las Islas Canarias, en el Océano Atlántico. Además, ejerce su soberanía en dos ciudades de la costa de Marruecos, Ceuta y Melilla, y no la ejerce en un peñón, en su propia costa, el Peñón de Gibraltar, que es una posesión inglesa.

El español, aunque tiene muy poco que ver en muchos aspectos con los habitantes del norte y centro de Europa, es europeo y latino, por su historia y por su cultura. A pesar de todo, algunos dicen que "África empieza en los Pirineos," y esto se debe a la influencia que tuvieron los casi ocho siglos de dominación árabe.

Para mucha gente, los españoles son personas pequeñas, morenas, que pasan la vida cantando y bailando flamenco, muy aficionadas a las corridas de toros, que les gusta mucho perder el tiempo hablando de todo en las tertulias y en la sobremesa y que cuando están contentas, que es muy frecuente, dicen: "olé." Esta idea es tan falsa como la que en España mucha gente también tiene de los estadounidenses. El estadounidense típico, para ellos, es el *cowboy*, el gangster o el artista de Hollywood. Sin embargo, hay españoles en los Estados Unidos que han visto, oído, cantado y bailado más flamenco aquí que en España, lo mismo que la mayoría de los estadounidenses no tienen nada que ver ni con un *cowboy*, ni con un gangster ni con Hollywood.

1. La superficie de España es de un tamaño

   (A) dos veces el tamaño de los Estados Unidos
   (B) dos veces el tamaño del estado de Wyoming
   (C) una vez y media el tamaño de California
   (D) igual al tamaño del Peñón de Gibraltar

A Handy Guide
They're called "guide words" for a reason! Look for key words that point to where you should look in the passage for the right answer.

Here's How to Crack It

The answer to this question is located in the beginning of the first paragraph. The guide word **superficie** is located only in that one area of the passage, and that's a big hint that they took the question from this area. The passage says that Spain is **dos veces la del estado de Wyoming** *(twice the size of Wyoming)*. Choice (B) is therefore the answer.

Try this next question.

2. ¿Cuál de los siguientes no es territorio español?

   (A) Las Islas Canarias
   (B) El Peñón de Gibraltar
   (C) Las Islas Baleares
   (D) Ceuta y Melilla

Here's How to Crack It

Notice that here we are looking for the choice that is not a part of Spain. The answer choices are mentioned in the first paragraph, so that's where you go to find the answer. Pay close attention to the wording of the last two sentences of the paragraph:

Su territorio está formado por la Península Ibérica, excepto Portugal, y los archipiélagos de las Islas Baleares, en el Mar Mediterráneo, y de las Islas Canarias, en el Océano Atlántico. Además, ejerce su soberanía en dos ciudades de la costa de Marruecos, Ceuta y Melilla, y no la ejerce en un peñón, en su propia costa, el Peñón de Gibraltar, que es una posesión inglesa.

Choices (A), (C), and (D) are cited as parts of Spain. Choice (B) is therefore the answer.

And finally, see whether you can answer the question on the next page.

3. ¿Cuál de las ideas siguientes tienen muchos estadounidenses de los españoles?

   (A) Que los españoles típicos son gangsters
   (B) Que las mujeres españolas están enamoradas de los *cowboys* estadounidenses
   (C) Que todos pasan el día bailando y cantando flamenco
   (D) Que quisieran vivir en Hollywood

Here's How to Crack It

This question doesn't have guide words, but since the entire third paragraph is about the mutual stereotypes to which Americans and Spaniards subscribe, it isn't too tough to locate the source of the question. You *do* have to read the question carefully, though, because some of the wrong answers are misconceptions Spaniards have about Americans—(A), (B), and (D) are variations on this idea—and the question asks for the opposite. Therefore, (C) is correct.

Question Order

The specific questions are best done in the order in which they appear (although you want to follow the golden rule of skipping any question that looks really difficult). This is because the order of the questions usually follows the progression of the passage—early questions come from the beginning of the passage, and subsequent questions come from the middle of the passage. Something that you read in the early part of the passage can sometimes help on a later question.

As with Part B of the exam, there is a tendency on Part C to feel as if you're not done until you've answered every question that pertains to a certain passage. You're done whenever you want to be done. In other words, if you've done all the questions that you understand and to which you can easily find answers, then move on to the next passage and see whether you can find a couple of easy questions there. To a certain extent, reading comprehension will be as easy (or as difficult) as you want to make it.

Drill 1: Reading Comprehension

Answers and explanations can be found in Part IV.

Part C

Directions: Read the following texts carefully for comprehension. Each passage is followed by a number of questions or incomplete statements. Select the answer or completion that is best according to the text and fill in the corresponding oval on the answer sheet.

Al pasar ante una granja, un perro mordió a mi amigo. Entramos a ver al granjero y le preguntamos si era suyo el perro. El granjero, para evitarse complicaciones, dijo que no era suyo.

—Entonces —dijo mi amigo— présteme una hoz para cortarle la cabeza, pues debo llevarla al Instituto para que la analicen.

En aquel momento apareció la hija del granjero y le pidió a su padre que no permitiera que le cortáramos la cabeza al perro.

—Si es suyo el perro —dijo mi amigo— enséñeme el certificado de vacunación antirrábica.

El hombre entró en la granja, y tardó largo rato en salir. Mientras tanto, el perro se acercó y mi amigo dijo:

—No me gusta el aspecto de este animal.

En efecto, babeaba y los ojos parecían arderle en las órbitas. Incluso andaba dificultosamente.

—Hace unos días —dijo la joven— le atropelló una bicicleta.

El granjero nos dijo que no encontraba el certificado de vacunación.

—Debo haberlo perdido.

—La vida de un hombre puede estar en juego —intervine yo. Díganos, con toda sinceridad, si el perro está vacunado o no.

El hombre bajó la cabeza y murmuró:

—Está sano.

1. ¿Qué les pasó a los tipos cuando pasaron por la granja?

   (A) A uno de ellos lo mordió un perro.
   (B) Un granjero les pidió direcciones.
   (C) Se evitaron complicaciones.
   (D) Perdieron su perro.

2. ¿Por qué el granjero les dijo que el perro no era suyo?

   (A) No sabía de quien era el perro.
   (B) No conocía a los tipos que vinieron a la puerta.
   (C) No quería echarse la culpa de lo que había hecho el perro.
   (D) No le gustaban los perros.

3. ¿Qué le pidió su hija al granjero?

   (A) Que sacara el perro a caminar
   (B) Que llevara el perro al médico
   (C) Que le diera comida al perro
   (D) Que no dejara que los hombres hirieran al perro

4. ¿Qué le pidieron los tipos al granjero?

   (A) Dinero para pagar un médico
   (B) El certificado de vacunación antirrábica
   (C) Un teléfono para llamar a la policía
   (D) Prueba de que verdaderamente era granjero

5. ¿Cómo parecía el perro del granjero?

   (A) Sano y de buen humor
   (B) Enfermo, como si tuviera rabia
   (C) Joven y lleno de energía
   (D) Serio y pensativo

6. ¿Qué razón dio la niña por la manera en que el perro se portaba?

   (A) Tuvo un accidente con una bicicleta.
   (B) Acaba de recibir su vacuna antirrábica.
   (C) Es un perro muy feroz.
   (D) Tenía mucha hambre.

7. En fin, ¿qué les dice el granjero a los tipos?

   (A) Que vayan al hospital
   (B) Que adopten un perro
   (C) Que se vayan de la granja ahora mismo
   (D) Que el perro no tiene ninguna enfermedad

Drill 2: Reading Comprehension

Answers and explanations can be found in Part IV.

Part C

Directions: Read the following texts carefully for comprehension. Each passage is followed by a number of questions or incomplete statements. Select the answer or completion that is best according to the text and fill in the corresponding oval on the answer sheet.

Hotel Marybel

Mendoza * Córdoba * Buenos Aires

¡Especiales del mes para todos! ¡Reserven con dos semanas de anticipación y reciban un descuento de 10%! Llamen al 239-7155—24 horas al día, 7 días a la semana.

Dirección de Internet: www.hotelmarybel.ar

Aire acondicionado en todos los cuartos, cafetería, bar, conexión de Internet gratis en los cuartos. No se pierdan esta oferta. Oferta vence a fin de mes.

---

1. ¿Este anuncio es para qué tipo de servicio?

   (A) Un hotel
   (B) Una cadena de hoteles
   (C) Una tienda
   (D) Un aviso de servicios gratis

2. ¿Cuánto dura esta oferta?

   (A) Un día
   (B) Un mes
   (C) Un año
   (D) Dos semanas

3. ¿Qué tiene que hacer el cliente para recibir un descuento?

   (A) Reservar dos semanas antes de llegar
   (B) Reservar por dos semanas
   (C) Reservar con un mes de anticipación
   (D) Reservar con una semana de anticipación

4. ¿Cuál de los siguientes servicios ofrece el hotel?

   (A) Aire acondicionado solamente en los cuartos grandes
   (B) Piscina de natación
   (C) Internet en el bar
   (D) Un lugar para comer

Drill 3: Reading Comprehension

Answers and explanations can be found in Part IV.

Part C

Directions: Read the following texts carefully for comprehension. Each passage is followed by a number of questions or incomplete statements. Select the answer or completion that is best according to the text and fill in the corresponding oval on the answer sheet.

Para los arqueólogos y los historiadores, la civilización maya es, sin duda ninguna, la que alcanzó un mayor nivel de desarrollo entre todas las civilizaciones que existían antes de la llegada de Colón. Aunque todavía hay muchos secretos que no se han descifrado con relación a los mayas, parece que esta civilización empezó varios siglos antes del nacimiento de Cristo. Sin embargo, se sabe que los mayas abandonaron los grandes centros ceremoniales en el siglo X de nuestra era.

Los primeros templos que construyeron son de forma de pirámide de cuatro lados con una gran escalinata. Sobre la pirámide hay un edificio de un piso normalmente, y en algunos casos de dos, y en él podemos ver relieves de arcilla y esculturas de madera y piedra caliza. Las figuras son siempre de perfil y en ellas se puede apreciar los adornos y joyas que usaban. En la clasificación que se ha hecho de las épocas de esta civilización, se llama preclásica a la época primera, que se desarrolla en Guatemala y Honduras, y que según los arqueólogos duró hasta el fin del siglo III de nuestra era.

1. ¿Qué piensan los arqueólogos y los historiadores de la civilización maya?

   (A) Que era una civilización muy avanzada.
   (B) Que los maya escribieron libros magníficos.
   (C) Que conocieron a Colón.
   (D) Que tenían muchos secretos.

2. ¿Cuándo empezó la civilización maya?

   (A) En el siglo X de nuestra era
   (B) Inmediatamente antes de la llegada de Colón
   (C) Bastante más temprano que el nacimiento de Cristo
   (D) Varios siglos después del nacimiento de Cristo

3. ¿Cómo parecían los primeros templos de los mayas?

   (A) Eran edificios muy bajos.
   (B) Eran hechos de madera y piedra caliza.
   (C) Eran pirámides de cuatro lados.
   (D) Eran casas corrientes, como las que tenemos hoy.

4. ¿Qué se puede decir de las esculturas que hicieron los mayas?

   (A) Tenían escalinatas grandes.
   (B) Dan información sobre las joyas y adornos que usaban.
   (C) Cuesta mucho comprarlas.
   (D) Se puede encontrarlas en los museos famosos.

5. ¿Aproximadamente cuanto tiempo pasó desde que terminó la era preclásica hasta que los mayas abandonaron sus centros ceremoniales?

   (A) Cien años
   (B) Tres siglos
   (C) Siete siglos
   (D) Diez siglos

6. El pasaje se trata de

   (A) la civilización y arquitectura maya
   (B) la influencia de Cristo sobre la civilización maya
   (C) las diferencias entre nuestra civilización y la de los mayas
   (D) los adornos y las joyas que usaban los mayas

Drill 4: Reading Comprehension

Answers and explanations can be found in Part IV.

Part C

Directions: Read the following texts carefully for comprehension. Each passage is followed by a number of questions or incomplete statements. Select the answer or completion that is best according to the text and fill in the corresponding oval on the answer sheet.

En 1992, se cumplieron cinco siglos ya del encuentro de Europa con América. Fue poco después de la medianoche del 11 al 12 de octubre de 1492, cuando Rodrigo de Triana, un tripulante de la carabela *La Niña*, la cual se había adelantado a *La Santa María*, donde iba Colón, dio el grito de "¡Tierra! ¡Tierra!" El lugar estaba muy cercano a la Florida, era una pequeña isla llamada Guanahaní que Colón llamó San Salvador y que pertenece al archipiélago de las Lucayas, o Bahamas.

Lo que Colón encontró y describe en sus cartas a los Reyes Católicos fue mucha pobreza y gente que iba desnuda, como su madre los parió, todos jóvenes, con hermosos cuerpos, cabellos gruesos como los de los caballos y cortos, que les caían por encima de las cejas y otros largos por detrás.

Pocos días después, descubrió la costa de Cuba, que llamó Juana, por la hija de los reyes. Por entonces, Martín Alonso Pinzón, que mandaba *La Pinta*, se separó de la expedición, lo cual consideró Colón como una deserción, aunque lo disimuló por mantener la unidad de la expedición. Al cabo de unos días llegó a Haití, que llamó la Hispaniola, pero debido a los muchos bajos y arrecifes que había, *La Santa María* encalló.

1. ¿Quién fue el primero que vio tierra en la expedición?

    (A) Un tripulante que se llamaba Rodrigo de Triana
    (B) Colón
    (C) *La Niña*
    (D) Guanahaní, el mejor amigo de Colón

2. ¿Cómo era la gente que Colón encontró?

    (A) Muy pobre, pero también hermosa
    (B) Violenta y agresiva
    (C) Más inteligente que los tripulantes
    (D) Muy miedosa y confundida

3. ¿Qué descubrió Colón unos días después de que descubrió San Salvador?

    (A) El archipiélago de las Bahamas
    (B) La isla que hoy se llama Cuba
    (C) Haití
    (D) Cabellos gruesos

4. ¿Cuál fue la reacción de Colón cuando Martín Alonso Pinzón se separó de la expedición?

    (A) Se puso furioso.
    (B) Empezó a llorar.
    (C) Dio la impresión de que no sabía lo que había pasado.
    (D) Mandó otra carabela tras él.

5. ¿Cómo terminó *La Santa María*?

    (A) Regresó a España.
    (B) Se perdió y nunca la han encontrado.
    (C) Se hundió.
    (D) Embarrancó como resultado de los bajos y arrecifes.

Drill 5: Reading Comprehension

Answers and explanations can be found in Part IV.

Part C

Directions: Read the following texts carefully for comprehension. Each passage is followed by a number of questions or incomplete statements. Select the answer or completion that is best according to the text and fill in the corresponding oval on the answer sheet.

Si no fuera por el gusto exigente de los bebedores de café de Arabia Saudita, el pueblo guatemalteco de Cobán, al otro lado del mundo, estaría en problemas.

Cobán, capital de la región montañosa de Alta Verapaz, en Guatemala, es la fuente de la mayor parte del cardamomo que consume el mundo árabe: una especia dulce, picante y sumamente aromática que se emplea en la cocina de la India. De hecho, el café de cardamomo, conocido en el mundo árabe como *kahwe hal*, es considerado un símbolo de hospitalidad en todo el Medio Oriente.

En Cobán, famoso por su iglesia católica del siglo XVI y las ruinas mayas que se encuentran en los alrededores, prácticamente nadie habla árabe y ninguno de sus 125.000 habitantes pone cardamomo en el café. Sin embargo, todos conocen perfectamente la conexión que existe entre la especia y el mundo árabe. "El cardamomo es la base de nuestra economía, y Guatemala es el principal exportador del mundo."

1. ¿En qué país en particular toman el café de cardamomo?

    (A) En Guatemala
    (B) En Arabia Saudita
    (C) En la Alta Verapaz
    (D) En el Medio Oriente

2. ¿Qué es el cardamomo?

    (A) Un tipo de café raro
    (B) Una especia
    (C) Un estilo de cocinar indio
    (D) Un tipo de árbol

3. ¿Cómo sabe el cardamomo?

    (A) Picante, pero también dulce
    (B) Un poco amargo
    (C) Casi no tiene sabor
    (D) Sabe como el café colombiano

4. ¿Por qué es conocida la ciudad de Cobán?

    (A) Por el cardamomo
    (B) Por el mejor café en América del Norte
    (C) Por sus ruinas, y por su iglesia del siglo XVI
    (D) Por la comida india

5. ¿Cuál es la conexión entre el mundo árabe y Guatemala?

    (A) En Guatemala todos hablan árabe.
    (B) En los dos lugares les encanta el café de cardamomo.
    (C) Guatemala exporta mucha especia al mundo árabe.
    (D) De verdad no hay conexión entre los dos lugares.

6. ¿Cuál sería un buen título para el pasaje?

    (A) "Cobán: la ciudad en las montañas"
    (B) "La economía de Guatemala"
    (C) "Los cafés del mundo"
    (D) "Cardamomo: lo que une a Guatemala con el mundo árabe"

Summary

o   Choose the order in which you want to do the passages. Read a couple of sentences to see whether the writing style is easy to follow and the vocabulary is manageable. If so, go for it. If not, look ahead for something easier.

o   Read the passage for topic and structure only. Don't read for detail, and don't try to memorize the entire thing. The first read is for you to get a sense of the subject and the overall structure—that's all.

o   Go straight to the general questions. If you read correctly, you should be able to answer any general questions without looking back to the passage. Very few passages have general questions, so don't expect to find many.

o   Then do the specific questions in order. For these, you're going to let the guide words in the question tell you where to look in the passage. Then slowly and carefully read the area that the question comes from. Find an answer choice that basically says the same thing in slightly different language. These questions are about paraphrasing, not about comprehension.

o   Avoid specific answers on general questions, and on specific questions avoid answers that are reasonable but aren't from the passage.

o   Don't be afraid to leave blanks if there are questions that stump you. You're done with a passage whenever you've answered all the questions that you can answer. Instead of banging your head against a wall trying to do the last remaining question on a passage, go on to the next passage and find an easier question.

Part IV
Drill Answers
and
Explanations

CHAPTER 3 DRILLS

Drill 1: Process of Elimination

1. **B**   **Limpia** *(cleans)* would make **casa** *(house)* a very good guess. The other answers—**libro** *(book)*, **huesos** *(bones)*, and **lluvia** *(rain)*—are not clearly related to cleaning.

2. **D**   **Revistas** *(magazines)* would match up with **artículos interesantes** *(interesting articles)* better than it would with any of the other choices offered (**vacaciones** = *vacation*, **obras de teatro** = *plays*, **conciertos** = *concerts*).

3. **C**   This is a pretty tough one, but you can still take a good guess. **Salir** *(to go out)*, combined with the **no** that precedes it, gives you *not go out*. Are any of the answers something that might keep you from going out? Yes, **nieve** *(snow)*. None of the others really makes sense (**comida** = *food*, **dinero** = *money*, **hambre** = *hunger*).

4. **C**   **Postre** means dessert, and there is only one answer that is a dessert: **helado** *(ice cream)*. **Arroz con pollo** *(chicken with rice)*, **vitaminas** *(vitamins)*, and **agua** *(water)* are all edible, but they aren't desserts.

5. **A**   If you put **película** *(movie)* and **miedo** *(fear)* together, what do you get? A scary movie! The closest guess would be **violenta** *(violent)*. **Graciosa** means *funny*, **corta** means *short*, and **tremenda** means *huge* or *grand*.

6. **C**   **Sueño** *(sleepiness)* would be a good fit because we know that the little girl is crying. **Feliz** *(happy)* and **corriendo** *(running)* could describe a little girl, but wouldn't make a great fit with crying. **Silla** *(chair)* would not fit with any of the clues.

Drill 2: Sentence Completion

1. **B**   **Translation:** My girlfriend's shirt is made of ------- .

    (A) roses
    (B) cotton
    (C) wood
    (D) blue

    The key words in the sentence are **camisa** *(shirt)* and **hecha de** *(made of)*. **Rosas** *(roses)* and **madera** *(wood)* do not work; **azul** *(blue)* could describe the color of the shirt, but not what the shirt is made of. Therefore, **algodón** *(cotton)* is the correct answer.

2.   **B**   **Translation:** I was looking/looked for medicine for my grandfather in the ------- on the corner.

(A) bookstore
(B) pharmacy
(C) office
(D) bakery

The clue in this question is a cognate (remember those?), **medicinas**, so that even if the rest of the sentence was a blur you could tell that the answer had something to do with medicine. The answer also happens to be a cognate and is the only choice that relates to medicine.

3.   **A**   **Translation:** I was ------- because my employees arrived late for the fourth time in the same week.

(A) furious
(B) delighted
(C) very happy
(D) open

Unless you were some sort of lunatic, you'd be pretty peeved if your staff was late all the time. Although three of the answers are emotions, only one of the three is a negative emotion.

4.   **D**   **Translation:** A good way to improve your grades in school is ------- a lot.

(A) to teach
(B) to understand
(C) to speak
(D) to practice

The key words in the sentence are **mejorar** *(to improve)* and **notas** *(grades)*. **Practicar** *(to practice)* is the best answer choice. **Enseñar** *(to teach)*, **entender** *(to understand)*, and **hablar** *(to speak)* all have to do with school, but they don't quite fit in with what is described.

5.   **A**   **Translation:** He is an extremely vain man; he's always looking at himself in the ------- .

(A) mirror
(B) glass
(C) glasses
(D) self

Vanidoso is one clue in this one, but that's a pretty tough vocabulary word (add it to your list). You've also got **mirarse** *(to look at oneself)* later in the sentence to tell you that the best answer is **espejo. Cristal** means plain old *glass,* as in a window or a bottle, or fine glass.

6. **C** **Translation:** Old people have more ------- than young people because they've had more experiences.

(A) time
(B) to eat
(C) wisdom
(D) appetite

Older people probably have more of everything than young people, but what might they have more of based on experience? Not time, food, or appetite, which leaves you with only (C). We know this is a hard word, but you could have used POE to get this question right without knowing **sabiduría**.

7. **B** **Translation:** It's evident enough that Alejandro likes doing his homework; he always does it ------- .

(A) reluctantly
(B) with enthusiasm
(C) very slowly
(D) without taste

Likes implies a positive answer, such as (B). The others are all negative things, and if you could determine that much, you could eliminate them without knowing their precise meanings.

8. **D** **Translation:** Pedro ------- very happy when his child was born.

(A) changed
(B) gave himself
(C) made himself
(D) became

Choices (A) and (B) are really awkward, and although (C) seems like it could work, the verb **ponerse** is generally used to indicate a change of emotions. **Hacerse** is not.

9. **B** **Translation:** I want you to ------- notes about the lecture.

(A) take (simple present)
(B) take (present subjunctive)
(C) used to take (imperfect)
(D) took (preterite)

The phrase that starts the sentence, **Quiero que,** tells you that you should use the subjunctive. Choices (C) and (D) both refer to the past, so if you at least know you need to stay in the present tense, then you can eliminate two choices.

CHAPTER 4 DRILLS

Ser vs. *Estar* Drill

1. está
2. está
3. estoy
4. es
5. son
6. estoy
7. son
8. estamos
9. Estuve/Estaba/Estoy

Conocer vs. *Saber* Drill

1. sabe
2. Conoces
3. saben
4. conocen
5. saber
6. sé
7. conozcas (present subjunctive)
8. conocen
9. Sé

Drill 1: Pronouns

1. **B** **Translation:** If he can do it alone, I don't have to help ------- .

   (A) her
   (B) him (direct object)
   (C) him (indirect object)
   (D) them

   Whom do I have to help? *Him*, which is the direct object.

2. **A** **Translation:** We asked for seats near a window, but they gave ------- these.

   (A) **us**
   (B) them (indirect object)
   (C) ours
   (D) me

   Pedimos tells you that the subject of the sentence is **nosotros**. Since you are trying to say *they gave us these,* the correct pronoun is **nos**.

3. **B** **Translation:** When her students misbehave, the professor punishes ------- .

   (A) them (feminine, direct object)
   (B) **them (masculine, direct object)**
   (C) to them (indirect object)
   (D) to him (indirect object)

   Estudiantes is masculine and plural, so (A) and (D) are incorrect. (Remember that in Spanish the masculine pronoun is used whenever the gender of a group is mixed, even if the majority of the group is female. Also, when the gender of the people in the group is unknown [as it is in this question], the male pronoun is used.) Whom does the professor punish? *Them,* which is the direct object; therefore, (B) is the answer.

4. **C** **Translation:** Are those gloves that are on the armchair ------- ?

   (A) mine (masculine, singular)
   (B) mine (feminine, singular)
   (C) **mine (masculine, plural)**
   (D) mine (feminine, plural)

   Guantes is a masculine plural word, so the correct form of the possessive adjective is **míos**, which is (C).

5. **B** **Translation:** For your birthday, I'll give ------- a new horse.

   (A) him (indirect object)
   (B) **you**
   (C) to you
   (D) me

   The person whose birthday it is in the sentence is **tú**, so **te** is the correct indirect object pronoun. It is indirect in this case because it receives the direct object *horse.* Choice (C) is incorrect because it is an expression of emphasis that complements an indirect object pronoun. However, there is no indirect object pronoun to complement, so it cannot be right. The indirect object pronoun itself is necessary, so (B) is the best answer.

6. **A** Translation: ------- is your favorite singer?

    (A) **Who (singular)**
    (B) Which
    (C) Who (plural)
    (D) What

Since the question refers to a single person (**el cantante**), **quién** is the correct pronoun.

7. **B** Translation: ------- do you prefer? The blue one or the red one?

    (A) What
    (B) **Which (singular)**
    (C) Which (plural)
    (D) That one

In this question a choice is being given, so **cuál** is used instead of **qué**. Eliminate (A) and (D). **Cuáles** is incorrect because the choice is between two singular things. Therefore, (B) is correct.

Drill 2: Verbs

1. **A** Translation: When I have money, I ------- you a luxury car.

    (A) **will buy (yo)**
    (B) bought (yo)
    (C) would buy (yo, él/ella/Ud.)
    (D) bought (tú)

The sentence refers to something that will happen in the future, so the correct answer will be in either the future or the conditional tense. In this case, the event is certain (*I will buy you a luxury car);* therefore, the future (A) is correct.

2. **D** Translation: I want you to ------- the homework before going to bed.

    (A) did (tú)
    (B) does (él/ella/Ud.)
    (C) do (yo, él/ella/Ud., subjunctive)
    (D) **do (tú, subjunctive)**

Quiero que is one of those expressions that tells you to use the subjunctive. In this case, the expression is in the present tense, so the present subjunctive is correct. If the expression were in the past (**quería que**), you'd use the imperfect subjunctive. The reason (D) is correct is that **te** is the direct object pronoun in the sentence, so you want the **tú** form of the verb.

3.   C   **Translation:** I don't ------- my friend's mother.

(A) knew (él/ella/Ud.)

(B) know (tú)

(C) know (yo)

(D) know (tú, subjunctive)

The key to answering this correctly is to look at the subject of the sentence, *I*. Since *I* is the subject, the only choice that works is (C). Even if you don't know that the verb **conocer** means *to know,* you can get to the right answer simply by using POE!

4.   D   **Translation:** If they had (were to have) time, they ------- pass the time relaxing.

(A) want to (present)

(B) wanted to (imperfect)

(C) want to (present subjunctive)

(D) would want to (conditional)

Si tuvieran tells you to use the conditional tense (in fact, **si** often precedes use of the conditional because it introduces a condition that doesn't currently exist). The only answer that's in the conditional tense is **querrían** (D).

5.   A   **Translation:** Do you ------- the phone number for the train station?

(A) know (tú)

(B) will know (yo)

(C) will know (ellos/ellas/Uds.)

(D) know (yo)

This sentence uses the second-person singular **tú**. Choices (B), (C), and (D) are in the wrong forms and, therefore, not correct. Choice (A) is the correct answer.

6.   D   **Translation:** Carlos ------- much time studying biology lately.

(A) spent (preterite)

(B) would spend (conditional)

(C) spent (imperfect)

(D) has spent (present perfect)

Lately suggests the past tense, but a more recent past tense. Choices (A) and (C) place the action too far in the past, while (B) is not a past tense. Therefore, (D) is the answer.

Drill 3: Prepositions

1. **A**   **Translation:** I want to arrive at the party ------- María.

    (A) **before**
    (B) before (preceding a verb)
    (C) before at
    (D) before without

    In the original sentence, you're given **antes** followed by a blank, leaving it up to you to fill in the correct preposition. **Antes** tells you that you're going for *before*, so **de** is the correct preposition. Choice (B) (**de que**) is one of those expressions that needs to be followed by a verb (in the subjunctive) because the word **que** always begins a new clause. The others are way off in terms of meaning.

2. **B**   **Translation:** The coffee shop is ------- the library.

    (A) around
    (B) **in front of**
    (C) underneath
    (D) on

    We can deduce from the sentence that the coffee shop and the library are in some kind of physical relation to each other. Choice (A) does not work grammatically in this sentence, and (C) and (D) do not make logical sense. The correct answer is (B).

3. **A**   **Translation:** My school is ------- the bus station.

    (A) **far from**
    (B) for
    (C) inside of
    (D) on top of

    As in the previous question, this sentence involves a geographical relationship between two places, the school and the bus station. Choice (B), **por**, does not make sense grammatically, and (C) and (D) do not make sense logically. Therefore, (A) is correct.

4. **D**   **Translation:** ------- a little luck, it will not rain on the day of the wedding!

    (A) More than
    (B) For
    (C) For (expressing point of reference)
    (D) **With**

This sentence can be a little tricky, since **por** (B) and **para** (C) are both choices. However, we wouldn't say "For a little luck"; therefore, neither (B) nor (C) is correct. Choice (A) also does not work in this context. Choice (D), *With a little luck,* is clear and conveys the correct meaning, so it is the correct answer.

5. **A** **Translation:** Next week they are going ------- play here.

(A) **to**
(B) of
(C) with
(D) for

This one is nice and easy, no tricks or traps, and it translates straight from English. This is an example of the use of **ir a**. Notice that **ir** is conjugated to agree with the subject of the sentence (**ellos**).

6. **D** **Translation:** I don't like to see horror films ------- the night.

(A) behind
(B) on
(C) in
(D) **during**

This one is a pretty tough call between (C) and (D) because both sound fine in the blank, but one of them makes a little more sense than the other if you think carefully about the difference in meaning. Do you see films *in* (as in, *inside*) the night, or *during* the night? They're sort of close, and the exact English idiom would be *at night,* but *during* makes a bit more sense.

7. **C** **Translation:** I am going on an excursion to Italy ------- to be able to learn Italian faster.

(A) for
(B) in
(C) **for (destination)**
(D) to

Here we have **para** versus **por** again! In this case, the sentence states a clear purpose. Thus, choices (A) and (B) do not work. Choice (D) means *to,* but the the sentence states that someone is going on a trip to Italy for a specific reason. We have to use **para**, which is (C).

CHAPTER 5 DRILLS

Drill 1: Paragraph Completion

Translation:

Emma dropped the paper. Her first *impression* was of uneasiness in her belly and in her knees, then of blind guilt, of unreality, of coldness, of *fear*; then she wanted *to* already *be* in the next day. Immediately afterwards she understood that that wish was futile because *the* death of her father was the only thing that *had happened* in the world and it *would continue* happening endlessly. She picked up the paper and went to her room. Furtively, she *saved* it in a drawer, as if somehow she already *knew* the subsequent facts.

1. **D**   (A) time
             (B) sight
             (C) place
             (D) impression

In this sentence, Emma's initial reaction to a letter is being described. The word that makes sense in the blank has to be something along the lines of *reaction*. Of the choices offered, only **impresión** is even remotely similar to *reaction*.

2. **B**   (A) youth
             (B) fear
             (C) joy
             (D) hunger

At this point in the paragraph, you know from the rest of Emma's reactions that she's not feeling so well, and the blank should be filled with a word that's consistent with her bad reactions. The only really negative choice is **temor**. If you weren't sure whether she was feeling good or bad, you should have skipped this and read on—later we find out that her father has died, which tells you for sure how she's feeling.

3. **A**   **(A) to be (estar)**
             (B) to be (ser)
             (C) will be (estar)
             (D) to go

So we know Emma isn't happy. It makes sense that she'd want *to be* in the next day. That eliminates (C) and (D), but does this situation call for **estar** or **ser**? Being in the next day is a location in time, so **estar** is correct. Another approach to this question is to use the preposition that follows the blank (en). **Ir en** means *to go via* (as in **ir en avión**…), which makes no sense at all in this blank. Also, **quiso** *(wanted to)* implies the past, so **estaré** is wrong because it's in the future tense.

4. **C**   (A) it
            (B) the (masculine, singular)
            (C) the (feminine, singular)
            (D) the (feminine, plural)

Muerte is a singular feminine noun, so the proper article is **la**.

5. **D**   (A) entered
            (B) grew
            (C) had finished
            (D) had happened

It doesn't make sense that the death of her father would *enter* or *grow,* so cross out (A) and (B). **Había terminado** is possible, but if you read on, you find out that in fact Emma feels that her father's death will go on affecting her, so the best choice is (D).

6. **A**   **(A) would continue**
            (B) would stop
            (C) would change
            (D) would feel

This is sort of a continuation of the last question. The expression **sin fin** *(without end)* is a big clue because it tells you that Emma's going to be unhappy for a long time. The fact that her grief is on-going, without end, really only leaves one possible answer, and that's **seguiría** (A).

7. **B**   (A) took out
            (B) saved
            (C) found
            (D) took away

In this sentence, Emma does something with her letter. Because we know she already has it and has read it, (A) and (C) don't make sense. **Quitó** is just strange, so that leaves us with (B).

8. **C**   (A) knows
            (B) knew (imperfect indicative)
            (C) knew (imperfect subjunctive)
            (D) would know

The saving grace on this question is the **como si** that comes just before the blank, which tells you to use the imperfect subjunctive, since it is a hypothetical event. Luckily, only (C) is in the imperfect subjunctive because this would be a very tough question to do based on meaning alone.

Drill 2: Paragraph Completion

Translation:

After having led two expeditions to explore the coast of Mexico, the governor of Cuba *organized* another expedition under the command of Hernán Cortés in 1519. A soldier whose *name was* Bernal Díaz del Castillo *took* part in the three expeditions. *This* soldier, when he was almost an old man and *lived* retired in Guatemala, *wrote* his memoirs of the Mexican wars, which form the best narrative *about* the conquest of Mexico and are titled "The True History of the Conquest of New Spain."

Cortés's expedition consisted of eleven ships that *carried* little more than six hundred men and sixteen *horses*. When Cortés was ready *to* leave, the governor tried to take command from him, but he decided to set out to sea.

1. **B**   (A) that
        (B) of
        (C) to
        (D) for

The preposition that follows **después** to mean *after* is **de** (B). It's on your list of prepositions.

2. **D**   (A) put an end to
        (B) rehearsed
        (C) asked
        (D) organized

The only answers that make any kind of sense in the blank are (A) and (D). How do we know whether the governor organized or put an end to the next expedition? We know a third one happened because in the very next sentence it talks about three expeditions. Therefore, the answer is (D). By skipping a question and reading on, you can sometimes find a clue that helps answer an earlier question.

3. **D**   (A) made
        (B) gave
        (C) left
        (D) took

Although a couple of the choices are a bit awkward in the blank—namely, (A) and (C)—it really helps on this question if you know that the expression **tomar parte** means *to take part*. If you didn't know this expression, you should've eliminated (A) and (C) and guessed.

4. C (A) was named (preterite)
       (B) is named
       (C) was named (imperfect)
       (D) had been named

Here, what you want to say is *was named*. We know it's going to be some kind of past tense, but which past tense is appropriate? Well, a person's name goes on for a period of time, so it's not the regular past, which eliminates (A). Choice (D) doesn't make any sense because it implies that Castillo's name changed at some point in the past. That leaves the imperfect, which is (C).

5. A **(A) This (masculine)**
       (B) That (feminine)
       (C) A (masculine)
       (D) The (feminine)

Soldado is masculine, so (B) and (D) are immediately out. The sentence goes on to discuss the soldier in question, who was mentioned and named in the previous sentence, so what you want to say is *this soldier,* making (A) correct.

6. D (A) stopped
       (B) thought
       (C) heard
       (D) lived

Look at the adjective that follows the blank (**retirado**). Even if you've never seen this word before, you can tell what it means because it looks like the English equivalent. Does a person *stop* retired, *think* retired, or *hear* retired? None of those makes sense, so that leaves only (D).

7. A **(A) wrote**
       (B) ran
       (C) lost
       (D) asked for

The blank in this case precedes **recuerdos**, which can mean *memories*. However, in this case it means *memoirs,* which is a hint that something having to do with writing (like **escribió**) would be the correct answer, (D). If you missed **recuerdos**, the word **titula** is mentioned later on, followed by a title with quotes. Look around for clues; don't just stick to the immediate area where the blank is.

8. C (A) on top of
       (B) next to
       (C) on; about
       (D) instead of

The meaning you want for this blank is roughly *about* (C) because you're providing a preposition that describes the relationship between the memoirs and their subject (memoirs are *about* a subject). **Encima de** means *on,* like *on top of* or *above,* not *about.* **En vez de** and **junto a** don't mean anything close to *about.*

9. **C** (A) carried (singular imperfect)
   (B) carried (plural preterite)
   (C) carried (plural imperfect)
   (D) carry

The verb (**llevar**) in this blank refers back to the plural subject **navíos**, so you know the answer must be plural, which leaves (B), (C), and (D). If you back up just a bit earlier in the sentence, you notice that we're in the imperfect tense (**constaba** tells you). Even if you only knew it was some type of past tense, you could eliminate (D) (**llevan** is present tense) and guess. You'd have a fifty-fifty chance of guessing (C), which is correct.

10. **C** (A) cars
    (B) airplanes
    (C) horses
    (D) gloves

The big hint on this question is that the passage deals with events that happened in the early sixteenth century (1519), before the invention of the airplane and the automobile. *Gloves* could work, but *horses* (a means of transportation) is a much more likely answer, leaving (C) as the correct choice.

11. **B** (A) for
    (B) to
    (C) in
    (D) of

This question asks for the preposition that precedes **salir**. Although (C) and (D) do not make sense, you are still left with a decision between **para** and **por**. In this case, we are concerned with the narrator's purpose *(to leave)*, so we should use **para** (B).

Drill 3: Paragraph Completion

Translation:

But today, on this cold morning, in which we're in a bigger hurry than ever, the girl and I *passed by* the tempting line of stopped cars. For the *first* time in our lives we're going to school...I tell her, *you cannot* go to school by taxi. You have to run through the streets a bit, you have to take the subway, then you have to *walk* to a specific place for a bus.... It's true that I've chosen a school that is very *far* for my daughter, a school that *I like* very much, but it is very far away. However, I'm not impatient today, nor *tired*, and the girl knows it. It is now she who initiates a timid caress with her little hand *inside* mine, and for the first time, I realize that her four-year-old hand is *the same as* my adult one: just as resolute, just as soft, and just as nervous as mine.

1. **A** **(A) we passed**
        (B) we entered
        (C) we gave
        (D) we paid

    The preposition **delante de** *(in front of)* that comes shortly after the blank is the main clue on this question. The only verb that makes sense before this expression is (A).

2. **B** (A) none
        (B) first
        (C) always
        (D) habit

    The word **vez** *(time, occasion)* immediately follows the blank, and the only choice that forms an expression in conjunction with **vez** is (B).

3. **C** (A) tricks herself
        (B) we know
        (C) one can
        (D) have left over

    The sentence is about getting to school by taxi. Earlier in the passage it says that they passed by a row of taxis. But that only gets rid of (A) and (D) because we don't know why they passed by the taxis. Choice (B) doesn't make sense because we'd use **saber** (**sabemos**), not **conocer**, to say we know how to do something like get to school in a taxi.

4. **D** (A) to sleep
        (B) to touch
        (C) to play
        (D) to walk

    You wouldn't *sleep, touch,* or *play* to get to a bus stop. Walking (D), however, seems likely.

5. **B** (A) closed
        (B) far away
        (C) dark
        (D) difficult

    This blank describes the type of school that the mother chose for her daughter. Common sense eliminates (A) and (C). If you're stuck at this point, you just need to look forward a little to find the clue that singles out (B) as the best answer: **está muy lejos.**

6. A   (A) I like
        (B) I hate
        (C) I don't know
        (D) we doubt

The blank is followed by the expression **pero está muy lejos**. The **pero** tells you that a positive quality about the school came immediately before the expression (the word **pero** indicates a contrast, as in "strict *but* fair"). This gets rid of (B) and (D), and (C) doesn't make sense because the mother in the passage chose this school for her daughter, whom she seems to love very much. Would she send her daughter to a school she didn't know? Probably not.

7. C   (A) old
        (B) tall
        (C) tired
        (D) fresh

The verb **estar** is used in this sentence, and that eliminates **vieja** because **vieja** would be used with **ser** (ella *es* **vieja**). The same is true for **alta** (ella *es* **alta**). **Fresca** is a word you are more likely to use when referring to fruit or vegetables. Therefore, (C) is correct.

8. A   **(A) inside**
        (B) outside
        (C) close to
        (D) without

Here the daughter is making an affectionate gesture (**caricia**) toward her mom by putting her hand somewhere in relation to her mom's hand. Choices (B) and (D) suggest just the opposite, as if she were making a negative gesture. Choice (C) is fine, but it really doesn't make a lot of sense if you think about it: You wouldn't put your hand *close to* someone else's to show affection; you'd put your hand *in* someone else's. That's (A).

9. B   (A) different from
        (B) equal to; the same as
        (C) close to
        (D) on top of

The giveaway for this question follows the blank: **tan**. **Tan** by itself means *so,* but the expression **tan...como** means *as...as.* The correct answer, therefore, is (B).

CHAPTER 6 DRILLS

Drill 1: Reading Comprehension

Translation:

Upon passing in front of a farm, a dog bit my friend. We went in to see the farmer and asked him if the dog was his. The farmer, in order to avoid trouble, said it was not his.

"Then," said my friend, "lend me a sickle to cut off his head, since I should take it to the Institute so they can analyze it."

At that moment the farmer's daughter appeared and asked her father not to let us cut off the dog's head.

"If the dog is yours," said my friend, "show me the certificate of rabies vaccination."

The man went into the farmhouse and took a long time to come back out. Meanwhile, the dog approached, and my friend said:

"I don't like the way this animal looks."

Essentially, he foamed at the mouth and his eyes seemed to burn in their sockets. He also walked with difficulty.

"A few days ago," said the girl, "a bicycle hit him."

The farmer told us that he didn't find the certificate of vaccination.

"I must have lost it."

"The life of a man may be at stake," I interjected. "Tell us, in all honesty, if the dog is vaccinated or not."

The man bowed his head and murmured:

"He's healthy."

1. **A** **Translation:** What happened to the men when they passed by the farm?

   (A) **A dog bit one of them.**
   (B) A farmer asked them for directions.
   (C) They avoided complications.
   (D) They lost their dog.

The answer to this question, (A), is in the first sentence of the passage. Normally the progression of the questions follows the progression of the passage. The earlier a question is, the earlier in the passage you'll find its answer.

2. C   Translation: Why did the farmer tell them that the dog wasn't his?

    (A) He didn't know whose dog it was.
    (B) He didn't know the men who came to the door.
    (C) He didn't want to take blame for what the dog had done.
    (D) He didn't like dogs.

In the passage (third line) it says that the farmer wanted to **evitarse complicaciones** *(avoid trouble)*. The answer closest to that in meaning is (C). Some of the other answers are reasonable, but they aren't in the passage.

3. D   Translation: What did the farmer's daughter ask of him?

    (A) That he take the dog out for a walk
    (B) That he take the dog to the doctor
    (C) That he give food to the dog
    (D) That he not let the men hurt the dog

The guide word for this question is **hija.** The first place where **hija** appears (and the source of the answer) is toward the beginning of the passage, where you will find that (D) is correct.

4. B   Translation: What did the men ask the farmer for?

    (A) Money to pay for a doctor
    (B) The certificate of rabies vaccination
    (C) A telephone to call the police
    (D) Proof that he was really a farmer

The certificate of rabies vaccination, and whether the farmer has it, is the focus of most of the passage, so (B) is the answer.

5. B   Translation: How did the farmer's dog seem?

    (A) Healthy and in good humor
    (B) Sick, as if it had rabies
    (C) Youthful and full of energy
    (D) Serious and thoughtful

Most of the passage is concerned with vaccinations (**vacunas**) and whether or not to cut off the dog's head and have it inspected. You probably wouldn't do this to a happy, healthy dog (unless you're some kind of sick weirdo), so you can eliminate (A) and (C) immediately. You probably wouldn't decapitate a dog for being **serio y pensativo** either, so (D) is out. That leaves you with (B).

6. A **Translation:** What reason did the girl give for the way the dog behaved?

(A) **It had an accident with a bicycle.**
(B) It just had its rabies shot.
(C) It's a very ferocious dog.
(D) It was very hungry.

Once again, this question deals with the daughter, who is referred to as **la joven,** as well as **hija** and **niña,** in different parts of the passage. Choice (A) is the answer you're looking for.

7. D **Translation:** Finally, what does the farmer tell the men?

(A) To go to a hospital
(B) To adopt a dog
(C) That they should leave the farm right now
(D) **That the dog has no disease**

En fin is a pretty strong hint that the answer is toward the end. The correct answer is (D).

Drill 2: Reading Comprehension

Translation:

Hotel Marybel

Mendoza * Cordoba * Buenos Aires

Monthly specials for everyone! Reserve two weeks in advance and receive a 10% discount!

Call 239-7155—24 hours a day, 7 days a week.

Website: www.hotelmarybel.ar

Air conditioning in all rooms, café, bar, free Internet connection in rooms. Don't lose out on this offer. Offer expires at the end of the month.

1. B **Translation:** This announcement is for what type of service?

(A) A hotel
(B) **A chain of hotels**
(C) A store
(D) An ad for free services

At the top of the announcement, below the name of the hotel, are three cities: Mendoza, Cordoba, and Buenos Aires. This indicates that Hotel Marybel is a chain rather than one hotel. Choice (B) is the correct answer.

2. **B** **Translation:** How long does the offer last?

(A) A day
(B) A month
(C) A year
(D) Two weeks

The announcement starts off by mentioning the hotel's *monthly specials,* and at the bottom it states that the offer expires at the end of the month. Choice (B) is the correct answer.

3. **A** **Translation:** What does the client have to do in order to receive a discount?

(A) Reserve two weeks prior to arrival
(B) Reserve for two weeks
(C) Reserve with a month's notice
(D) Reserve with a week's notice

The announcement states that reservations should be made at least two weeks before arrival in order for a discount to apply, so (A) is the correct answer.

4. **D** **Translation:** Which of the following services does the hotel offer?

(A) Air conditioning in the larger rooms only
(B) Swimming pool
(C) Internet in the bar
(D) A place to eat

The announcement states that the hotel offers air conditioning in all rooms, as well as a café, a bar, and free Internet connection in the room. It does not mention Internet in the bar, a swimming pool, or air conditioning being available only in the larger rooms. Since a café is a place to eat, (D) is the correct answer.

Drill 3: Reading Comprehension

Translation:

For archaeologists and historians, the Mayan civilization is, without a doubt, the one that reached the highest level of development among all the civilizations that existed before the arrival of Columbus. Although there are still many secrets that have not been deciphered with regard to the Mayas, it seems that this civilization began many centuries before the birth of Christ. However, it's known that the Mayas abandoned their large ceremonial centers in the tenth century of our era.

The first temples they built were pyramid-shaped, with four sides and a huge outside stairway. On top of the pyramid there is an edifice that is normally one story, and in some cases two, and in it we can see clay reliefs and statues made of wood and limestone. The figures are always in profile, and in them one can appreciate the adornments and jewels that they used. In the classification that has been made of the epochs of this civilization, the first, which developed in Guatemala and Honduras, is called the pre-classic era and, according to archaeologists, it lasted until the end of the third century of our era.

1. **A**   **Translation:** What do the archaeologists and historians think of the Mayan civilization?

   (A) **That it was a very advanced civilization**
   (B) That the Mayas wrote wonderful books
   (C) That they knew Columbus
   (D) That they had many secrets

   Arqueólogos and **historiadores** are the guide words; use them to lead you to the correct answer, which is (A).

2. **C**   **Translation:** When did the Mayan civilization begin?

   (A) In the tenth century of our era
   (B) Immediately before Columbus's arrival
   (C) **Quite a while before Christ's birth**
   (D) Many centuries after Christ's birth

   It's technically not a guide word, but **cuando** tells you that you want to look for a period in time. The correct answer is (C).

3. **C**   **Translation:** What did the first Mayan temples look like?

   (A) They were very short buildings.
   (B) They were made of wood and limestone.
   (C) **They were pyramids with four faces.**
   (D) They were ordinary houses, like the ones we have today.

   Templos is your guide for this question, and the answer is (C).

4. **B**   **Translation:** What can be said about the sculptures that the Mayas made?

   (A) They had large outside staircases.
   (B) **They give information about the jewels and adornments that they used.**
   (C) It costs a lot to buy them.
   (D) One can find them in famous museums.

   Esculturas tells you where to look, but you still must read with care in order to determine that (B) is the correct answer.

5. **C** **Translation:** Approximately how much time passed between the end of the pre-classic era and when the Mayans abandoned their ceremonial centers?

(A) One hundred years
(B) Three centuries
(C) Seven centuries
(D) Ten centuries

The end of the pre-classic era was in the third century (see the end of the second paragraph), and the Mayans abandoned their ceremonial centers in the tenth century (see the end of the first paragraph). This puts the gap at about seven centuries (C).

6. **A** **Translation:** The passage deals with

(A) Mayan civilization and architecture
(B) Christ's influence on Mayan civilization
(C) the differences between our civilization and Mayan civilization
(D) the adornments and jewels that the Mayas used

This one's a little tricky. The passage does mention Christ (**Cristo**), whose name appears in (B), and adornments and jewels (**adornos y joyas**), which appear in answer (D), but it also deals with other stuff. Choices (B) and (D) are too specific. Omit them. The passage doesn't specifically compare Mayan culture to any other culture, including ours, so (C) is out. That leaves (A), a nice, general, correct answer.

Drill 4: Reading Comprehension

Translation:

In 1992, five centuries were completed since the meeting of Europe and America. It was shortly after midnight between the 11th and 12th of October in 1492 when Rodrigo de Triana, a crew member of the ship *The Niña*, which had gone ahead of *The Santa María*, where Columbus was, shouted "Land! Land!" The place was very close to Florida, a small island named Guanahaní, which Columbus called San Salvador and which belongs to the Lucayan, or Bahama, archipelago.

What Columbus found and describes in his letters to the Catholic king and queen was much poverty and people who went about naked, as their mothers bore them, all young, with beautiful bodies, thick heads of hair like a horse's that fell over their eyebrows and that others wore long in back.

A few days later, he discovered the coast of Cuba, which he called Juana, after the daughter of the king and queen. At that point, Martín Alonso Pinzón, who captained *The Pinta*, pulled away from the expedition, which Columbus considered an act of desertion, although he overlooked it to maintain the unity of the expedition. At the end of a few days he reached Haiti, which he called

Hispaniola, but because of the many sandbanks and reefs that were there, *The Santa María* ran aground.

1. **A** Translation: Who was the first to see land in the expedition?

    (A) A sailor named Rodrigo de Triana
    (B) Columbus
    (C) *The Niña*
    (D) Guanahaní, Columbus's best friend

    You can knock off (C) without looking back at the passage. Once you look back, the answer, (A), is in the sentence containing **tierra**.

2. **A** Translation: What were the people whom Columbus found like?

    (A) Very poor, but also beautiful
    (B) Violent and aggressive
    (C) Smarter than the sailors
    (D) Very scared and confused

    This question doesn't really have guide words, but luckily there is an entire paragraph about this topic, so it shouldn't have been too tough to locate the answer to the question, which is (A).

3. **B** Translation: What did Columbus discover a few days after he discovered San Salvador?

    (A) The Bahama archipelago
    (B) The island that today is called Cuba
    (C) Haiti
    (D) Thick hair

    This is a tricky question, because it's easy to think that **San Salvador** is the guide, when actually **pocos días después** is your clue on this one. The correct answer is (B), but remember, if you ever have trouble locating the source of a question, just skip it and come back to it later.

4. **C** Translation: What was Columbus's reaction when Martín Alonso Pinzón separated from the expedition?

    (A) He became furious.
    (B) He started to cry.
    (C) He gave the impression that he didn't know what had happened.
    (D) He sent another ship after him.

    The name Martin Alonso Pinzón is the guide, and it only appears once. The answer is (C).

5. **D** Translation: How did *The Santa María* end up?

    (A) It returned to Spain.

    (B) It was lost and they have never found it.

    (C) It sank.

    (D) It ran aground as a result of reefs and shallows.

The name of the ship is the big clue. The location of the question tells you to look toward the end of the passage, where you will find that (D) is the correct answer.

Drill 5: Reading Comprehension

Translation:

If it weren't for the demanding taste of the coffee drinkers of Saudi Arabia, the Guatemalan town of Cobán, on the other side of the world, would be in big trouble.

Cobán, capital of the mountainous region of Alta Verapaz, in Guatemala, is the source of the majority of cardamom that the Arab world consumes: a sweet, sharp, and extremely aromatic spice that is used in Indian cooking. As a matter of fact, coffee with cardamom, known in the Arab world as *kahwe hal*, is considered a symbol of hospitality in all of the Middle East.

In Cobán, famous for its sixteenth-century Catholic church and the Mayan ruins that are found in its environs, practically no one speaks Arabic, and none of its 125,000 inhabitants puts cardamom in his/her coffee. However, they all know perfectly well the connection that exists between the spice and the Arab world. "Cardamom is the base of our economy, and Guatemala is the principal exporter in the world."

1. **B** Translation: In which country in particular do they drink coffee with cardamom?

    (A) In Guatemala

    (B) In Saudi Arabia

    (C) In Alta Verapaz

    (D) In the Middle East

A couple of answers, namely, (C) and (D), can be eliminated right away, since they aren't countries. Choice (B) is the correct answer here.

2. **B** Translation: What is cardamom?

    (A) A rare type of coffee

    (B) A spice

    (C) An Indian style of cooking

    (D) A type of tree

Even if you'd never seen the word **especia**, POE works really well on this question and will help you choose (B) as your answer.

3. A   Translation: How does cardamom taste?

(A) **Hot, but also sweet**
(B) A bit bitter
(C) It hardly has any flavor
(D) It tastes like Colombian coffee

The answer to this one is in the paragraph that describes the spice. Choice (A) is correct.

4. C   Translation: For what is the city of Cobán known?

(A) For cardamom
(B) For the best coffee in North America
(C) **For its ruins, and for its sixteenth-century church**
(D) For the Indian food

Choice (A) is an easy trap to fall for if you're lazy on this one and don't look back. For those who aren't lazy, the answer, (C), is right at the top of the final paragraph. Look back to the passage on the specific questions.

5. C   Translation: What is the connection between the Arab world and Guatemala?

(A) In Guatemala everyone speaks Arabic.
(B) In both places they love coffee with cardamom.
(C) **Guatemala exports much spice to the Arab world.**
(D) There really is no connection between the two places.

Although the answer to this one, (C), is in the last paragraph (**conexión** is your guide), the relationship is mentioned earlier in the passage as well.

6. D   Translation: What would be a good title for the passage?

(A) "Cobán: The City in the Mountains"
(B) "The Economy of Guatemala"
(C) "The Coffees of the World"
(D) **"Cardamom: What Joins Guatemala with the Arab World"**

Remember, the answer to a question like this must include the ideas of the whole passage. Choice (B) is only partially correct; it's not wrong, but it doesn't tell the whole story. You want to go with (D).

Part V
Additional
Practice Tests

Practice Test 2

SPANISH SUBJECT TEST 2

Your responses to Spanish Subject Test 2 questions must be filled in on Test 2 of your answer sheet (at the back of the book). Marks on any other section will not be counted toward your Spanish Subject Test score.

When your supervisor gives the signal, turn the page and begin the Spanish Subject Test.

SPANISH SUBJECT TEST

PLEASE NOTE THAT YOUR ANSWER SHEET HAS FIVE ANSWER POSITIONS MARKED A, B, C, D, E, WHILE THE QUESTIONS THROUGHOUT THIS TEST CONTAIN ONLY FOUR CHOICES. BE SURE <u>NOT</u> TO MAKE ANY MARKS IN COLUMN E.

Part A

Directions: This part consists of a number of incomplete statements, each having four suggested completions. Select the most appropriate completion and fill in the corresponding oval on the answer sheet.

---

1. Hay siete días en una semana y cuatro semanas en ------- .

   (A) un siglo
   (B) una estación
   (C) un mes
   (D) una década

2. Me gustaría realmente comprar un traje nuevo, pero ¡me encantan estos zapatos! ¿ ------- ?

   (A) Cómo son
   (B) Cuáles son
   (C) Cuándo cuestan
   (D) Cuántos cuestan

3. Mi abuela me tejía un suéter y ------- una revista a la vez.

   (A) leyera
   (B) leía
   (C) había leído
   (D) lee

4. Los pulmones están ------- del pecho.

   (A) debajo
   (B) arriba
   (C) en medio
   (D) dentro

5. Los empleados no han trabajado desde el miércoles pasado, porque ------- un incendio ese día que destruyó el edificio donde trabajan.

   (A) hubo
   (B) haya
   (C) habría
   (D) hay

6. Aunque no teníamos mucho dinero, no había ------- problema con pagar nuestra cuenta.

   (A) algún
   (B) alguna
   (C) ninguna
   (D) ningún

7. Tú ------- a Francisco en el estadio durante el partido de fútbol el sábado pasado.

   (A) conociste
   (B) conoces
   (C) conozcas
   (D) conocerás

8. ¿ ------- dónde son los Gutiérrez? Me parece que son guatemaltecos, pero no sé con toda seguridad.

   (A) Para
   (B) A
   (C) De
   (D) En

9. La música cubana fue ------- muy bien por la orquesta del Hotel Playa de Oro.

   (A) oída
   (B) hecha
   (C) leída
   (D) tocada

GO ON TO THE NEXT PAGE →

10. Después de que yo los esperé una hora y media, ------- llegaron mis hermanos a visitarme.

    (A) por casualidad
    (B) por fin
    (C) por supuesto
    (D) por favor

11. Es ridículo que las naciones del mundo no ------- vivir en paz.

    (A) podían
    (B) puedan
    (C) pudieron
    (D) pueden

12. Me alegro que Ud. esté en casa, Don Alejandro, quería ------- un favor.

    (A) sacarte
    (B) pedirlo
    (C) pedirle
    (D) prestarle

13. Uds. vivirían en una mansión gigante y espléndida si ------- millonarios.

    (A) son
    (B) habrían sido
    (C) sean
    (D) fueran

14. ------- tú no entiendes es que odio las alcachofas.

    (A) Que
    (B) Cual
    (C) Lo que
    (D) Como

15. Después de nadar un poco, Marta se secó porque estaba muy ------- .

    (A) mojada
    (B) molesta
    (C) enferma
    (D) lista

16. Nuestro primo es famoso porque ------- el papel de Don Quijote en una obra de teatro hace muchos años.

    (A) tocó
    (B) puso
    (C) jugó
    (D) hizo

17. Yo tengo diecisiete años, pero mi hermana ------- sólo tiene quince años.

    (A) mayor
    (B) mejor
    (C) menor
    (D) peor

18. Cuando vayamos de compras el lunes que viene, ------- a las tiendas más exclusivas.

    (A) vayamos
    (B) iremos
    (C) fuimos
    (D) vamos

19. Ricardo habla alemán y ruso muy ------- .

    (A) malos
    (B) malas
    (C) mal
    (D) maldad

20. Uds. están furiosos que nosotros no ------- nada de la cultura puertorriqueña.

    (A) sabemos
    (B) supimos
    (C) hemos sabido
    (D) sepamos

21. Allí está el paraguas de Alicia, pero ¿dónde está ------- ?

    (A) el tuyo
    (B) tuyo
    (C) la tuya
    (D) tuya

22. Ramón compró un anillo para su amiga y ------- dio a ella para su cumpleaños.

    (A) lo
    (B) le
    (C) se la
    (D) se lo

GO ON TO THE NEXT PAGE

23. Ya que has pasado tanto tiempo en el campo, ahora te ------- las montanas.

   (A) encantas
   (B) encantan
   (C) encanta
   (D) encantes

24. La prestigiosa familia contrató al pintor para pintar ------- de su matriarca, la Sra. Pedregal.

   (A) un retrato
   (B) un vaso
   (C) un césped
   (D) un recado

25. Aunque Lucía y Roberto no querían hacer su trabajo, lo hicieron ------- .

   (A) de todos modos
   (B) a primera vista
   (C) al azar
   (D) por desgracia

26. Después de recibir una mala nota en su examen final, Manuel ------- muy enojado y se fue del cuarto.

   (A) se volvió
   (B) se hizo
   (C) se puso
   (D) llegó a ser

27. Las butacas mejores ------- en el fondo del teatro, porque se puede ver toda la pantalla desde allí.

   (A) son
   (B) están
   (C) hay
   (D) hayan

28. El papá de Joaquín es un abogado que se especializa en ------- de los impuestos.

   (A) la piedra
   (B) el ajo
   (C) el sótano
   (D) la ley

29. Desde que me mudé a la Argentina, paso mucho tiempo pensando ------- mis amigos en Paraguay.

   (A) de
   (B) en
   (C) que
   (D) con

GO ON TO THE NEXT PAGE

Part B

Directions: In each of the following passages, there are numbered blanks indicating that words or phrases have been omitted. For each numbered blank, four completions are provided. First read through the entire paragraph. Then, for each numbered blank, choose the completion that is most appropriate given the context of the entire paragraph and fill in the corresponding oval on the answer sheet.

La Sra. Jensen llegó el primer día a la clase diciendo que (30) aprender español. Era obviamente una persona alerta y vivaz. Lo único que (31) distinguía de los otros estudiantes era su (32) : en ese momento tenía sesenta y nueve años. Su historia es interesante. El esposo de la Sra. Jensen (33) inesperadamente de un ataque cardíaco cuando ella tenía apenas treinta años, dejándola sola con cuatro hijos y ningún oficio para ganarse la vida. Sus padres habían muerto, los abuelos paternos de sus hijos tenían muy pocos recursos, y ella no tenía otros (34) que la ayudaran. En efecto, la muerte de su esposo (35) destruyó la vida. (36) ver bien su situación, ella (37) que tenía que volver a pensar todos sus planes y rehacer su vida sobre otras bases.

30. (A) querría
    (B) quiera
    (C) quiere
    (D) quería

31. (A) la
    (B) lo
    (C) los
    (D) le

32. (A) ropa
    (B) edad
    (C) comportamiento
    (D) mochila

33. (A) nació
    (B) murió
    (C) habló
    (D) oyó

34. (A) brazos
    (B) cuentos
    (C) mapas
    (D) parientes

35. (A) la
    (B) lo
    (C) le
    (D) se

36. (A) Al
    (B) Para
    (C) Antes de
    (D) A

37. (A) reconoce
    (B) reconozca
    (C) reconocerá
    (D) reconoció

—Cuando te sientas mal, mi hijita, le (38) consejos al retrato. El (39) dará. Puedes rezarle, ¿acaso no rezas a los santos?

Este (40) de proceder le pareció extraño a Alejandrina. Mi vida transcurría monótonamente, pues tengo un testigo constante que me prohibe la felicidad: mi dolencia. El doctor Edgardo es la única persona que lo (41) . Hasta el momento de conocerlo, (42) ignorando que algo (43) mi organismo me carcomía. Ahora conozco todo lo que sufro: el doctor Edgardo me lo (44) . Es mi naturaleza. Algunos (45) con ojos negros, otros con ojos azules. Parece imposible que, siendo tan joven, él (46) tan sabio; (47) , me he enterado de que no es precisa ser un anciano para serlo. Su piel lisa, sus ojos de niño, su cabellera rubia, ensortijada, son para (48) el emblema de la sabiduría.

38. (A) pidas
    (B) pedirás
    (C) pides
    (D) pediste

39. (A) me lo
    (B) me las
    (C) te los
    (D) te la

40. (A) guante
    (B) tópico
    (C) modo
    (D) relato

41. (A) sabe
    (B) anuncia
    (C) ignora
    (D) muestra

42. (A) viviera
    (B) viví
    (C) vivo
    (D) viva

43. (A) fuera de
    (B) al lado de
    (C) dentro de
    (D) alrededor de

44. (A) ha explicado
    (B) hubiera explicado
    (C) habré explicado
    (D) haya explicado

45. (A) salen
    (B) andan
    (C) mueren
    (D) nacen

46. (A) sería
    (B) fue
    (C) es
    (D) sea

47. (A) porque
    (B) sin embargo
    (C) además
    (D) entonces

48. (A) yo
    (B) mi
    (C) mí
    (D) mío

GO ON TO THE NEXT PAGE

Cortejar es pretender en matrimonio a una señorita.
En la España del siglo XIX, y en particular, en la clase
media, existían ciertas costumbres muy _(49)_ que se
observaban durante el cortejo. Así, un joven y una joven
eran presentados el uno al otro en un evento _(50)_, por
ejemplo, en un baile o una fiesta. Si ellos se gustaban
y querían verse otra vez, tenían que _(51)_ una ocasión
para un nuevo encuentro. Cuando se veían, a la salida
de la misa, durante el intermedio de una obra de teatro,
o en el paseo de la tarde, intercambiaban cartitas _(52)_.

La mujer joven informó al pretendiente _(53)_ la
hora en la cual ella _(54)_ al balcón para verse o hablarse
calladamente o cuándo iría al paseo, con quién estaría
acompañada, dónde se sentaría, y las demás señas
necesarias.

Una vez que la joven pareja decidía _(55)_, el joven
hacía una cita con los padres de la novia y les pedía la
mano de su hija en matrimonio. _(56)_ ese momento, se
les permitía a los novios verse más a menudo.

Pero, por supuesto, la novia siempre era
acompañada de una hermana mayor, una tía, una dueña,
un hermano u otra persona mayor hasta el día de _(57)_.

49. (A) perturbadores
    (B) tradicionales
    (C) chocantes
    (D) tontas

50. (A) social
    (B) secreto
    (C) sombrío
    (D) inapropiado

51. (A) olvidar
    (B) mencionar
    (C) buscar
    (D) recordar

52. (A) amorosas
    (B) profesionales
    (C) antiguas
    (D) odiosas

53. (A) para
    (B) de
    (C) a
    (D) con

54. (A) salga
    (B) habían salido
    (C) saldría
    (D) saldrá

55. (A) casarse
    (B) despedirse
    (C) divorciarse
    (D) enfadarse

56. (A) Antes de
    (B) A partir de
    (C) Para
    (D) Con

57. (A) la fiesta
    (B) la boda
    (C) la muerte
    (D) el baile

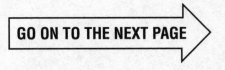

GO ON TO THE NEXT PAGE

Part C

Directions: Read the following texts carefully for comprehension. Each passage is followed by a number of questions or incomplete statements. Select the answer or completion that is best according to the text and fill in the corresponding oval on the answer sheet.

Pasaron días terribles sin que llegara respuesta. Le envié una segunda carta y luego una tercera y una cuarta, diciendo siempre lo mismo, pero cada vez con mayor desolación. En la última, decidí relatarle todo lo que había pasado aquella noche que siguió a nuestra separación. No escatimé detalle ni bajeza, como tampoco dejé de confesarle la tentación de suicidio. Me dio vergüenza usar eso como arma, pero la usé. Debo agregar que, mientras describía mis actos más bajos y la desesperación de mi soledad en la noche frente a su casa de la calle Posadas, sentía ternura para conmigo mismo y hasta lloré de compasión. Tenía muchas esperanzas de que María sintiese algo parecido al leer la carta, y con esa esperanza me puse bastante alegre.

Cuando despaché la carta, certificada, estaba francamente optimista. A vuelta de correo llegó una carta de María, llena de ternura. Sentí que algo de nuestros primeros instantes de amor volvería a reproducirse...Quería que fuera a la estancia. Como un loco, preparé una valija, una caja de pinturas, y corrí a la estación Constitución.

58. ¿Cómo se describiría el estado mental del narrador al principio de este pasaje?

(A) Optimista
(B) Contento
(C) Impaciente
(D) Triste

59. ¿A quién le está enviando el narrador sus cartas?

(A) Al correo
(B) A la Srta. Posadas
(C) A su prima en la estación Constitución
(D) A su novia lejana

60. ¿Por qué está escribiendo el narrador estas cartas?

(A) Quiere visitar a María en su casa.
(B) Quiere jactarse de las cosas malas que ha hecho.
(C) Quiere escribirle a María tantas veces como sea posible.
(D) Quiere explicarse para que María lo entienda mejor.

61. ¿Cómo se ha sentido el narrador desde su confrontación con María?

(A) Avergonzado
(B) Tranquilo
(C) Irritado
(D) Estable

62. ¿Por qué está feliz el narrador cuando envía su carta?

(A) Recibe una carta afectuosa de María.
(B) Piensa que la carta le va a inspirar el amor a María.
(C) No tiene que escribir cartas nunca más.
(D) Sabe que María va a llorar de compasión.

63. ¿Cuál es la reacción del narrador cuando lee la respuesta de María?

(A) Quiere pensar un largo rato en sus sentimientos.
(B) Decide mudarse.
(C) Sale para la estación.
(D) Corre una milla.

GO ON TO THE NEXT PAGE

Los mayas eran oriundos de Guatemala. De Guatemala pasaron a la península de Yucatán en México, a Belice y Honduras. La cultura de los mayas era aún más avanzada que la de los aztecas, a quienes encontró Cortés cuando llegó a México. La arquitectura de los mayas era notable, como atestiguan las famosas ruinas de templos y pirámides en Palenque, Uxmal, Tikal y Copán. Se sitúa el apogeo de su cultura y civilización en el año 250 D.C. Poco antes del año 900 D.C. desaparecieron. Su desaparición ha sido un enigma. No se sabe precisamente por qué desaparecieron. Nuevos descubrimientos arqueológicos indican que existe la posibilidad de que los mayas quisieran lograr una gran expansión territorial y que las confrontaciones bélicas que acompañaban esa expansión fueran la causa más importante de la decadencia del Imperio Maya.

64. Belice y Honduras

(A) son partes de la cultura azteca
(B) son los sitios de los templos de los mayas
(C) están cerca de la península de Yucatán
(D) están en Guatemala

65. El Imperio Maya

(A) no existió después del año 900 D.C.
(B) fue una expansión territorial
(C) fue destruido por Cortés cuando llegó a México
(D) era mejor que el Imperio Azteca

66. El gran misterio de los mayas es

(A) su apogeo
(B) sus ruinas
(C) su éxito
(D) su desaparición

67. La belicosidad de los mayas se debe a

(A) los nuevos descubrimientos arqueológicos
(B) las famosas ruinas de templos
(C) la decadencia de su imperio
(D) su deseo de ampliar la extensión de su imperio

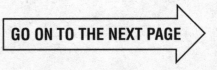
GO ON TO THE NEXT PAGE

Nos conviene pensar en los inmigrantes como miembros de tres grupos. El primer grupo consiste en los que vinieron aquí cuando eran adultos y ya hablaban su lengua materna. El segundo grupo consiste en los que nacieron aquí o vinieron aquí cuando eran niños; son hijos del primer grupo. El tercer grupo consiste en los que nacieron aquí, hijos del segundo grupo.

El primer grupo suele aprender un inglés funcional. Es decir, aprenden a expresarse y a comprender bastante bien pero casi nunca aprenden a hablar sin errores y sin acento. El segundo grupo aprende a hablar inglés perfectamente bien, sin ningún acento extranjero. Pero como hijos de inmigrantes, este grupo retiene algo de su primera lengua y muchas veces es bilingüe. El tercer grupo suele estar lingüísticamente asimilado, con poco conocimiento funcional de la lengua de sus abuelos.

La asimilación de los hispanos se ha estudiado mucho, y se ha visto repetidas veces que la gran mayoría de los inmigrantes hispanos siguen exactamente el mismo patrón que todos los demás inmigrantes. Por lo tanto, la percepción de que los inmigrantes hispanos no quieren aprender inglés es totalmente falsa. Como en el caso de cualquier grupo de inmigrantes, casi todo depende del tiempo que lleve su generación en este país.

68. ¿Qué determina el grupo al cual pertenece el/la inmigrante?

(A) Su deseo de aprender inglés
(B) El alcance de su conocimiento de inglés
(C) El país de donde vino originalmente
(D) El número de idiomas en que puede se comunicar

69. ¿Por qué no pierden sus acentos los miembros del primer grupo?

(A) Su conocimiento de su lengua nativa es más fuerte.
(B) No tienen deseo de aprender una lengua nueva.
(C) No necesitan aprender inglés.
(D) No se han asimilado bien a la cultura nueva.

70. ¿Cuál es una característica principal del segundo grupo?

(A) Aprendieron la lengua nueva de sus padres.
(B) Nacieron en este país.
(C) Tiene facilidad en dos idiomas.
(D) Han pasado muy poco tiempo en Estados Unidos.

71. ¿Cuál es la gran similitud entre el primer y el tercer grupo?

(A) No están bien asimilados lingüísticamente en este país.
(B) Solamente pueden hablar un idioma sin error.
(C) No creen que haya necesidad de aprender inglés.
(D) Son inmigrantes a este país.

72. ¿Cuál es el patrón que siguen casi todos inmigrantes?

(A) Sus oportunidades de aprender la lengua no son muchas.
(B) Se dividen en tres grupos que hablan sus propios idiomas.
(C) Tienen la misma percepción de que a ellos les falta el deseo de aprender inglés.
(D) El alcance de su asimilación lingüística depende de cuánto tiempo han vivido aquí.

73. ¿Cuál sería un buen título para este pasaje?

(A) "Generaciones de asimilación"
(B) "Dificultades con un idioma nuevo"
(C) "Inmigrantes que han aprendido inglés"
(D) "Percepciones erróneas de los inmigrantes"

GO ON TO THE NEXT PAGE

Los estudiantes se pusieron a reír. Primero, me molestaron los modales del profesor —era mi segundo día en un país extranjero— pero ahora me daba cólera que me pusiera en ridículo. No dije nada.

—¿Tal vez, continuó, nos hará el honor de tocar "Souvenir de Spa"?

Se trataba de una composición superficialmente brillante, popular en la escuela belga. Contesté que sí, que la tocaría.

—Estoy seguro de que vamos a oír algo asombroso de este joven que lo sabe todo. Pero, ¿y en qué va a tocar?

Más risa entre los estudiantes. Yo estaba tan furioso que estuve a punto de irme. Pero, recapacité. Quiera o no quiera, me dije, me va a escuchar. Le arrebaté el violoncelo al estudiante que estaba a mi lado y empecé a tocar. Se produjo un gran silencio en la sala. Cuando concluí, no se oía un ruido. El profesor me observaba intensamente, tenía una rara expresión en la cara.

—¿Quiere venir a mi oficina? —preguntó el profesor.

74. ¿Quién es el narrador?

(A) Un músico professional
(B) Un estudiante de un país extranjero
(C) Alguien que está perdido
(D) Un empleado de la escuela

75. ¿Qué es "Souvenir de Spa"?

(A) Es una obra de música bien conocida.
(B) Es una pieza maestra de literatura.
(C) Es una escultura magnífica.
(D) Es un poema clásico.

76. ¿Cuál es la actitud del maestro hacia el narrador al principio del pasaje?

(A) Respeto profundo
(B) Apoyo humillado
(C) Condescendencia entretenida
(D) Desprecio abierto

77. ¿Cómo reaccionan los estudiantes cuando oyen el narrador tocar el instrumento musical?

(A) No dicen nada.
(B) Empiezan a aplaudir.
(C) Se ríen.
(D) Salen de la clase.

78. ¿Qué característica del narrador se destaca más?

(A) Su timidez
(B) Su bondad
(C) Su humildad
(D) Su determinación

79. ¿Qué sería un buen título para esta narración?

(A) "Una Manzana al Día Mantiene Alejado al Doctor"
(B) "Las Grandes Mentes Piensan Igual"
(C) "No Juzgue un Libro por Su Cubierta"
(D) "El Amor No Tiene Precio"

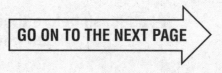

GO ON TO THE NEXT PAGE

25 de Marzo de 2014
Londres, Inglaterra
Reino Unido

Querido Abuelo:

¡Hola! ¡Tanto tiempo que no te escribo! Espero que te sientas bien y que tu pierna ya se haya curado. ¡Cuidado con el hielo abuelo! Es muy resbaladizo.

Los estudios van muy bien y realmente me gusta mucho Oxford. Es una universidad muy popular pero los profesores dan mucho trabajo, y eso no me gusta. El fin de semana pasado, me tomé un tren a Londres. ¡Que lindo que es! Visité los grandes museos, el palacio de Buckingham, el río Thames y las Casas de Parlamento. Realmente fue una experiencia. Las cafeterías son bastante caras, pero sin embargo me he juntado con muchos amigos para cenar. Me gusta mucho la comida. Espero poder volver el próximo año por última vez antes de volver para casa. ¿Están planeando en visitarnos el próximo año? Me gustaría verte a vos y a la abuela. Ya sé que el viaje de Alaska a Oregón no es nada fácil. A lo mejor podemos planear en encontrarnos en California.

Mañana empiezo una nueva clase de arte. Quería otro curso de arte artesanal, pero no tenían espacio. Me anoté en un curso de arte moderno. ¡Estoy muy entusiasmada! Te voy a mandar unos de mis grandes dibujos—¡algún día los podrás vender!

¡Te mando muchos abrazos y besos! Espero verte pronto. ¡Te quiero mucho!

Ana

80. ¿Qué no le gusta a Ana?

(A) La Universidad de Oxford
(B) La cantidad de tarea que dan los profesores
(C) La cuidad de Londres
(D) La popularidad de Oxford

81. ¿Cómo se lastimó la pierna el abuelo?

(A) Fue a patinar en Alaska.
(B) Se cayó.
(C) Se cayó sobre el hielo.
(D) Se quebró la pierna.

82. ¿Que se puede decir de las cafeterías?

(A) Son caras.
(B) No están cerca de el centro de Londres.
(C) No aceptan reservaciones.
(D) No le gusta la comida a Ana.

83. ¿Por qué fue a Londres?

(A) Para estudiar
(B) Para encontrarse con el abuelo
(C) Para encontrarse con amigos
(D) En excursión de turista

84. ¿Dónde y cuándo se quiere encontrar Ana con su Abuelo?

(A) En Oregón el próximo año
(B) En Oregón el próximo mes
(C) En Alaska el próximo año
(D) En California el próximo año

85. ¿Qué tipo de curso quería tomar Ana?

(A) Un curso de arte moderna
(B) Un curso de arte artesanal
(C) Un curso de arte general
(D) Un curso de arte especial

STOP
**If you finish before time is called, you may check your work on this test only.
Do not work on any other test in this book.**

Practice Test 2:
Answers and
Explanations

- Practice Test 2 Answer Key
- Practice Test 2 Explanations
- How to Score Practice Test 2

PRACTICE TEST 2 ANSWER KEY

Question Number	Correct Answer	Right	Wrong	Question Number	Correct Answer	Right	Wrong	Question Number	Correct Answer	Right	Wrong
1	C	___	___	33	B	___	___	65	A	___	___
2	D	___	___	34	D	___	___	66	D	___	___
3	B	___	___	35	C	___	___	67	D	___	___
4	D	___	___	36	A	___	___	68	B	___	___
5	A	___	___	37	D	___	___	69	A	___	___
6	D	___	___	38	B	___	___	70	C	___	___
7	A	___	___	39	C	___	___	71	B	___	___
8	C	___	___	40	C	___	___	72	D	___	___
9	D	___	___	41	A	___	___	73	A	___	___
10	B	___	___	42	B	___	___	74	B	___	___
11	B	___	___	43	C	___	___	75	A	___	___
12	C	___	___	44	A	___	___	76	C	___	___
13	D	___	___	45	D	___	___	77	A	___	___
14	C	___	___	46	D	___	___	78	D	___	___
15	A	___	___	47	B	___	___	79	C	___	___
16	D	___	___	48	C	___	___	80	B	___	___
17	C	___	___	49	B	___	___	81	C	___	___
18	B	___	___	50	A	___	___	82	A	___	___
19	C	___	___	51	C	___	___	83	D	___	___
20	D	___	___	52	A	___	___	84	D	___	___
21	A	___	___	53	B	___	___	85	B	___	___
22	D	___	___	54	C	___	___				
23	B	___	___	55	A	___	___				
24	A	___	___	56	B	___	___				
25	A	___	___	57	B	___	___				
26	C	___	___	58	C	___	___				
27	B	___	___	59	D	___	___				
28	D	___	___	60	D	___	___				
29	B	___	___	61	A	___	___				
30	D	___	___	62	B	___	___				
31	A	___	___	63	C	___	___				
32	B	___	___	64	C	___	___				

PRACTICE TEST 2 EXPLANATIONS

Part A

1. C **Translation:** There are seven days in a week and four weeks in ------- .

    (A) a century
    (B) a season
    (C) a month
    (D) a decade

    The key to this question is time, but all the answers are expressions for specific lengths of time. What to do? Vocabulary knowledge is important when choosing an answer. We might use POE to eliminate (B) because it's a length of time that's a little more obscure than the rest of the answers, but the only logical answer is (C).

2. D **Translation:** I really would like to buy a new suit, but I love these shoes! ------- ?

    (A) How are they?
    (B) Which are they?
    (C) When much are they?
    (D) How much are they?

    The implication here is that I want to buy the shoes instead of a suit. What is the most appropriate question that follows? Choice (A) sounds as if I am asking for a description of the shoes, but if I love them, I must be able to see them! Likewise, (B) does not make sense, unless I am extremely forgetful, and (C) is just silly and grammatically incorrect. The correct answer, then, is (D).

3. B **Translation:** My grandmother knitted/was knitting me a sweater and ------- a magazine at the same time.

    (A) read/was reading (subjunctive)
    (B) read/was reading (indicative)
    (C) had read
    (D) reads

    The verb **tejía** places the action of the sentence in the past, so (D) (the present) does not correspond. Choice (C) (the pluperfect) places the act of reading the magazine before that of knitting the sweater, but the sentence says **a la vez**, so this is incorrect. Choices (A) and (B) are both in the past tense, but there is no cue for the use of the subjunctive in this sentence, so (A) is out. The correct answer is (B).

4. **D** **Translation:** The lungs are ------- the chest.

    (A) under
    (B) above
    (C) in the middle of
    (D) inside

    This is a basic anatomy question, as long as you know what the prepositions mean. Choice (D) is obviously correct.

5. **A** **Translation:** The employees haven't worked since last Wednesday because ------- a fire on that day which destroyed the building where they work.

    (A) there was
    (B) there is (subjunctive)
    (C) there would be
    (D) there is (indicative)

    The fire occurred last Wednesday, which is in the past, so (B) and (D) can be eliminated. The conditional tense in (C) does not apply because the fire doesn't depend on anything (it already happened), so (A) is the correct answer.

6. **D** **Translation:** Although we didn't have a lot of money, there was not ------- problem with paying our bill.

    (A) any (masculine, affirmative)
    (B) any (feminine, affirmative)
    (C) any (feminine, negative)
    (D) any (masculine, negative)

    Translation doesn't really help, as you can see. Remember the double negative rule in Spanish—it's mandatory, so (A) and (B) are gone because they are affirmative words, which cannot be used in a negative sentence. The word *any* is an adjective in this sentence, and so it must agree in number and gender with the word it modifies, **problema**, which in Spanish is singular and masculine (even though it ends in an **a**), so (C) is eliminated and the correct answer is (D).

7. **A** **Translation:** You ------- Francisco in the stadium during the soccer game last Saturday.

    (A) met
    (B) meet (indicative)
    (C) meet (subjunctive)
    (D) will meet

    El sábado pasado indicates that the action took place in the past, so (B) and (C) (the present) and (D) (the future) are eliminated. Choice (A) is correct.

8.   C   **Translation:** ------- where are the Gutiérrezes? It seems to me that they are Guatemalan, but I don't know for sure.

(A) For
(B) To
(C) From
(D) In

The sentence is speaking of the nationality of the family—their country of origin. Choices (A) and (B) imply destination, or movement toward something instead of away from it. Because these choices would also require the use of **estar** to make any grammatical sense, they are wrong. Likewise, (D) suggests their current location, and also requires the use of **estar**, so it is incorrect as well. Choice (C) is correct.

9.   D   **Translation:** The Cuban music was ------- very well by the orchestra of the Hotel Playa de Oro.

(A) heard
(B) made
(C) read
(D) played

An orchestra doesn't generally listen to its own or other people's music, so (A) makes no sense whatsoever. *To make music* would make sense in English, but it is better represented in Spanish by the verb **componer**, *to compose,* so (B) is eliminated. Does an orchestra read music? Sure, and one supposes that if it reads music well, then it might be a pretty decent orchestra, but that's not the main function of an orchestra, so (C) is out. Only (D) is right on target.

10. B   **Translation:** After I waited an hour and a half for them, ------- my brothers arrived to visit me.

(A) by chance
(B) finally
(C) of course
(D) please

The sentence indicates that the reason I was waiting was that my brothers were supposed to come, so (A) is silly, unless their visit is an unbelievable coincidence. Choice (C) indicates that there was never any doubt they would come, but I waited an hour and a half—surely I must have started second-guessing at some point. In the context of the sentence, (D) makes no sense. Only (B) puts an end to the waiting.

11. **B**   **Translation:** It is ridiculous that the nations of the world ------ not live in peace.

    (A) could (imperfect)
    (B) can (subjunctive)
    (C) could (preterite)
    (D) can (indicative)

The implication of both (A) and (C) is that the nations of the world were unable to coexist only in the past (or perhaps that these nations don't even exist anymore), which is not the case, so those choices are wrong. The present tense is used in (B) and (D), but remember that the subjunctive is used with impersonal expressions that characterize the opinion of the speaker. **Es ridículo** is obviously a personal opinion, not a general truth, so the subjunctive is needed and (B) is the answer.

12. **C**   **Translation:** I'm glad you (formal) are home, Don Alejandro, I wanted to ------- a favor.

    (A) extract from you (informal)
    (B) ask it
    (C) ask you (formal)
    (D) lend you (formal)

This question hinges on a student's knowledge of the indirect pronoun to use in formal situations. Choice (B) is a trap for those who attempt to match the pronoun to the direct object **favor**, which, as it's used in this context, does not need one. The correct answer is (C).

13. **D**   **Translation:** You (plural) would live in a gigantic and splendid mansion if ------- millionaires.

    (A) you (plural) are (indicative)
    (B) you (plural) would have been
    (C) you (plural) are (subjunctive)
    (D) you (plural) were (subjunctive)

The use of the conditional tense in combination with the word **si** tells us that we are talking about something that is not currently true—it has the condition of already being a millionaire attached. Placing the action in the present tense, then, would be incorrect, which eliminates (A) and (C). Choice (B) is simply not logical; it is awkward and grammatically incorrect. When you speak about something hypothetical in Spanish, the imperfect subjunctive is always used to indicate such situations, so (D) is correct.

14.   C   **Translation:** ------- you don't understand is that I hate artichokes.

(A) That
(B) Which
(C) What
(D) As

Choice (B) makes absolutely no sense, while (D) would make sense only if we eliminated the words **es que.** Choice (A) might seem to make sense if you translate **que** to mean *what,* but this is only correct when **que** has an accent mark, which indicates that it is being used as an interrogative (question) word. In this instance, **que** (no accent) is a conjunction (connecting word) that should join the two parts of the sentence together logically, which doesn't happen here. Choice (C) means literally *that which* or *the thing which,* and this is correct in the context of the sentence.

15.   A   **Translation:** After swimming a little, Marta dried off because she was very ------- .

(A) wet
(B) bothered
(C) sick
(D) ready

Choice (C) is a basic word of high school Spanish and does not make sense in the context of this sentence, so it's out. Choice (B) is a pseudo-cognate that indicates someone is doing something to someone else that he/she doesn't appreciate, which does not make sense. That leaves (A) and (D). She didn't dry off because she was ready to do so but rather because of the normal reason—she was wet. The correct answer is (A).

16.   D   **Translation:** Our cousin is famous because ------- the role of Don Quijote in a play many years ago.

(A) he played
(B) he played
(C) he played
(D) he played

Translation doesn't help at all, as all these verbs mean the same thing in English; however, they have a variety of meanings in Spanish. Choice (A) means *to play (an instrument),* while (B) means *to play (a record or compact disc).* Choice (C) means *to play (a game),* while (D) carries the appropriate meaning of *to play (a role)* and is correct.

17. **C** **Translation:** I am seventeen years old but my ------- sister is only fifteen.

    (A) older
    (B) better
    (C) younger
    (D) worse

Many people confuse the meanings of (A) and (B) because they seem so similar in spelling, but (A) and (C) and (B) and (D) are actually pairs of opposites. Unless I regularly compare my sisters, (B) and (D) really don't make any sense here. Choice (A) defies logic, so (C) is the appropriate response.

18. **B** **Translation:** When we go shopping next Monday, ------- to the most exclusive stores.

    (A) we go/are going (subjunctive)
    (B) we will go
    (C) we went
    (D) we go/are going (indicative)

Since the shopping trip will take place next Monday, a specific day in the future, we want to avoid verbs that use the present tense, such as (A) **vayamos** (present subjunctive) and (D) **vamos** (present indicative). Likewise, we don't want to use the past tense, which leads us to eliminate (C) **fuimos.** Choice (B) is the only option that speaks of the future. Note that we could also say **vamos a ir** *(we are going to go),* which is not the same as saying simply **vamos** *(we go/we are going).*

19. **C** **Translation:** Ricardo speaks German and Russian very ------- .

    (A) bad (masculine, plural)
    (B) bad (feminine, plural)
    (C) badly
    (D) evil

Choices (A) and (B) are incorrect because they modify the wrong part of the sentence—the languages. Choice (D) is way off. The answer is (C), an adverb modifying how Ricardo speaks.

20. **D** **Translation:** You (plural) are furious that we don't ------- anything about Puerto Rican culture.

    (A) know (indicative)
    (B) knew
    (C) have known
    (D) know (subjunctive)

The verb **están** places the action in the present, thus eliminating (B). Remember that the subjunctive is used with expressions of emotion, and the word **furioso** is definitely an emotion, so the use of the indicative in (A) and (C) is incorrect. Choice (D) is correctly in the present tense and the subjunctive mood.

21.   **A**   **Translation:** There is Alicia's umbrella, but where is ------- ?

(A) **yours (masculine, pronoun)**
(B) yours (masculine, adjective)
(C) yours (feminine, pronoun)
(D) yours (feminine, adjective)

The word **tuyo** cannot be used by itself. It is a possessive adjective and must be used in conjunction with the noun that it modifies, so (B) and (D) are incorrect. In the case of (A) and (C), adding **el** and **la** to the possessive adjectives **tuyo** and **tuya** turns them into possessive pronouns, which are appropriate. Remembering that pronouns agree in number with the nouns they replace, and seeing from the sentence that **el paraguas** is a masculine noun, you can figure out that (A) is correct.

22.   **D**   **Translation:** Ramón bought a ring for his friend and gave ------- for her birthday.

(A) it (masculine)
(B) to her
(C) it (feminine) to her
(D) **it (masculine) to her**

Choice (B) eliminates important information—gave her what? The sentence requires a direct object pronoun. Choice (A) may seem correct, but it also eliminates important information—gave it to whom? Remember that in Spanish the indirect object pronoun must be included, even if the indirect object itself is also present. Since Ramón gave his friend **un anillo**—a masculine noun—the direct object pronoun must be masculine. Eliminate (C). Choice (D) is correct.

23.   **B**   **Translation:** Since you have spent so much time in the country, the mountains now ------- you.

(A) (you) enchant (indicative)
(B) **(they) enchant**
(C) (he/she/it) enchants
(D) (you) enchant (subjunctive)

Encantar is a verb like **gustar**, which confuses many. Generally, this sentence would translate, *now you love the mountains,* but one loses the thread of who/what the subject is and who/what the object is with this translation. *The mountains* is the subject of the sentence, so the verb must correspond to the third-person plural conjugation, which is (B). Choice (A) is a common mistake, which comes from not understanding how this verb type functions. Choice (C) is way off base, while (D) is out because there are no cues in the sentence that require the use of the subjunctive.

24. A **Translation:** The prestigious family commissioned the painter to paint ------- of its matriarch, Mrs. Pedregal.

(A) **a portrait**
(B) a glass
(C) a lawn
(D) a message

Choice (B) is a relatively common vocabulary word in high school Spanish, while (C) is a little less common but still within reach. Both can be eliminated readily. Choices (A) and (D) sound very similar, but the proper response is (A).

25. A **Translation:** Although Lucía and Roberto did not want to do their work, they did it ------- .

(A) **anyway**
(B) at first sight
(C) at random
(D) unfortunately

This question relies on a knowledge of idioms. Choice (B) makes absolutely no sense in the context of this sentence. One would hope that (C) were simply not true, but it is actually incorrect because the conjunction **aunque** doesn't lead logically to the second part of the sentence—**porque** would make more sense. While (D) may be the opinion of Lucía and Roberto, it doesn't make any sense either. Choice (A) is the appropriate response.

26. C **Translation:** After receiving a bad grade on his final exam, Manuel ------- very angry and left the room.

(A) became
(B) became
(C) **became**
(D) became

Again, translating doesn't help at all, as all the verbs mean the same thing in English, though very different things in Spanish. Choice (A) means not only that he became angry, but also that he was never happy again—his anger is a permanent condition. Choices (B) and (D) are essentially interchangeable, as they mean *became* in the sense of moving to a new social position or status (*he became a doctor* or *he became a success*). Choice (C) indicates a temporary change in emotional condition, which is the intention of the sentence, and it is thus correct.

27. **B**   **Translation:** The best seats ------- at the back of the theater, because one can see the entire screen from there.

(A) are (ser)
(B) are (estar)
(C) there is/are (haber)
(D) they have (haber, subjunctive)

This sentence locates the best seats, so this question hinges around the sometimes confusing **ser** versus **estar** issue. Choice (C) is not correct because **hay** is used only to indicate the general existence of something, not its specific location. Choice (D) does not make sense at all, first because it is an auxiliary (helping) verb, which requires another verb afterward, second because there are no cues in the sentence that require the use of the subjunctive. The verb **ser** is used to describe permanent characteristics, so (A) is incorrect. **Estar** is used to locate things, so (B) is the answer.

28. **D**   **Translation:** Joaquín's father is an attorney who specializes in tax ------- .

(A) stone
(B) garlic
(C) basement
(D) law

This is another vocabulary question, just to prove that no matter how much you think you know, there is always something you might *not* know. Choice (D) is the only one that makes sense.

29. **B**   **Translation:** Since I moved to Argentina, I spend a lot of time thinking ------- my friends in Paraguay.

(A) of
(B) about
(C) that
(D) with

Prepositions in Spanish can often change the meaning of a verb very subtly, as is the case in this sentence. Choice (D) is obviously wrong, and we can use the literal translation to get rid of it. Choice (C) is incorrect because the word **que** must introduce a new clause. Choices (A) and (B) can both be translated as *of,* but the preposition **de** can only be used with the verb **pensar** in a question. Choice (B) gives the appropriate meaning of the verb.

Part B

Passage:

La Sra. Jensen llegó el primer día a la clase diciendo que <u>quería</u> aprender español. Era obviamente una persona alerta y vivaz. Lo único que <u>la</u> distinguía de los otros estudiantes era su <u>edad</u>: en ese momento tenía sesenta y nueve años. Su historia es interesante. El esposo de la Sra. Jensen <u>murió</u> inesperadamente de un ataque cardíaco cuando ella tenía apenas treinta años, dejándola sola con cuatro hijos y ningún oficio para ganarse la vida. Sus padres habían muerto, los abuelos paternos de sus hijos tenían muy pocos recursos, y ella no tenía otros <u>parientes</u> que la ayudaran. En efecto, la muerte de su esposo <u>le</u> destruyó la vida. <u>Al</u> ver bien su situación, ella <u>reconoció</u> que tenía que volver a pensar todos sus planes y rehacer su vida sobre otras bases.

Translation:

Mrs. Jensen arrived to class the first day saying that *she wanted* to learn Spanish. She was obviously an alert and lively person. The only thing that distinguished *her* from the other students was her *age*: at that moment she was seventy-nine years old. Her story is interesting. Mrs. Jensen's husband *died* unexpectedly of a heart attack when she was scarcely thirty, leaving her alone with four children and no job with which to earn a living. Her parents were dead, the children's paternal grandparents had very few resources, and she did not have other *relatives* to help her. In effect, the death of her husband destroyed life for *her*. *Upon* looking well at her situation, she *recognized* that she had to rethink all her plans and remake her life upon other foundations.

30. D (A) would want
        (B) wants (subjunctive)
        (C) wants (indicative)
        (D) wanted

The action of the first sentence is in the past, so the verb **querer** must correspond, thus eliminating (B) and (C). Choice (A) does not make sense in the context of the sentence, as the conditional is most often used in hypothetical situations or situations of conjecture. The class is happening—it is not hypothetical, so (A) is incorrect. Choice (D) is in the past and is the correct response.

31. A **(A) her**
        (B) him
        (C) them (masculine)
        (D) (to) her/him

Distinguished what? Distinguished *her*—Mrs. Jensen receives the action of the verb. A direct object pronoun is needed, thus eliminating (D), which is indirect. Choice (B) suggests that there is a man in this passage. Unless we're talking about the deceased Mr. Jensen being in the class, this is incorrect. Likewise, the only noun to which (C) might be referring is **los estudiantes**, which would not make sense in the context of the sentence. Choice (A) is correct.

32. **B** (A) clothes

     (B) age

     (C) behavior

     (D) knapsack

The clue to the answer of this problem follows the colon: **en ese momento tenía sesenta y nueve años.** This is a pretty distinguishing characteristic, and (B) is the correct answer.

33. **B** (A) was born

     (B) died

     (C) spoke

     (D) heard

Important words in this sentence are **ataque cardíaco** and **dejándola sola.** People are not *born* of a heart attack, so (A) is incorrect. Likewise, it hardly seems possible that Mr. Jensen unexpectedly *spoke* or *heard* of a heart attack and then left his family almost fifty years ago. Choice (B) is the only one that makes any sense.

34. **D** (A) arms

     (B) stories

     (C) maps

     (D) relatives

The sentence before says that Mrs. Jensen was with **ningún oficio para ganarse la vida.** What are some things, then, that could help Mrs. Jensen financially following the death of her husband? Certainly not (B), and probably not (A) or (C) (unless it's a treasure map and they'll dig for the gold...), and so we are left with (D), the only choice that could offer this type of help.

35. **C** (A) her

     (B) him

     (C) (for) her/him

     (D) itself

Destroyed what? Destroyed *life*—*life* is the direct object, receiving the action of the verb directly. We are not, then, looking for a direct object pronoun, because the direct object is already in the sentence, so (A) and (B) are incorrect. Is life destroying *itself*? That doesn't make much sense, so (D) is out, as well. Choice (C) is correct, as Mrs. Jensen is the person who receives the effect of the destroyed life—she is the indirect object of the sentence.

36. **A**   (A) **Upon**
        (B) In order to
        (C) Before
        (D) Let's

This question depends on a knowledge of idiomatic expressions. Choices (B) and (C) present situations that are backwards in their logic: *to* see (or *before* seeing) her situation well, she has to rethink her life. It's the other way around, so both choices are out. **A ver** in Spanish means *Let's see* and does not fit in the sentence, so (D) is eliminated. Choice (A) presents a logical introduction to the situation in the sentence and is correct.

37. **D**   (A) recognizes (indicative)
        (B) recognizes (subjunctive)
        (C) will recognize
        (D) **recognized**

The verb **tenía** tells us that we are in the past, so (A), (B), and (C) are all incorrect because they don't correspond to the proper tense. Choice (D) is the answer.

Passage:

   —Cuando te sientas mal, mi hijita, le <u>pedirás</u> consejos al retrato. El <u>te los</u> dará. Puedes rezarle, ¿acaso no rezas a los santos?
   Este <u>modo</u> de proceder le pareció extraño a Alejandrina. Mi vida transcurría monótonamente, pues tengo un testigo constante que me prohibe la felicidad: mi dolencia. El doctor Edgardo es la única persona que lo <u>sabe</u>. Hasta el momento de conocerlo, <u>viví</u> ignorando que algo <u>dentro de</u> mi organismo me carcomía. Ahora conozco todo lo que sufro: el doctor Edgardo me lo <u>ha explicado</u>. Es mi naturaleza. Algunos <u>nacen</u> con ojos negros, otros con ojos azules. Parece imposible que, siendo tan joven, él <u>sea</u> tan sabio; <u>sin embargo</u>, me he enterado de que no es precisa ser un anciano para serlo. Su piel lisa, sus ojos de niño, su cabellera rubia, ensortijada, son para <u>mí</u> el emblema de la sabiduría.

Translation:

"When you feel bad, my little girl, *you will ask* the portrait for advice. It will give *it to you*. You can pray to it—perhaps you don't pray to the saints?"

This *way* of proceeding seemed strange to Alejandrina. My life was passing monotonously, as I have a constant witness which prohibits happiness for me: my ailment. Dr. Edgardo is the only person who *knows* it. Until the time I met him, *I lived* ignoring the fact that something *inside* my body was consuming me. Now I know all that I suffer: Dr. Edgardo *has explained* it to me. It is my nature. Some *are born* with dark eyes, others with blue eyes. It seems impossible that, being so young, *he is* so wise; *however*, I have gotten to know that you don't need to be old to be wise. His smooth skin, his childlike eyes, his blond, curly head of hair are for *me* the emblem of wisdom.

38. **B** (A) you ask for (subjunctive)

      (B) you will ask for

      (C) you ask for (indicative)

      (D) you asked for

Cuando anticipates a time in the future when the narrator will feel bad (the use of the subjunctive tells us this, also), so the answer must be in the future tense. Choice (D) is thus incorrect. You can use the present tense to speak of the near future, but it is already used in the subjunctive with **sientas** and would indicate the present if used again in a different part of the sentence, so (A) and (C) are out. Only (B) is in the appropriate future tense.

39. **C** (A) it (masculine) to me

      (B) them (feminine) to me

      (C) them (masculine) to you

      (D) it (feminine) to you

Will give what? Will give advice. **Consejos**, the direct object, is replaced by the masculine plural pronoun **los**. This eliminates everything except (C), which is the answer.

40. **C** (A) glove

      (B) topic

      (C) way

      (D) story

The word **este** refers to what immediately precedes it—the first paragraph, which involves someone telling the narrator to pray to a portrait when she feels bad. Which word would describe this situation best? Choice (A) is obviously quite silly and can be eliminated. The answer must also be an adjective that is logical with the word **proceder**—*proceeding*—so (D) seems silly. Because the person speaking seems to be suggesting a method of reaction to illness, (C) is the most logical fit.

41. **A** **(A) knows**

      (B) announces

      (C) ignores

      (D) shows

A doctor who *announces* patients' illnesses? Or *ignores* them? Choices (B) and (C) are eliminated for making no sense whatsoever. Choice (D) is a little strange—Dr. Edgardo is the only person who *shows* it. To whom? When? Where? Why? The most logical answer is (A).

42. B (A) I lived (imperfect subjunctive)
       (B) **I lived (preterite indicative)**
       (C) I live (indicative)
       (D) I live (subjunctive)

The narrator already knows that she is sick, so her life **ignorando** obviously took place in the past (before she knew), thus eliminating (C) and (D). There are no cues in the sentence that require the use of the subjunctive, so (B) is the correct answer.

43. C (A) outside
       (B) next to
       (C) **inside**
       (D) around

Where is the illness that is consuming the narrator's body? Obviously inside the body; therefore, (C) is the correct answer. All the other choices are prepositions referring to the *outside* of the body, which is hard to imagine, and would be even harder to ignore.

44. A (A) **has explained (indicative)**
       (B) had explained (subjunctive)
       (C) will have explained
       (D) has explained (subjunctive)

If the narrator now understands **todo lo que sufro**, then the doctor has already explained it to her. We need the past tense, which eliminates (C). There are no cues in the sentence that require the use of the subjunctive, thus eliminating (B) and (D), so (A) is the answer.

45. D (A) leave
       (B) walk
       (C) die
       (D) **are born**

Dark eyes and blue eyes are relatively permanent conditions throughout one's life, so (A), (B), and (C) seem rather silly. Choice (D) establishes this permanent condition for life, and, therefore, it is the answer.

46. D (A) would be
       (B) was
       (C) is (indicative)
       (D) **is (subjunctive)**

The verb **parece** places the action in the present tense, eliminating (A) and (B). The phrase **Parece imposible que** is an impersonal expression of opinion on the part of the speaker (not a statement of general fact), and thus requires the use of the subjunctive. Choice (D) is correct.

47. **B** (A) because
     (B) however
     (C) furthermore
     (D) then

Look at what's happening on either side of the semicolon: It seems impossible for him to be so wise / you don't have to be old to be wise. Which conjunction most logically connects these two ideas? They seem not to be saying the same thing, which eliminates (A), (C), and (D). Choice (B) gives us the proper word to show the contradiction between the two parts of the sentence.

48. **C** (A) I
     (B) my
     (C) me
     (D) mine

Para is a preposition, and nouns/pronouns in prepositional phrases are the objects of those prepositions. Choice (A) is a subject pronoun and can be eliminated. Choices (B) and (D) are out because they are types of possessive pronouns. The proper response is (C).

Passage:

     Cortejar es pretender en matrimonio a una señorita. En la España del siglo XIX, y en particular, en la clase media, existían ciertas costumbres muy <u>tradicionales</u> que se observaban durante el cortejo. Así, un joven y una joven eran presentados el uno al otro en un evento <u>social</u>, por ejemplo, en un baile o una fiesta. Si ellos se gustaban y querían verse otra vez, tenían que <u>buscar</u> una ocasión para un nuevo encuentro. Cuando se veían, a la salida de la misa, durante el intermedio de una obra de teatro, o en el paseo de la tarde, intercambiaban cartitas <u>amorosas</u>.
     La mujer joven informó al pretendiente <u>de</u> la hora en la cual ella <u>saldría</u> al balcón para verse o hablarse calladamente o cuándo iría al paseo, con quién estaría acompañada, dónde se sentaría, y las demás señas necesarias.
     Una vez que la joven pareja decidía <u>casarse</u>, el joven hacía una cita con los padres de la novia y les pedía la mano de su hija en matrimonio. <u>A partir de</u> ese momento, se les permitía a los novios verse más a menudo.
     Pero, por supuesto, la novia siempre estaba acompañada de una hermana mayor, una tía, una dueña, un hermano u otra persona mayor hasta el día de <u>la boda</u>.

Translation:

Courtship is to seek a woman for marriage. In nineteenth-century Spain, and in particular in the middle class, there existed certain very *traditional* customs that one observed during courtship. Thus, a young man and a young woman were presented to each other at a *social* event, for example, at a dance or a party. If they liked each other and wanted to see each other again, they had to *look for* an occasion for a new encounter. When they saw each other, at departure from Mass, during the intermission of a play, or on an afternoon walk, they exchanged *love* letters.

The young woman informed the suitor *of* the hour at which she *would go out* onto the balcony to see him or talk to him quietly, or when she would go for a walk, by whom she would be accompanied, where she would sit, and other necessary signs.

Once the young couple decided *to be married*, the young man made an appointment with the young woman's parents and asked them for their daughter's hand in marriage. *From* that moment, they would allow the couple to see each other more often.

But, of course, the young woman was always accompanied by an older sister, an aunt, a chaperone, a brother, or another older person until the day of *the wedding*.

49. **B** (A) disturbing
         (B) traditional
         (C) shocking
         (D) stupid

Customs are customs because of their tradition, so (B) is the answer. The other three terms would not normally be applied to customs.

50. **A** **(A) social**
         (B) secret
         (C) somber
         (D) inappropriate

What kind of events are dances and parties? They involve being with other people, and thus are *social,* so (A) is the answer. The other three terms are not normally associated with dances and parties.

51. **C** (A) forget
         (B) mention
         (C) look for
         (D) remember

If the two people want to see each other again, they have to be reasonably active in setting up another meeting. Choices (B) and (D) are a little too passive, and (A) would certainly defeat their purpose. Choice (C) makes sense—they would try to find another time to meet.

52. **A** **(A) love**
         (B) professional
         (C) ancient
         (D) hateful

What kinds of letters would two people who like each other a lot exchange? The answer is understandably (A).

53. **B**   (A) for
            (B) of
            (C) to
            (D) with

This is a question regarding the use of idiomatic expressions. Luckily, the expression in Spanish is the same as that in English. You inform someone *about* or *of* something, so (B) is correct.

54. **C**   (A) goes out (subjunctive)
            (B) had gone out
            (C) would go out
            (D) will go out

The use of the verb **informaba** puts us in a tense that corresponds with the past, so (A) and (D) are eliminated. Look at the tense of the other verbs in this sentence: **iría, estaría, sentaría**. They are all in the conditional, as they are speaking of anticipated events, not events that have already happened. Choice (B) is the conditional perfect, which is only used to describe an event occurring in the past before another past event (and is thus not anticipated). Choice (C) corresponds to the other verbs in the sentence and speaks of anticipated events.

55. **A**   **(A) to be married**
            (B) to say good-bye
            (C) to be divorced
            (D) to become angry

The key phrase in this sentence is **les pedía la mano de su hija en matrimonio**. These people obviously like each other a lot. Choice (A) describes the next logical step in their relationship. The other three choices don't really describe what a couple in love would want to do.

56. **B**   (A) Before
            (B) From
            (C) For
            (D) With

Logic is important. Would the young woman's parents allow the two to see each other more often *before* he asks for her hand? Probably not, so (A) is out. Likewise, (C) is eliminated because it would not be for that moment only that they would allow it, especially because the sentence continues by suggesting various chaperones for their future dates. Choice (D) doesn't really make a whole lot of sense either, so (B) is the proper answer—from that moment on.

57.   **B**   (A) the party

(B) **the wedding**

(C) death

(D) the dance

We've been clobbered over the head with the words **matrimonio** and **amor** in this passage. What's the obvious conclusion we can draw? Choice (B) is correct.

Part C
Passage:

Pasaron días terribles sin que llegara respuesta. Le envié una segunda carta y luego una tercera y una cuarta, diciendo siempre lo mismo, pero cada vez con mayor desolación. En la última, decidí relatarle todo lo que había pasado aquella noche que siguió a nuestra separación. No escatimé detalle ni bajeza, como tampoco dejé de confesarle la tentación de suicidio. Me dio vergüenza usar eso como arma, pero la usé. Debo agregar que, mientras describía mis actos más bajos y la desesperación de mi soledad en la noche frente a su casa de la calle Posadas, sentía ternura para conmigo mismo y hasta lloré de compasión. Tenía muchas esperanzas de que María sintiese algo parecido al leer la carta, y con esa esperanza me puse bastante alegre.

Cuando despaché la carta, certificada, estaba francamente optimista. A vuelta de correo llegó una carta de María, llena de ternura. Sentí que algo de nuestros primeros instantes de amor volvería a reproducirse...Quería que fuera a la estancia. Como un loco, preparé una valija, una caja de pinturas, y corrí a la estación Constitución.

Translation:

Awful days passed without a response arriving. I sent her a second letter and then a third and a fourth, always saying the same thing, but each time with greater despair. In the last one, I decided to relate to her all that had happened that night that followed our separation. I didn't skimp on detail or baseness, as I also didn't neglect to confess to her the temptation of suicide. I was ashamed to use that as a weapon, but I used it. I should add that, while I described my lowest acts and the desperation of my solitude on that night in front of her house on Posadas Street, I felt tenderness toward myself and I almost cried in pity. I had much hope that María would feel something similar on reading the letter, and with that hope I became quite happy.

When I sent the letter, certified, I was honestly optimistic. Once back from the post office, a letter from María arrived, full of tenderness. I felt that something of our first moments of love would start to happen again...I wished that I were at the hacienda. Like a fool, I prepared a suitcase, a box full of paints, and I ran to Constitution Station.

58.   C   **Translation:** How would one describe the mental state of the narrator at the beginning of this passage?

(A) Optimistic
(B) Content
(C) Impatient
(D) Sad

The guy has sent four letters to the same person and is complaining that he has not received a response yet. He is certainly not content with or optimistic about the situation, so (A) and (B) are gone. While he may be sad that María has not responded, one doesn't sense this emotion as much as his impatience (four letters?). Choice (C) is correct.

59.   D   **Translation:** To whom is the narrator sending his letters?

(A) To the post office
(B) To Miss Posadas
(C) To his cousin at Constitution Station
(D) To his estranged girlfriend

We know that María is receiving the letters and that the narrator once had a relationship with her that he wants to recapture. He is sending the letters from, not to, the post office, so (A) is incorrect. Posadas is the name of María's street, so (B) is wrong, and there is no cousin mentioned in the passage, so (C) is incorrect as well. Choice (D) describes the narrator's relationship with María well.

60.   D   **Translation:** Why is the narrator writing these letters?

(A) He wants to visit María in her home.
(B) He wants to brag about the bad things he has done.
(C) He wants to write to María as many times as possible.
(D) He wants to explain himself so that María understands him better.

The narrator does not want to visit María—he already did that when they separated, so (A) is out. He doesn't necessarily want to brag about his deeds as much as he wants to explain them to her, so (B) is not correct. While it may seem that the narrator is going for the world record in letter writing, this is not his intention in writing them either. He wants María to understand him, so (D) is the correct response.

61.   A   **Translation:** How has the narrator felt since his confrontation with María?

(A) **Ashamed**
(B) Calm
(C) Irritated
(D) Stable

In addition to seeming a little desperate, the narrator does not seem at all proud of his actions. Why else would he write four letters trying to explain himself and his actions to María? He is certainly not stable (he thought about suicide), nor is he calm (he's a nervous wreck waiting for her response), so (B) and (D) are eliminated. While he may be a little irritated that he hasn't received a response to his letters, the focus of the passage is on his motive for writing the letters, which is his shame; thus, (A) is the answer.

62.   B   **Translation:** Why is the narrator happy when he sends his letter?

(A) He receives an affectionate letter from María.
(B) **He thinks that the letter will inspire María's love.**
(C) He doesn't have to write letters anymore.
(D) He knows that María is going to cry in pity.

Choice (A) is incorrect because he receives the letter after he returns from the post office. Choice (D) is a misreading of the passage—it is the narrator who cried when he wrote the letter. Choice (C) is a little strange when it seems that the narrator didn't seem to mind writing four letters to get a response. The second-to-last sentence says that he hoped that María would feel tenderness toward him upon reading the letter, so (B) is the answer.

63.   C   **Translation:** What is the narrator's reaction when he reads Maria's response?

(A) He wants to think for a long while about his feelings.
(B) He decides to move.
(C) **He leaves for the station.**
(D) He runs a mile.

While it is true that the narrator packed his suitcase, it's not because he has decided to move (B). He also didn't need to think a long while about his feelings (A) because he knows what he feels and can't wait to see his beloved. We don't know whether he runs a mile (D), but he does leave for the station (C).

Passage:

Los mayas eran oriundos de Guatemala. De Guatemala pasaron a la península de Yucatán en México, a Belice y Honduras. La cultura de los mayas era aún más avanzada que la de los aztecas, a quienes encontró Cortés cuando llegó a México. La arquitectura de los mayas era notable, como atestiguan las famosas ruinas de templos y pirámides en Palenque, Uxmal, Tikal y Copán. Se sitúa el apogeo de su cultura y civilización en el año 250 D.C. Poco antes del año 900 D.C. desaparecieron. Su desaparición ha sido un enigma. No se sabe precisamente por qué desaparecieron. Nuevos descubrimientos arqueológicos indican que existe la posibilidad de que los mayas quisieran lograr una gran expansión territorial y que las confrontaciones bélicas que acompañaban esa expansión fueran la causa más importante de la decadencia del Imperio Maya.

Translation:

The Mayas were natives of Guatemala. From Guatemala they moved to the Yucatán Peninsula in Mexico, to Belize and Honduras. The culture of the Mayas was even more advanced than that of the Aztecs, whom Cortés encountered when he arrived in Mexico. The architecture of the Mayas was notable, as the famous ruins of temples and pyramids in Palenque, Uxmal, Tikal, and Copán prove. The apex of their culture and civilization is situated in the year 250 A.D. A little before 900 A.D. they disappeared. Their disappearance has been an enigma. It is not known precisely why they disappeared. New archaeological discoveries indicate that the possibility exists that the Mayas wanted to achieve a great territorial expansion and that the warlike confrontations that accompanied that expansion were the most important cause of the decline of the Mayan Empire.

64.   C   **Translation:** Belize and Honduras

(A)   are parts of the Aztec culture
(B)   are the sites of the Mayan temples
(C)   **are near the Yucatán Peninsula**
(D)   are in Guatemala

The passage does not focus on the Aztecs at all; therefore, (A) is incorrect. The Mayas moved from Guatemala—they left, so Belize and Honduras cannot be in Guatemala; thus, (D) is incorrect. The sites of the Mayan temples and pyramids are the four cities mentioned, not these two countries, so (B) is incorrect. That leaves (C) as the answer.

65.   A   **Translation:** The Mayan Empire

(A)   **didn't exist after 900 A.D.**
(B)   was a territorial expansion
(C)   was destroyed by Cortés when he arrived in Mexico
(D)   was better than the Aztec Empire

The Empire was not a territorial expansion and was not destroyed by Cortés, so (B) and (C) are incorrect. Although the passage says that **La cultura de los mayas era aún más avanzada** than that of the Aztecs, it doesn't say that it was better, so (D) is incorrect. Choice (A) corresponds with the time of the disappearance of the Mayan civilization and is correct.

66. **D** Translation: The great mystery of the Mayas is

(A) their apex
(B) their ruins
(C) their success
(D) their disappearance

Nearly the entire second half of the passage talks about the disappearance of the Mayas and says that it has been **un enigma**. Choice (D) is correct.

67. **D** Translation: The bellicosity (tendency to be warlike) of the Mayas is due to

(A) the new archaeological discoveries
(B) the famous ruins of temples
(C) the decline of their empire
(D) their desire to increase the extent of their empire

The passage says that **las confrontaciones bélicas...acompañaban esa expansión**—that is, they became more aggressive in trying to expand their empire. Choice (D) summarizes this nicely.

Passage:

Nos conviene pensar en los inmigrantes como miembros de tres grupos. El primer grupo consiste en los que vinieron aquí cuando eran adultos y ya hablaban su lengua materna. El segundo grupo consiste en los que nacieron aquí o vinieron aquí cuando eran niños; son hijos del primer grupo. El tercer grupo consiste en los que nacieron aquí, hijos del segundo grupo.

El primer grupo suele aprender un inglés funcional. Es decir, aprenden a expresarse y a comprender bastante bien pero casi nunca aprenden a hablar sin errores y sin acento. El segundo grupo aprende a hablar inglés perfectamente bien, sin ningún acento extranjero. Pero como hijos de inmigrantes, este grupo retiene algo de su primera lengua y muchas veces es bilingüe. El tercer grupo suele estar lingüísticamente asimilado, con poco conocimiento funcional de la lengua de sus abuelos.

La asimilación de los hispanos se ha estudiado mucho, y se ha visto repetidas veces que la gran mayoría de los inmigrantes hispanos sigue exactamente el mismo patron que todos los demás inmigrantes. Por lo tanto, la percepción de que los inmigrantes hispanos no quieren aprender inglés es totalmente falsa. Como en el caso de cualquier grupo de inmigrantes, casi todo depende del tiempo que lleve su generación en este país.

Translation:

It is fitting for us to think about immigrants as members of three groups. The first group consists of those who came here when they were adults and already spoke their mother language. The second group consists of those who were born here or who came here when they were children; they are children of the first group. The third group consists of those who were born here, children of the second group.

The first group usually learns a functional English. That is to say, they learn to express themselves and to understand well enough but almost never learn to speak without errors or without accent. The second group learns to speak English perfectly well, without any foreign accent. But as children of immigrants, this group retains something of its first language and is often bilingual. The third group is usually linguistically assimilated, with little functional knowledge of their grandparents' language.

The assimilation of Hispanics has been much studied, and it has been seen repeatedly that the great majority of Hispanic immigrants follows exactly the same pattern as all the rest of the immigrants. Therefore, the perception that Hispanic immigrants don't want to learn English is totally false. As in the case of any group of immigrants, almost everything depends on the time that their generation has been in this country.

68. **B** Translation: What determines the group to which an immigrant belongs?

(A) His/her desire to learn English
(B) The extent of his/her knowledge of English
(C) The country from which he/she came originally
(D) The number of languages in which he/she can communicate

The focus of this passage is on an immigrant's relative knowledge of English, as it is explained extensively in the second paragraph, so (B) is the correct answer.

69. **A** Translation: Why don't the members of the first group lose their accents?

(A) Their knowledge of their native language is stronger.
(B) They don't have the desire to learn a new language.
(C) They don't need to learn English.
(D) They haven't assimilated well in the new culture.

Choice (B) is a myth that this passage hopes to end, so it is incorrect. Choice (C) is negated by the phrase **suele aprender un inglés funcional**. If they don't need to, why bother? Choice (D) really has nothing to do with their accents, so (A) is the correct answer. Remember: When they came to this country **ya hablaban su lengua materna**.

70. **C** Translation: What is a principal characteristic of the second group?

(A) They learned the new language from their parents.
(B) They were born in this country.
(C) They have facility in two languages.
(D) They have spent very little time in the United States.

Choice (A) is incorrect because their parents speak only **un inglés funcional**. Choice (B) is not necessarily correct: They could have come here at an early age. If they were born here or came here early, then (D) is also incorrect. Choice (C) is the correct answer—**son bilingüe**.

71.　**B**　**Translation:** What is the great similarity between the first and third groups?

(A) They are not well assimilated linguistically in this country.

(B) They can only speak one language without error.

(C) They don't believe that there is a necessity to learn English.

(D) They are immigrants to this country.

The third group was born in the United States, so (A), (C), and (D) are all illogical, so (B) is the answer. The first group only speaks Spanish well, the third group only English.

72.　**D**　**Translation:** What is the pattern that almost all immigrants follow?

(A) Their opportunities to learn the language are not many.

(B) They divide themselves into three groups that speak their own languages.

(C) They have the same perception that they lack a desire to learn English.

(D) The extent of their linguistic assimilation depends on how much time they have lived here.

Again, (C) is a point the passage is trying to disprove, so it is incorrect. Choice (A) is not logical, given the fact that even the first generation has to learn **un inglés funcional** to survive in the country. Choice (B) is a misunderstanding—these are not physical groups that the immigrants themselves form. They are groups formed theoretically to allow us to understand how generations of immigrants differ. Choice (D) is the ultimate point of the passage, expressed in the final sentence.

73.　**A**　**Translation:** What would be a good title for this passage?

(A) "Generations of Assimilation"

(B) "Difficulties with a New Language"

(C) "Immigrants who Have Learned English"

(D) "Erroneous Perceptions of Immigrants"

The main idea of the passage is that of linguistic assimilation, so (A) is the answer. The other choices are either too narrow in scope, like (B) and (D), or completely off the map (C).

Passage:

　　　　Los estudiantes se pusieron a reír. Primero, me molestaron los modales del profesor
—era mi segundo día en un país extranjero— pero ahora me daba cólera que me pusiera en
ridículo. No dije nada.
　　　　—¿Tal vez, continuó, nos hará el honor de tocar "Souvenir de Spa"?
　　　　Se trataba de una composición superficialmente brillante, popular en la escuela belga.
Contesté que sí, que la tocaría.
　　　　—Estoy seguro de que vamos a oír algo asombroso de este joven que lo sabe todo. Pero,
¿y en qué va a tocar?
　　　　Más risa entre los estudiantes. Yo estaba tan furioso que estuve a punto de irme. Pero,
recapacité. Quiera o no quiera, me dije, me va a escuchar. Le arrebaté el violoncelo del
estudiante que estaba a mi lado y empecé a tocar. Se produjo un gran silencio en la sala.
Cuando concluí, no se oía un ruido. El profesor me observaba intensamente, tenía una rara
expresión en la cara.
　　　　—¿Quiere venir a mi oficina? —preguntó el profesor.

Translation:

The students started to laugh. First, the professor's manner bothered me—it was my second day in a foreign country—but now it angered me that he ridiculed me. I said nothing.

"Perhaps," he continued, "you will do us the honor of playing 'Souvenir de Spa'?"

He was talking about a superficially brilliant composition, popular in the Belgian school. I answered that yes, I would play it.

"I am sure that we are going to hear something amazing from this young man who knows it all. But, on what are you going to play?"

More laughter among the students. I was so furious that I was at the point of leaving. But I thought things over. Like it or not, I told myself, he is going to listen to me. I snatched the cello from the student that was at my side and began to play. A great silence came over the room. When I finished, not a sound was heard. The professor was observing me intensely; he had a strange expression on his face.

"Do you want to come to my office?" he said.

74. **B** **Translation:** Who is the narrator?

(A) A professional musician
(B) A student from a foreign country
(C) Someone who is lost
(D) An employee of the school

In the first paragraph, the narrator says **era mi segundo día en un país extranjero**. There is no indication that he is lost or an employee of the school, so we can eliminate (C) and (D). And although he can play a musical instrument, we do not know whether he is a professional musician (A). Choice (B) is the correct answer.

75. **A** **Translation:** What is "Souvenir de Spa"?

(A) It is a well-known work of music.
(B) It is a masterpiece of literature.
(C) It is a magnificent sculpture.
(D) It is a classic poem.

The word **composición** may fool some people into picking (B) or (D). When we see, however, the words **violoncelo** and **tocar**, we should realize that we are talking about music, making (A) the answer.

76.   **C**   **Translation:** What is the attitude of the teacher toward the narrator at the beginning of the passage?

(A) Profound respect
(B) Humbled support
(C) **Amused condescension**
(D) Open disdain

The passage begins with the teacher having just ridiculed the narrator, so (A) and (B) seem unlikely. Choice (D) is a little too extreme an answer; the point is that the teacher is subtly questioning the ability of the narrator, not openly saying that he hates him. Choice (C) is the proper response.

77.   **A**   **Translation:** How do the students react when they hear the narrator play the musical instrument?

(A) **They don't say anything.**
(B) They begin to applaud.
(C) They laugh.
(D) They leave the classroom.

In the second-to-last paragraph, the narrator says that when he finished playing, **no se oía ni un ruido**. The students don't applaud, laugh, or leave the room, so (B), (C), and (D) are incorrect. Choice (A) is the correct answer.

78.   **D**   **Translation:** What trait about the narrator stands out the most?

(A) His timidity
(B) His kindness
(C) His humility
(D) **His determination**

To stand up to a condescending teacher is anything but timid, so that eliminates (A). Nothing indicates that the narrator is kind or humble, which rules out (B) and (C). Choice (D) is the best answer.

79.   **C**   **Translation:** What would be a good title for this passage?

(A) "An Apple a Day Keeps the Doctor Away"
(B) "Great Minds Think Alike"
(C) **"Don't Judge a Book by Its Cover"**
(D) "Love Has No Price"

Neither (A) nor (D) has any relevance to the passage. We can also eliminate (B); clearly the teacher and the narrator don't see eye to eye. Choice (C) is the best answer because the teacher assumes without any real basis that the narrator can't play the song.

Passage:

25 de Marzo de 2014
Londres, Inglaterra
Reino Unido

Querido Abuelo:

¡Hola! ¡Tanto tiempo que no te escribo! Espero que te sientas bien y que tu pierna ya se haya curado. ¡Cuidado con el hielo abuelo! Es muy resbaladizo.

Los estudios van muy bien y realmente me gusta mucho Oxford. Es una universidad muy popular pero los profesores dan mucho trabajo, y eso no me gusta. El fin de semana pasado, me tomé un tren a Londres. ¡Que lindo que es! Visité los grandes museos, el palacio de Buckingham, el río Thames y las Casas de Parlamento. Realmente fue una experiencia. Las cafeterías son bastante caras, pero sin embargo me he juntado con muchos amigos para cenar. Me gusta mucho la comida. Espero poder volver el próximo año por última vez antes de volver para casa. ¿Están planeando con la abuela visitarnos el próximo año? Me gustaría verte a vos y a la abuela. Ya sé que el viaje de Alaska a Oregón no es nada fácil. A lo mejor podemos planear en encontrarnos en California.

Mañana empiezo una nueva clase de arte. Quería otro curso de arte artesanal, pero no tenían espacio. Me anoté para un curso de arte moderno. ¡Estoy muy entusiasmada! Te voy a mandar unos de mis grandes dibujos—¡algún día los podrás vender!
¡Te mando muchos abrazos y besos! Espero verte pronto. ¡Te quiero mucho!

Ana

Translation:

March 25, 2014
London, England
United Kingdom

Dear Grandpa:

Hello! It's been a long time since I wrote you. I hope you are feeling good and that your leg has healed. Careful with the ice, Grandpa! It's very slippery.

My studies are going really well and I really like Oxford. It's a very popular university, but the professors give a lot of work, and I don't like that. Last weekend, I took a train to London. It's so pretty! I visited the grand museums, Buckingham Palace, the Thames River, and the Houses of Parliament. It really was an experience. The cafes are very expensive, but nevertheless I met up with a lot of my friends for dinner. I really love the food. I hope to be able to go back once more next year before returning home. Are you planning to visit us next year? I would like to see you and Grandma. I know that the trip from Alaska to Oregon is not easy. Maybe we can plan to meet up in California.

Tomorrow I start a new art class. I wanted another course on artisanal art, but there was no room. I signed up for a course on modern art. I am very excited! I will send you some of my grand drawings—someday you might be able to sell them!

I send you lots of hugs and kisses! I hope to see you soon. I love you very much!

Ana

80. **B**   **Translation: What does Ana not like?**

(A) Oxford University
(B) The amount of work that the professors give
(C) The city of London
(D) Oxford's popularity

In her postcard, Ana makes reference to liking Oxford very much but not the amount of work that the professors give her. Choice (B) is the correct answer.

81. **C**   **Translation: How did the grandfather hurt his leg?**

(A) He went ice skating in Alaska.
(B) He fell.
(C) He fell on the ice.
(D) He broke his leg.

At the beginning of the her letter, Ana sends her good wishes to her grandfather about his leg. She says to be cautious of ice because it's slippery. However, it's not clear whether the accident involved ice skating or whether her grandfather broke his leg, so we have to eliminate (A) and (D). Also, (B) is not specific enough, since we know ice was the cause of the incident. Therefore, (C) is the correct answer.

82. **A**   **Translation: What can be said of the cafes?**

(A) They are expensive.
(B) They are not close to central London.
(C) They don't take reservations.
(D) She doesn't like the food they serve.

Ana states that the cafes are expensive. She makes no mention of the distance to central London (B) or reservations (C), and she mentions loving the food in London. Therefore, (A) is the correct answer.

83. **D**   **Translation: Why did she go to London?**

(A) To study
(B) To meet up with her grandfather
(C) To meet up with her friends
(D) To go on a tourist excursion

Ana is already studying at Oxford and finishing up her studies next year. She is sending her grandfather a postcard, so we can eliminate (A) and (B). She mentions meeting up with her friends for dinner, but that does not seem to be the main reason for her trip, so we can eliminate (C). However, we know that Ana visited numerous tourist attractions, so (D) is the correct answer.

84. **D**   **Translation:** Where and when does Ana want to meet up with her grandfather?

(A) Next year in Oregon

(B) Next month in Oregon

(C) Next year in Alaska

(D) Next year in California

Ana is visiting London, but she lives in Oregon. We know her grandfather lives in Alaska, as Ana mentions that the trip from Alaska to Orgeon is not easy. This probably explains why she suggests that they meet up in California next year, making (D) the correct answer.

85. **B**   **Translation:** What type of course did Ana want to take?

(A) A course in modern art

(B) A course in artisanal art

(C) A course in general art

(D) A course in special art

Ana writes that she has started a new class. She wanted an artisanal art class, but it was full, so she registered for a course in modern art instead. Choice (B) is the correct answer, as it represents what she *wanted* to take, not what she ended up taking.

HOW TO SCORE PRACTICE TEST 2

When you take the real exam, the proctors take away your exam and your bubble sheet and send it to a processing center, where a computer looks at the pattern of filled-in ovals on your exam and gives you a score. We couldn't include even a small computer with this book, so we are providing this more primitive way of scoring your exam.

Determining Your Score

STEP 1   Using the answer key, determine how many questions you got right and how many you got wrong on the test. Remember, questions that you do not answer do not count as either right answers or wrong answers.

STEP 2   List the number of right answers here.

(A) _____

STEP 3   List the number of wrong answers here. Now divide that number by 3.

(B) _____ ÷ 3 _____ = (C) _____

STEP 4   Subtract the number of wrong answers divided by 3 (C) from the number of correct answers (A). Round this score to the nearest whole number. This is your raw score.

(A) – (C) = _____

STEP 5   To determine your real score, take the number from Step 4 above and look it up in the left column of the Score Conversion Table on the next page; the corresponding score on the right is your score on the exam.

PRACTICE TEST 2
SCORE CONVERSION TABLE

Raw Score	Scaled Score	Raw Score	Scaled Score	Raw Score	Scaled Score
85	800	47	590	9	360
84	800	46	580	8	360
83	800	45	570	7	350
82	800	44	570	6	350
81	790	43	560	5	340
80	790	42	550	4	340
79	780	41	550	3	330
78	780	40	540	2	320
77	770	39	530	1	320
76	770	38	530	0	310
75	760	37	520	−1	310
74	760	36	520	−2	300
73	750	35	510	−3	290
72	750	34	500	−4	290
71	740	33	500	−5	280
70	730	32	490	−6	270
69	730	31	490	−7	260
68	720	30	480	−8	260
67	720	29	470	−9	250
66	710	28	470	−10	240
65	700	27	460	−11	230
64	700	26	460	−12	220
63	690	25	450	−13	220
62	680	24	450	−14	220
61	680	23	440	−15	210
60	670	22	430	−16	210
59	670	21	430	−17	210
58	660	20	420	−18	200
57	650	19	420	−19	200
56	650	18	410	−20	200
55	640	17	410	−21	200
54	630	16	400	−22	200
53	630	15	400	−23	200
52	620	14	390	−24	200
51	620	13	390	−25	200
50	610	12	380	−26	200
49	600	11	380	−27	200
48	590	10	370	−28	200

Practice Test 3

SPANISH SUBJECT TEST 3

Your responses to Spanish Subject Test 3 questions must be filled in on Test 3 of your answer sheet (at the back of the book). Marks on any other section will not be counted toward your Spanish Subject Test score.

When your supervisor gives the signal, turn the page and begin the Spanish Subject Test.

SPANISH SUBJECT TEST

PLEASE NOTE THAT YOUR ANSWER SHEET HAS FIVE ANSWER POSITIONS MARKED A, B, C, D, E, WHILE THE QUESTIONS THROUGHOUT THIS TEST CONTAIN ONLY FOUR CHOICES. BE SURE <u>NOT</u> TO MAKE ANY MARKS IN COLUMN E.

Part A

Directions: This part consists of a number of incomplete statements, each having four suggested completions. Select the most appropriate completion and fill in the corresponding oval on the answer sheet.

---

1. Manuel no pudo comer ------- porque estaba demasiado caliente.

   (A) la naranja
   (B) las medias
   (C) la sopa
   (D) la acera

2. Mis amigos van de compras ------- : cada lunes, jueves y sábado.

   (A) a menudo
   (B) de mala gana
   (C) diariamente
   (D) poco

3. Comeríamos mucho menos si no ------- comida en casa.

   (A) hay
   (B) haya
   (C) habría
   (D) hubiera

4. Cuando el fin de semana venga, ------- tiempo para hacer tus deberes en casa.

   (A) tienes
   (B) tenías
   (C) tendrías
   (D) tendrás

5. Como ella trabaja en Nueva York y Connecticut, tiene que pagar ------- en los dos estados.

   (A) ingresos
   (B) impuestos
   (C) deudas
   (D) luto

6. El equipo tuvo que cancelar el partido ------- la lluvia.

   (A) para
   (B) sin
   (C) a causa de
   (D) dentro de

7. Mi sofá es muy cómodo porque es viejo; ------- es nuevo y no muy cómodo.

   (A) el suyo
   (B) la suya
   (C) los suyos
   (D) las suyas

8. Mi mamá fue al dentista porque le dolían los dientes. El dentista necesitó sacarle ------- .

   (A) las carteras
   (B) las muelas
   (C) los techos
   (D) los hombros

9. Rodrigo sabe esquiar muy bien, pero yo no. Él es mejor ------- yo.

   (A) que
   (B) como
   (C) para
   (D) de

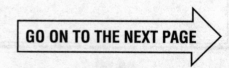

GO ON TO THE NEXT PAGE

10. A Susana no le gusta que casi todo el mundo ------- todo lo que pasa en su vida.

    (A) sabe
    (B) sepa
    (C) conoce
    (D) conozca

11. Fue imposible sacar agua del pozo porque el pozo estaba completamente ------- .

    (A) alto
    (B) fresco
    (C) anaranjado
    (D) seco

12. El policía va a dudar que le ------- la verdad si nos detiene.

    (A) digamos
    (B) decimos
    (C) diríamos
    (D) habremos dicho

13. La tienda está en ------- de la Calle Santo Tomás y la Avenida de Toros.

    (A) el pasillo
    (B) la esquina
    (C) la red
    (D) el rincón

14. Bárbara y Nicolás siempre quieren dar su ayuda. Cuando ------- la dan a sus compañeros de clase, ellos están muy alegres.

    (A) le
    (B) se
    (C) les
    (D) lo

15. ¿ ------- cuántas horas trabaja tu esposa todos los días?

    (A) Por
    (B) Para
    (C) Antes de
    (D) Desde

16. Si Uds. no se acuestan más temprano, estarán muy ------- mañana.

    (A) borrachas
    (B) cansadas
    (C) activas
    (D) heridas

17. ¡No me ------- cuenta de que él era tu tío hasta este momento!

    (A) he dado
    (B) había dado
    (C) habría dado
    (D) habré dado

18. Roberto perdió la voz anoche, entonces no podrá ------- hoy.

    (A) correr
    (B) respirar
    (C) cantar
    (D) barrer

19. ¿No puedes encontrar tu anillo? Creo que lo ------- en la cocina cerca del fregadero.

    (A) vi
    (B) fui
    (C) di
    (D) oí

20. Si tengo un paquete, compro estampillas, y entonces se lo envío a alguien, probablemente estoy en la oficina de ------- .

    (A) correos
    (B) platos
    (C) educación
    (D) regalos

21. Cuando una película nos confunde, la ------- después para entenderla mejor.

    (A) discutes
    (B) discute
    (C) discutimos
    (D) discuten

GO ON TO THE NEXT PAGE

22. El jefe me sigue como si ------- que yo hiciera algo malo.

    (A) esperó
    (B) esperara
    (C) espera
    (D) espere

23. Cuando el profesor terminó su lección, borró ------- y se fue de la sala de clase.

    (A) la pizarra
    (B) la basura
    (C) el escritorio
    (D) a la alumna

24. ¿Necesitas tomates y lechuga en la ensalada? Te ------- traeré en seguida.

    (A) lo
    (B) la
    (C) los
    (D) las

25. ¿Le ------- a Ud. un poco extraño que ellos no llevaran zapatos en la nieve?

    (A) veía
    (B) miraba
    (C) buscaba
    (D) parecía

26. ¿ ------- quién estaban preparando un pavo grande y puré de papas?

    (A) De
    (B) Dónde
    (C) A
    (D) Para

27. Estas dos rosas huelen exactamente similares, entonces esta rosa es ------- esa.

    (A) poco aromática a
    (B) menos aromática que
    (C) más aromática que
    (D) tan aromática como

28. Nadie ------- los tambores como Tito Puente.

    (A) jugaba
    (B) hacía
    (C) tocaba
    (D) ponía

29. Cuando la compañía ------- quién ganó el premio, estoy segura que seré yo.

    (A) anuncia
    (B) anuncie
    (C) anunció
    (D) anunciara

GO ON TO THE NEXT PAGE

SPANISH SUBJECT TEST—*Continued*

Directions: In each of the following passages, there are numbered blanks indicating that words or phrases have been omitted. For each numbered blank, four completions are provided. First read through the entire paragraph. Then, for each numbered blank, choose the completion that is most appropriate given the context of the entire paragraph and fill in the corresponding oval on the answer sheet.

En cada segundo, vivimos un momento nuevo y único del universo, un momento que no existió (30) y no existirá otra vez. ¿Y qué (31) enseñamos a los niños en las escuelas? Enseñamos que dos más dos es cuatro y que París es la capital de Francia. ¿Cuándo enseñamos (32) ellos son? Deberíamos decirle a cada niño: ¿Sabes lo que eres? Eres una maravilla. Único. No (33) en todo el mundo otro niño exactamente como (34) . Todos debemos trabajar para hacer que este mundo (35) digno de sus niños. (36) familia es una sola. Cada uno de nosotros tiene un deber (37) sus hermanos. Todos somos (38) de un solo árbol y ese árbol es la humanidad.

30. (A) nada
    (B) nunca
    (C) siempre
    (D) alguna vez

31. (A) los
    (B) lo
    (C) le
    (D) les

32. (A) que
    (B) cuando
    (C) lo que
    (D) donde

33. (A) hay
    (B) está
    (C) esté
    (D) es

34. (A) ti
    (B) tú
    (C) tuyo
    (D) suyo

35. (A) es
    (B) sea
    (C) era
    (D) fuera

36. (A) Nosotros
    (B) Nos
    (C) Nuestra
    (D) Ningún

37. (A) para
    (B) con
    (C) desde
    (D) sin

38. (A) ruedas
    (B) hojas
    (C) pastillas
    (D) albóndigas

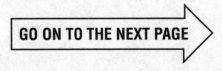
GO ON TO THE NEXT PAGE

Una mañana, se levantó y fue a buscar al amigo al otro lado de la valla. Pero el amigo no (39) , y cuando volvió, le dijo la madre:

—El amigo se murió. Niño, no pienses más (40) él y busca otros para jugar.

El niño se sentó en el quicio de la puerta con la cara (41) las manos y los codos en las rodillas.

"Él (42) ", pensó. Porque no podía ser que allí (43) las canicas, el camión, la pistola de hojalata y el reloj que ya no andaba, y el amigo no viniera a buscarlos. Vino la noche, con (44) muy grande, y el niño no quería entrar a comer.

—Entra niño, que (45) el frío—dijo la madre. Pero (46) entrar, el niño se levantó del quicio y se fue en busca del amigo. Pasó buscándole toda la noche. Cuando llegó el sol, el niño pensó: "Qué tontos y pequeños son (47) juguetes. Y ese reloj que no anda, (48) sirve para nada." (49) tiró al pozo y volvió a la casa, con mucha hambre.

39. (A) había
    (B) era
    (C) iba
    (D) estaba

40. (A) de
    (B) en
    (C) que
    (D) sobre

41. (A) entre
    (B) arriba de
    (C) debajo de
    (D) sin

42. (A) volvió
    (B) vuelva
    (C) volviera
    (D) volverá

43. (A) estaban
    (B) estuvieron
    (C) estuvieran
    (D) están

44. (A) una estrella
    (B) un sol
    (C) una flor
    (D) un océano

45. (A) lleva
    (B) llega
    (C) llueve
    (D) llora

46. (A) además
    (B) al
    (C) a pesar de
    (D) en lugar de

47. (A) esas
    (B) esos
    (C) esa
    (D) eso

48. (A) no
    (B) nadie
    (C) nada
    (D) ninguno

49. (A) La
    (B) Lo
    (C) Le
    (D) Les

GO ON TO THE NEXT PAGE

Hoy, con la facilidad de la fotografía, tendemos a olvidarnos (50) la importancia que tenía la pintura en el pasado como modo de conservar (51) de momentos históricos. El enorme (52), *La rendición de Breda,* fue pintado para conmemorar la victoria militar española de 1625 contra los holandeses. Velázquez (53) pintó diez años después del incidente y (54) que usar todo su ingenio para representar a personajes y un paisaje que nunca (55). Pero, ¡qué sorpresa! No es típico de las pinturas militares, porque (56) la violencia, la guerra y el orgullo nacional para evocar, en cambio, (57) de tranquilidad y compasión humana.

50. (A) con
    (B) a
    (C) de
    (D) en

51. (A) la basura
    (B) los recuerdos
    (C) la música
    (D) las muertes

52. (A) cuadro
    (B) abrazo
    (C) español
    (D) acontecimiento

53. (A) le
    (B) la
    (C) lo
    (D) se

54. (A) tuvo
    (B) tuviera
    (C) tendría
    (D) habría tenido

55. (A) ve
    (B) verá
    (C) habrá visto
    (D) había visto

56. (A) muestra
    (B) delinea
    (C) evita
    (D) adopta

57. (A) unos hechos
    (B) una salida
    (C) un mes
    (D) un sentido

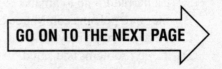

GO ON TO THE NEXT PAGE

Part C

Directions: Read the following texts carefully for comprehension. Each passage is followed by a number of questions or incomplete statements. Select the answer or completion that is best according to the text and fill in the corresponding oval on the answer sheet.

Se marchó y Luisa quedó sola. Absolutamente sola. Se sentó, desfallecida. Las manos dejaron caer el cuchillo contra el suelo. Tenía frío, mucho frío. Por el ventanuco, entraban gritos de los vencejos y el rumor del río entre las piedras. "Marcos, tú tienes la culpa...tú, porque Amadeo" ...De pronto, tuvo miedo, un miedo extraño, que hacía temblar sus manos. "Amadeo me quería. Sí: El me quería". ¿Cómo iba a dudarlo? Amadeo era brusco, desprovisto de ternura, callado, taciturno. Amadeo —a medias palabras, ella lo entendió— tuvo una infancia dura, una juventud amarga. Amadeo era pobre y ganaba su vida —la de él, la de ella y la de los hijos que hubieran podido tener— en un trabajo ingrato que destruía su salud. Y ella: ¿Tuvo ternura para él? ¿Comprensión? ¿Cariño? De pronto, vio algo. Vio su silla; su ropa allí, sucia, a punto de lavar; sus botas, en el rincón, aún llenas de barro. Algo le subió, como un grito. "Sí, me quería...acaso ¿será capaz de matarse?"

58. ¿Qué siempre ha dudado la narradora?

   (A) Que Amadeo tuviera sentimientos por ella
   (B) Que Marcos tuviera la culpa por sus problemas
   (C) Que Amadeo y ella pudieran tener hijos
   (D) Que Amadeo y ella fueran a ser ricos

59. ¿Qué tipo de persona es Amadeo?

   (A) Es muy amable y extrovertido.
   (B) Es profundamente cruel y violento.
   (C) Es apasionado y sensible.
   (D) Es bastante tranquilo y no muy
       bien refinado.

60. Según el pasaje, ¿por qué es la personalidad de Amadeo tal como es?

   (A) La narradora no lo amaba.
   (B) Siempre peleaba con Marcos.
   (C) Tuvo una vida muy difícil.
   (D) Tiene problemas de salud.

61. ¿Adónde piensa la narradora que Amadeo fue?

   (A) Al río para pescar
   (B) A su trabajo para ganar dinero
   (C) Afuera de la casa para suicidarse
   (D) Al cuarto de sus hijos

62. ¿Cuál es el punto central de este pasaje?

   (A) La narradora no ha sabido que Amadeo la ama
       hasta este momento.
   (B) Marcos es la causa de los problemas entre
       Amadeo y la narradora.
   (C) La vida de Amadeo y la narradora es
       increíblemente próspera.
   (D) Amadeo y Marcos se odian.

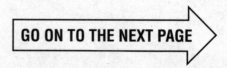

GO ON TO THE NEXT PAGE

Muchos científicos advierten con alarma que la Tierra está calentándose. Explican que esto podría significar un gran peligro debido al efecto invernadero. Un invernadero es un edificio donde se cultivan plantas usando el techo de vidrio (cristal) que permite la entrada de los rayos del sol, pero no deja que salga todo el calor reflejado. Según esta comparación, la atmósfera de nuestro planeta funciona como el techo de vidrio.

En realidad, el efecto invernadero, en proporciones moderadas, es positivo y aun necesario. Si no tuviera esta función nuestra atmósfera, la Tierra sufriría los radicales cambios de temperatura que ocurren en la luna, con un frío espantoso de noche y un calor insoportable de día. Mirándolo así, debemos darle gracias al efecto invernadero. Sin embargo, algunos expertos temen que la acumulación del dióxido de carbono, del metano y de otros gases producidos por las actividades humanas aumente la eficiencia de nuestro "techo de vidrio" a tal punto que atrape demasiado calor.

Muchos factores, como los terremotos y las erupciones de volcanes, influyen momentáneamente en el clima, pero el gradual calentamiento de la Tierra parece casi inevitable. De acuerdo con sus cálculos, los científicos afirman que desde el año 1850, el aumento de la temperatura global ha sido de uno a cinco grados centígrados, y que hacia el año 2030, podría llegar a aumentar entre 1,5 a 4,5 grados más. Junto con esta subida, se pronostican consecuencias drásticas en las economías de muchas regiones debido a fluctuaciones en la producción agrícola, pérdida o ganancia en el negocio del turismo y otros cambios.

63. ¿Cuál es la función de un efecto invernadero?

(A) Aumentar la temperatura de la Tierra
(B) Tener efectos positivos en la atmósfera del planeta
(C) Dejar que el sol entre, pero que el calor no salga
(D) Producir gases para el beneficio de la atmósfera

64. ¿Cuál es un resultado positivo del efecto invernadero?

(A) La temperatura de la Tierra no varía demasiado.
(B) El frío es espantoso y el calor insoportable.
(C) Atrapa el calor del sol para calentar el planeta.
(D) La producción agrícola fluctúa.

65. ¿Por qué piensan algunos expertos que la atmósfera es un "techo de vidrio"?

(A) Nos deja ver las estrellas.
(B) Encierra el planeta de manera efectiva.
(C) La temperatura fluctúa mucho.
(D) Causa problemas económicos.

66. ¿Cuál es el gran temor de algunos científicos?

(A) Que la situación empeore
(B) Que los gases producidos por la actividad humana desaparezcan
(C) Que no se pueda ver el universo fuera del "techo de vidrio"
(D) Que la temperatura baje drásticamente antes del año 2030

67. ¿Cuál podría ser el aumento total de la temperatura de la Tierra hacia el año 2030?

(A) Entre 1 y 5 grados centígrados
(B) Entre 1,5 y 4,5 grados centígrados
(C) Entre 2,5 y 9,5 grados centígrados
(D) Entre 5 y 15 grados centígrados

68. ¿Por qué la economía sufriría si el efecto invernadero continuara en el futuro?

(A) Los terremotos y los volcanes destruirían mucho del planeta.
(B) La cantidad de comida cultivada en la tierra podría bajar mucho.
(C) Los científicos necesitarían más dinero para investigar más este fenómeno.
(D) Necesitaríamos más industrias que no dependan tanto del tiempo.

GO ON TO THE NEXT PAGE

LA COCINA DE TOMAS

RESTAURANTE * CLUB DE BAILE

28 Elf Street, Lee, MA * 432-888-9090

El lugar mas lindo, original y lujoso de Massachusetts.

Comida Hispana con especialidad en: ¡empanadas y margaritas!

¡Venga a probar uno o todos los platos en el menú y quédese a bailar! ¡Música Latina para todos y mucho mas!

¡Abierto todo los días desde las 12 P.M. hasta amanecer!

¡Tenemos muchos grupos musicales que tocan todos los viernes!

La Cocina de Tomas presenta:

Junio 13: Orquesta Orlando—música de Argentina y Colombia
Junio 20: Los Lobos Locos—Mariachi
Junio 27: María Luz Roca—la Cantante Mejicana
Julio 4: Los Independientes—¡un grupo local que viene a festejar el día de la Independencia Americana! ¡Compre 2 entradas antes del 4 de julio y reciba una margarita gratis!

¡Reserve Hoy!

Mesas y asientos limitados.

69. ¿Que tipo de lugar es La Cocina de Tomas?

(A) Cocina
(B) Restaurante
(C) Restaurante y bar
(D) Restaurante y lugar de baile

70. ¿Quiénes son Los Independientes?

(A) Grupo musical de Argentina
(B) Grupo musical de los Estados Unidos
(C) Grupo musical local
(D) Grupo musical que festeja todo

71. ¿Cuándo hay que reservar y por que?

(A) Cuando se pueda porque hay muchas mesas
(B) Después de amanecer porque si no están cerrados
(C) Después de el 4 de Julio porque es un día feriado
(D) Inmediatamente porque no hay mucho lugar

72. ¿Cómo se describe el establecimiento?

(A) Lujoso
(B) Feo
(C) Famoso
(D) Lejano

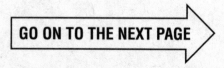

GO ON TO THE NEXT PAGE

73. ¿A que hora cerraría La Cocina de Tomas?

    (A) 12:00 A.M.
    (B) 2:00 A.M.
    (C) 6:00 A.M.
    (D) 12:00 P.M.

74. ¿Hay alguna ventaja por comprar las entradas temprano?

    (A) Si, pero hay que comprarlas el 4 de Julio.
    (B) Si, pero hay que comprarlas antes del 4 de Julio.
    (C) No, no hay ventaja.
    (D) No, no hay ninguna oferta especial.

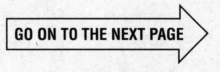

GO ON TO THE NEXT PAGE

Un producto de enorme importancia cultural y comercial en el mundo, el café tiene una historia pintoresca y de origen incierto. Según una conocida leyenda, fue en Etiopía, por el año 850, que un pastor observó que su rebaño se agitaba tras ingerir los frutos de un arbusto misterioso, el cafeto. Él mismo probó los frutos, y le gustó tanto la sensación, que compartió los frutos con otros en su poblado.

Varios siglos más adelante, el café llegó a Venecia por medio de los turcos. Desde esta ciudad italiana, el café pasó al resto de Europa, llegando primero a París y, pocos años después, a Londres. En el año 1723, Gabriel de Clieu llevó un cafeto al Caribe, y así llegó esta deliciosa bebida a las Américas. Hoy en día, el café es la bebida más popular del mundo.

Los expertos dicen que hay cuatro factores claves en la producción del café: el clima, es decir, la proporción de sol y lluvia; la altura (cuanto mayor sea, mejor es la calidad); el terreno (el suelo volcánico es el más rico en nutrientes); y el cuidado durante la cosecha. Cada árbol tarda entre tres y cuatro años antes de dar fruto, pero una vez maduro, el árbol permanece activo y productivo durante muchas décadas.

Así, lo que conocemos como el café tuvo que pasar por una interesante historia antes de llegar a la taza que nos tomamos.

75. ¿Dónde tiene el café su origen, supuestamente?

(A) En el Caribe
(B) En Etiopía
(C) En Turquía
(D) En Venecia

76. ¿Quién descubrió el café?

(A) Unos animales salvajes en el desierto
(B) Agricultores musulmanes
(C) Un pastor que observó cómo sus cabras se agitaban
(D) Unos pintores inciertos

77. ¿Cuál fue la reacción inicial al probar los frutos del cafeto?

(A) Repugnancia
(B) Confusión
(C) Satisfacción
(D) Indiferencia

78. Se podría deducir que el mejor sitio para cultivar el café sería

(A) la playa
(B) el desierto
(C) una gran ciudad
(D) las montañas

79. El árbol de café

(A) tiene una vida corta
(B) produce una libra de semillas desde el primer año
(C) puede ser productivo durante más de diez años
(D) tarda varias décadas en dar fruto

GO ON TO THE NEXT PAGE

Nos gustaba la casa porque, aparte de espaciosa y antigua, guardaba los recuerdos de nuestros bisabuelos, el abuelo paterno, nuestros padres y toda la infancia.

Nos habituamos Irene y yo a vivir solos en ella, lo que era una locura, pues en esa casa podían vivir ocho personas sin estorbarse. Hacíamos la limpieza por la mañana, levantándonos a las siete, y a eso de las once yo le dejaba a Irene las últimas habitaciones por repasar y me iba a la cocina. Almorzábamos a mediodía, siempre puntuales; ya no quedaba nada por hacer fuera de unos pocos platos sucios. Nos resultaba grato almorzar pensando en la casa profunda y silenciosa. A veces, llegamos a creer que era ella la que no nos dejó casarnos. Irene rechazó dos pretendientes sin mayor motivo. A mí se me murió María Esther antes que llegáramos a comprometernos. Entramos en los cuarenta años con la inexpresada idea de que el nuestro simple y silencioso matrimonio de hermanos era una clausura necesaria de la genealogía asentada por los bisabuelos en nuestra casa.

Pero es de la casa que me interesa hablar, de la casa y de Irene, porque yo no tengo importancia. Me pregunto qué hubiera hecho Irene sin el tejido. No necesitábamos ganarnos la vida. Todos los meses llegaba la plata de los campos y el dinero aumentaba. Pero a Irene solamente le entretenía el tejido. Mostraba una destreza maravillosa, y a mí se me iban las horas viéndole las manos. Era hermoso.

80. ¿Cómo es la vida del narrador e Irene?

    (A) Es excitante y llena de aventura.
    (B) Es repetitiva y bastante pasiva.
    (C) Es triste y muy deprimente.
    (D) No es muy próspera.

81. ¿Cómo es la casa del narrador e Irene?

    (A) Es pequeña y básicamente cómoda.
    (B) Está mal construida.
    (C) Está muy sucia.
    (D) Es enorme y está bastante vacía.

82. ¿Por qué rechazó Irene a sus dos novios?

    (A) No hay una razón aparente.
    (B) Al narrador no le gustaban.
    (C) Ellos no querían vivir en la casa.
    (D) Los padres de Irene los rechazaron también.

83. ¿Quién es María Esther?

    (A) Otra hermana del narrador
    (B) La madre del narrador
    (C) La novia muerta del narrador
    (D) La esposa del narrador

84. ¿Cuál es el estado financiero del narrador e Irene?

    (A) Son muy pobres porque no trabajan.
    (B) Tienen una vida difícil, pero tienen pocos problemas financieros.
    (C) No se puede determinar su estado financiero en el pasaje.
    (D) Ellos son muy ricos con el dinero de su propiedad.

85. ¿Cómo pasa el narrador su tiempo?

    (A) Sale con María Esther.
    (B) Investiga la genealogía de su familia.
    (C) Teje.
    (D) Mira a Irene hacer su propio trabajo.

STOP
**If you finish before time is called, you may check your work on this test only.
Do not work on any other test in this book.**

Practice Test 3: Answers and Explanations

- Practice Test 3 Answer Key
- Practice Test 3 Explanations
- How to Score Practice Test 3

PRACTICE TEST 3 ANSWER KEY

Question Number	Correct Answer	Right	Wrong	Question Number	Correct Answer	Right	Wrong	Question Number	Correct Answer	Right	Wrong
1	C	___	___	33	A	___	___	65	B	___	___
2	A	___	___	34	B	___	___	66	A	___	___
3	D	___	___	35	B	___	___	67	C	___	___
4	D	___	___	36	C	___	___	68	B	___	___
5	B	___	___	37	B	___	___	69	D	___	___
6	C	___	___	38	B	___	___	70	C	___	___
7	A	___	___	39	D	___	___	71	D	___	___
8	B	___	___	40	B	___	___	72	A	___	___
9	A	___	___	41	A	___	___	73	C	___	___
10	B	___	___	42	D	___	___	74	B	___	___
11	D	___	___	43	C	___	___	75	B	___	___
12	A	___	___	44	A	___	___	76	C	___	___
13	B	___	___	45	B	___	___	77	C	___	___
14	B	___	___	46	D	___	___	78	D	___	___
15	A	___	___	47	B	___	___	79	C	___	___
16	B	___	___	48	A	___	___	80	B	___	___
17	B	___	___	49	B	___	___	81	D	___	___
18	C	___	___	50	C	___	___	82	A	___	___
19	A	___	___	51	B	___	___	83	C	___	___
20	A	___	___	52	A	___	___	84	D	___	___
21	C	___	___	53	C	___	___	85	D	___	___
22	B	___	___	54	A	___	___				
23	A	___	___	55	D	___	___				
24	C	___	___	56	C	___	___				
25	D	___	___	57	D	___	___				
26	D	___	___	58	A	___	___				
27	D	___	___	59	D	___	___				
28	C	___	___	60	C	___	___				
29	B	___	___	61	C	___	___				
30	B	___	___	62	A	___	___				
31	D	___	___	63	C	___	___				
32	C	___	___	64	A	___	___				

PRACTICE TEST 3 EXPLANATIONS

Part A

1. **C**   **Translation:** Manuel couldn't eat ------- because it was too hot.

    (A) the orange
    (B) the stockings
    (C) the soup
    (D) the sidewalk

    Generally, we don't eat articles of clothing or parts of the street, so (B) and (D) are wrong. And because oranges are not usually heated, (C) is the correct answer.

2. **A**   **Translation:** My friends go shopping -------: every Monday, Thursday, and Saturday.

    (A) often
    (B) reluctantly
    (C) daily
    (D) little

    If my friends go shopping three days per week, we can hardly call that *reluctant* or *little,* so (B) and (D) are incorrect. Choice (C) also cannot be right because there are four days on which they *don't* go shopping, so the correct answer is (A).

3. **D**   **Translation:** We would eat much less if ------- no food at home.

    (A) there is (indicative)
    (B) there is (subjunctive)
    (C) there would be
    (D) there were (subjunctive)

    This sentence describes a situation that does not currently exist, so the present tense cannot be right—eliminate (A) and (B). The imperfect subjunctive is needed with the conditional to describe hypothetical events, so (D) is the correct answer.

4. **D**   **Translation:** When the weekend comes, ------- time to do your chores at home.

    (A) you have
    (B) you had
    (C) you would have
    (D) you will have

    The weekend is an anticipated event in the future, so (D) is the only answer that makes sense.

5.   **B**   **Translation:** Since she works in New York and Connecticut, she has to pay ------- in both states.

(A) income
(B) taxes
(C) debts
(D) mourning

This is a difficult question based on a student's knowledge of difficult vocabulary. While debts are certainly paid, **trabaja** is a clue that **impuestos** are what is at issue, so the correct answer is (B).

6.   **C**   **Translation:** The team had to cancel the game ------- the rain.

(A) for
(B) without
(C) because of
(D) inside of

Choice (B) can be quickly eliminated, as it's unlikely a team would cancel a game because it wasn't raining. Choices (A) and (D) also don't make a tremendous amount of sense, while (C) is quite logical. Therefore, (C) is correct.

7.   **A**   **Translation:** My sofa is very comfortable because it is old; ------- is new and not very comfortable.

(A) his/hers (masculine, singular)
(B) his/hers (feminine, singular)
(C) his/hers (masculine, plural)
(D) his/hers (feminine, plural)

Translating is not a big help in this case, as all the choices mean the same thing in English. Remember that stressed possessive pronouns agree in number and gender with the words they replace. In this case, the pronoun must agree with **sofá**, which is masculine and singular, so (A) is the answer.

8.   **B**   **Translation:** My mother went to the dentist because her teeth hurt her. The dentist needed to take out ------- .

(A) her wallets
(B) her molars
(C) her ceilings
(D) her shoulders

This is a vocabulary question. **Dentista** and **dientes** are big clues that we're looking for a type of tooth, so (B) is correct.

9.   A   **Translation:** Rodrigo knows how to ski very well, but I don't. He is better ------- I.

(A) **than**

(B) as

(C) for

(D) from

This is an idiomatic expression. Choices (C) and (D) are wrong because they are prepositions and would require the prepositional pronoun **mí** at the end of the sentence. **Mejor que** (A) is the proper expression.

10.   B   **Translation:** Susana doesn't like that almost everyone ------- everything that's happening in her life.

(A) knows (saber, indicative)

(B) **knows (saber, subjunctive)**

(C) knows (conocer, indicative)

(D) knows (conocer, subjunctive)

Our first hurdle here is the **saber/conocer** thing: Does everyone know a fact, or is everyone familiar with a person, place, or thing? **Todo lo que pasa en su vida** would be a series of *facts*, and we would thus use **saber**, which eliminates (C) and (D). Now, do we use the subjunctive or not? **No le gusta** is an expression of emotion, which always requires the subjunctive, so (B) is correct.

11.   D   **Translation:** It was impossible to take water from the well because the well was completely ------- .

(A) tall

(B) fresh

(C) orange

(D) **dry**

Even if you don't know what **pozo** means, the sentence has something to do with **agua**, so you should be looking for a word in the answer choices that relates to water. Choices (A) and (C) do not work. Choice (B) is possible and is a good second choice if you're unsure of the vocabulary, but it doesn't make as much sense as (D).

12.   A   **Translation:** The policeman is not going to believe that we ------- him the truth if he detains us.

(A) **are telling (subjunctive)**

(B) are telling (indicative)

(C) would tell

(D) will have told

The action of the sentence will occur in the *future*, and so (C)—which is used in the past or in hypothetical situations in the present—cannot be correct. The real key to this sentence is the expression **va a dudar**, which is an expression of doubt and, therefore, always requires the subjunctive. Choice (A) is the only choice in the subjunctive tense.

13. **B** **Translation:** The store is on ------- of Santo Tomás Street and the Avenue of Bulls.

   (A) the hallway
   (B) the corner
   (C) the net
   (D) the corner

If we are out on the street, then (A) can't be correct. Likewise, because we're not playing sports, (C) is not right. The answer here is tricky because it relies on a knowledge of the difference between a corner found *outside* a building (where two streets intersect), which is an **esquina**, and a corner found *inside* a building (where two walls intersect), which is a **rincón**. Thus, (B) is the answer.

14. **B** **Translation:** Bárbara and Nicolás always want to give help. When they give it ------- (their class-mates), they are very happy.

   (A) to him/her
   (B) to them/him/her
   (C) to them
   (D) it (masculine, singular)

What do they give? *Help*—a direct object. Who gets the help? Their *classmates*—an indirect object. (D) can be eliminated because it is not an indirect object pronoun. **A sus compañeros de clase** is the clarification of the identity of the indirect object, so we know that we need a plural pronoun, which eliminates (A). Remember that we cannot use **le** or **les** before a direct object pronoun that begins with **l**, like **la**. It changes to **se** in these cases, and so (B) is correct.

15. **A** **Translation:** ------- how many hours does your wife work every day?

   (A) For (por)
   (B) For (para)
   (C) Before
   (D) Since

Choices (C) and (D) are not really logical in this context, which brings us to the dreaded **para** versus **por** dilemma once again. Remember that **para** is used with destinations in time, which this sentence doesn't seem to be describing, while **por** is used with durations of time, which is the correct meaning here. Therefore, (A) is the answer.

16. **B** **Translation:** If you (pl.) don't go to bed earlier, you will be very ------- tomorrow.

   (A) drunk
   (B) tired
   (C) active
   (D) injured

   Vocabulary is important in this question as well. Not going to bed earlier means less sleep, which means less energy, thereby eliminating (C). Since no liquor or accidents are mentioned, eliminate (A) and (D); (B) is the only logical choice.

17. **B** **Translation:** I ------- that he was your uncle until this moment!

   (A) have not realized
   (B) had not realized
   (C) would not have realized
   (D) will not have realized

   When did this lack of realization take place? In the *past*, which eliminates (D). *When* in the past, though? Before or after this moment of realization that has just passed? *Before*. The tense that places past events before other past events is the pluperfect tense, which is (B).

18. **C** **Translation:** Roberto lost his voice last night, so he won't be able to ------- .

   (A) run
   (B) breathe
   (C) sing
   (D) sweep

   You need to know the word **voz** to be clued in on this question. Only (C) has anything to do with one's voice.

19. **A** **Translation:** You can't find your ring? I think I ------- it in the kitchen near the sink.

   (A) saw
   (B) went
   (C) gave
   (D) heard

   This question is playing tricks with verb forms that all sound similar, which may lead to confusion. Only (A) is logical.

20. **A** **Translation:** If I have a package, buy stamps, and then send it (the package) to someone, I am probably in the ------- office.

   (A) **post**
   (B) plates
   (C) education
   (D) presents

   Again, vocabulary is essential in this question. The words **paquete**, **estampillas**, and **envío** make it obvious that you are in the post office, so (A) is the answer.

21. **C** **Translation:** When a movie confuses us, ------- it afterward to understand it better.

   (A) you discuss
   (B) he/she discusses
   (C) **we discuss**
   (D) you (plural)/they discuss

   There has been no change in the subject that is apparent in the sentence. The indirect object pronoun **nos** gives us a "backdoor entry" into finding out the subject, **nosotros**, so (C) is correct.

22. **B** **Translation:** The boss follows me as if he ------- for me to do something bad.

   (A) waited (preterite indicative)
   (B) **were waiting (imperfect subjunctive)**
   (C) waits (indicative)
   (D) waits (subjunctive)

   Remember that the expression **como si** always requires the imperfect subjunctive, regardless of the tense of the sentence. The answer here is (B).

23. **A** **Translation:** When the professor finished the lesson, he erased ------- and left the classroom.

   (A) **the blackboard**
   (B) the garbage
   (C) the desk
   (D) the student (feminine)

   Borró is the key word, and the entire problem hinges on knowledge of this word. Only (A) makes sense.

24. **C** **Translation:** You need tomatoes and lettuce in the salad? I will bring ------- to you immediately.

   (A) it (masculine, singular)
   (B) it (feminine, singular)
   (C) them (masculine, plural)
   (D) them (feminine, plural)

   How many things am I bringing? *Two*, so I need a plural word, which eliminates (A) and (B). Remember that when a masculine and feminine noun are grouped together, the group retains the *masculine* article, so (C) is the answer.

25. **D** **Translation:** Did it ------- strange to you that they weren't wearing shoes in the snow?

   (A) see
   (B) look (at)
   (C) look for
   (D) seem

   This question is playing with the English translation of this idea: "Did it *look* strange to you..." While this is a proper translation, neither of the verbs that mean *look* can be used this way in Spanish. Only (D) is correct.

26. **D** **Translation:** ------- whom were you preparing a big turkey and mashed potatoes?

   (A) From
   (B) Where
   (C) To
   (D) For

   Think about meaning here. Only (C) and (D) are possibilities, but (D) is more appropriate.

27. **D** **Translation:** These two roses smell exactly similar, so this rose is ------- that one.

   (A) little aromatic to
   (B) less aromatic than
   (C) more aromatic than
   (D) as aromatic as

   If the roses are **exactamente similares**, then (B) and (C) do not make sense. Choice (A) is just awkward and means nothing, so (D) is correct.

28. **C** **Translation:** No one ------- the drums like Tito Puente.

    (A) played (a game)
    (B) played (a role)
    (C) played (an instrument)
    (D) played (a recording)

All of these verbs can mean *to play* in the appropriate contexts. Only (C) is used with musical instruments, however.

29. **B** **Translation:** When the company ------- who won the prize, I am sure it will be me.

    (A) announces (indicative)
    (B) announces (subjunctive)
    (C) announced (preterite indicative)
    (D) announced (imperfect subjunctive)

The future tense at the end of the sentence tells us what tense we're in, which eliminates (C) and (D). Since the event is not *currently* happening, however, we cannot use the present tense—only the present subjunctive lets us know that the event is not happening right now—it is merely anticipated at this point. Therefore, (B) is correct.

Part B

Passage:

En cada segundo, vivimos un momento nuevo y único del universo, un momento que no existió <u>nunca</u> y no existirá otra vez. ¿Y qué <u>les</u> enseñamos a los niños en las escuelas? Enseñamos que dos más dos es cuatro y que París es la capital de Francia. ¿Cuándo enseñamos <u>lo que</u> ellos son? Deberíamos decirle a cada niño: ¿Sabes lo que eres? Eres una maravilla. Único. No <u>hay</u> en todo el mundo otro niño exactamente como <u>tú</u>. Todos debemos trabajar para hacer que este mundo <u>sea</u> digno de sus niños. <u>Nuestra</u> familia es una sola. Cada uno de nosotros tiene un deber <u>con</u> sus hermanos. Todos somos <u>hojas</u> de un solo árbol y ese árbol es la humanidad.

Translation:

In every second, we live a new and unique moment of the universe, a moment that *never* existed and will not exist again. And what do we teach *(to them)* the children in the schools? We teach that two plus two is four and that Paris is the capital of France. When do we teach *what* they are? We ought to tell each child: Do you know what you are? You are a wonder. Unique. *There is* not another child exactly like *you* in all the world. We all should work to make sure this world *is* worthy of its children. *Our* family is one. Each one of us has a duty *to* his or her brothers and sisters. We are all *leaves* of a single tree and that tree is humanity.

30. **B** (A) nothing

       (B) never

       (C) always

       (D) sometime

We're talking about a **momento**, which is a measure of time, so we can get rid of (A). The expression **no existió** is very important because it begins a negative clause, which means that all other words that follow must also be negative. Choice (B) is the only negative word left.

31. **D** (A) them (masculine, plural)

       (B) it (masculine, singular)

       (C) to him/her

       (D) to them

What are we teaching? We are teaching **que dos más dos es cuatro y que París es la capital de Francia,** which would function as the direct object of the sentence (yes, the direct object can be more than one word). Who is receiving this teaching? **Los niños** is the indirect object, which is what we're looking for, so eliminate (A) and (B). Since **los niños** is plural, (D) is the correct answer.

32. **C** (A) that

       (B) when

       (C) what

       (D) where

Let's look at each choice: (A) can't be right because it would leave a sentence fragment. Choice (B) does not make sense. Choice (D) cannot be right because it would require the use of the verb **estar.** Choice (C) is the idiomatically correct way to say *what* in Spanish in this context.

33. **A** **(A) there is (haber)**

       (B) is (estar, indicative)

       (C) is (estar, subjunctive)

       (D) is (ser, indicative)

The key to this sentence is the expression **otro niño**, which is an *indefinite* expression. The verb **estar** is generally used with *definite* expressions, so (B) and (C) are not correct. **Ser** can be used with indefinite expressions, but not to express general existence, as this sentence does. The verb **haber** is used in such contexts, so (A) is the correct answer.

34. **B** (A) you
         (B) you
         (C) yours (fam.)
         (D) his/hers/yours (formal)

When making a comparison, the sentence is understood in the following way: *There is no other child exactly like you (are).* Therefore, we are looking for a subject pronoun to correspond with the verb, which is understood. Choice (B) is the only subject pronoun among the choices.

35. **B** (A) is (indicative)
         (B) is (subjunctive)
         (C) was (imperfect indicative)
         (D) was (imperfect subjunctive)

The key expression in this sentence is **hacer que**, which means *to make,* as in *to ensure that,* which is a way of exerting one's desire or wish over the actions of someone or something else. Such an expression requires the use of the subjunctive, so (A) and (C) are wrong. Because the sentence is in the present tense, the present subjunctive is appropriate, and (B) is the answer.

36. **C** (A) We
         (B) Us/To us
         (C) Our
         (D) No

In this sentence, we are looking for an adjective to modify the word **familia**. Since (A) and (B) are not adjectives, they are wrong. Choice (D) is incorrect because it is masculine, and we are looking for a feminine adjective, which (C) is.

37. **B** (A) for
         (B) with
         (C) since
         (D) without

Choices (C) and (D) really don't make a tremendous amount of sense. The *destination* of our duty is our brothers, and **para** is used in contexts of destination, but, idiomatically, the preposition used with **deber** is always **con**. Choice (B) is the correct answer.

38. **B** (A) tires
         (B) leaves
         (C) pills
         (D) meatballs

Choosing the right answer to this question all comes down to your vocabulary knowledge. Neither **ruedas** *(tires)*, **pastillas** *(pills),* nor **albóndigas** *(meatballs)* works here, but (B), **hojas** *(leaves),* does.

Passage:

Una mañana, se levantó y fue a buscar al amigo al otro lado de la valla. Pero el amigo no <u>estaba</u>, y cuando volvió, le dijo la madre:

—El amigo se murió. Niño, no pienses más <u>en</u> él y busca otros para jugar.

El niño se sentó en el quicio de la puerta con la cara <u>entre</u> las manos y los codos en las rodillas.

"Él <u>volverá</u>", pensó. Porque no podía ser que allí <u>estuvieran</u> las canicas, el camión, la pistola de hojalata y el reloj que ya no andaba, y el amigo no viniera a buscarlos. Vino la noche, con <u>una estrella</u> muy grande, y el niño no quería entrar a comer.

—Entra niño, que <u>llega</u> el frío—dijo la madre. Pero <u>en lugar de</u> entrar, el niño se levantó del quicio y se fue en busca del amigo. Pasó buscándole toda la noche. Cuando llegó el sol, el niño pensó: "Qué tontos y pequeños son <u>esos</u> juguetes. Y ese reloj que no anda, <u>no</u> sirve para nada." <u>Lo</u> tiró al pozo y volvió a la casa, con mucha hambre.

Translation:

One morning he got up and went to look for the friend on the other side of the fence. But the friend *was* not there, and when he returned, his mother said to him:

"The friend died. Child, don't think any more *about* him and look for others to play."

The child sat on the door frame with his face *between* his hands and his elbows on his knees.

"He *will return*," he thought. Because it couldn't be that the marbles, the truck, the tin pistol, and the watch that now didn't work *were there,* and the friend didn't come to look for them. Night came, with a very big *star*, and the child didn't want to go inside to eat.

"Come in child, it's *getting* cold," said the mother. But *instead of* entering, the child got up from the door frame and went to look for the friend. He spent all night looking for him. When the sun came up, the child thought: "How stupid and small *these* toys are. And that watch that doesn't work—it's *no* good for anything." He threw *it* into the well and returned home, very hungry.

39. **D** (A) there were

       (B) was

       (C) went

       (D) was (there)

The sentence is trying to say that the friend could not be located, which would require the use of the verb **estar**, which is (D).

40. **B** (A) of

       (B) about

       (C) that

       (D) above

Choice (C) cannot be right because the word **que** introduces clauses, and there is no clause in the second part of the sentence. The expression **pensar de** is generally used only in questions, while (D) does not make sense. The expression **pensar en** means *to think about,* and (B) is correct.

41.   A   (A) **between**
          (B) above
          (C) below
          (D) without

Imagine the boy's posture: He has his elbows on his knees. What might be the relation between his face and his hands? Choice (D) is silly, and (C) is only right if he is sitting upside down. While (B) makes sense, it seems more likely that the boy's head would be *between* his hands, since his mother just told him that his friend died. Choice (A) is the best answer.

42.   D   (A) returned (preterite indicative)
          (B) returns (subjunctive)
          (C) returned (imperfect subjunctive)
          (D) **will return**

The boy doesn't know where his friend is, and his friend doesn't appear in the rest of the passage, so neither the past nor the present would be logical in this sentence. Choices (A), (B), and (C) are all eliminated. The boy is hopeful that his friend will return in *the future*, so (D) is correct.

43.   C   (A) were (imperfect indicative)
          (B) were (preterite indicative)
          (C) **were (imperfect subjunctive)**
          (D) are

No podía ser que is an expression of *doubt*, which, you'll remember, requires the use of the subjunctive. Only (C) is in the subjunctive mood.

44.   A   (A) **a star**
          (B) a sun
          (C) a flower
          (D) an ocean

The night came *with* something—what is something that comes with the night? Even if you've never seen the word **estrella**, the other three answers don't make any sense. Choice (A) is correct.

45.   B   (A) it's carrying
          (B) **it's getting**
          (C) it's raining
          (D) it's crying

Does the cold *rain* or *cry*? No. Does it *carry* anything? Possibly, but the sentence doesn't tell us what it could be carrying. The only choice that is logical is (B).

46. **D**   (A) in addition to
     (B) upon
     (C) in spite of
     (D) instead of

Does the boy actually enter his house when his mother calls him? No, he goes to look for his friend. Choices (A), (B), and (C), which all suggest that he *has* entered the house, are wrong. Choice (D) is correct.

47. **B**   (A) those (feminine, plural)
     (B) those (masculine, plural)
     (C) that (feminine, singular)
     (D) that (neutral, singular)

We are looking for the correct demonstrative. Since the word being modified is **juguetes**, which is masculine and plural, (B) is the correct answer.

48. **A**   **(A) doesn't**
     (B) no one
     (C) nothing
     (D) none

You have to follow the logic of the sentence here: The boy is complaining about the watch, saying it doesn't work. Since he's limiting his commentary to just a watch, (C) is wrong because it implies that he's dissatisfied with *everything* in his life. Choice (D) implies that there is more than one watch that doesn't work, which isn't true. Choice (B) is silly, so (A) is correct.

49. **B**   (A) It (feminine, singular)
     (B) It (masculine, singular)
     (C) To him/her
     (D) To them

What did the boy throw? The *watch*, which is the direct object, so answers (C) and (D) are incorrect. Because **reloj** is masculine, (B) is correct.

Passage:

Hoy, con la facilidad de la fotografía, tendemos a olvidarnos <u>de</u> la importancia que tenía la pintura en el pasado como modo de conservar <u>los recuerdos</u> de momentos históricos. El enorme <u>cuadro</u>, *La rendición de Breda,* fue pintado para conmemorar la victoria militar española de 1625 contra los holandeses. Velázquez <u>lo</u> pintó diez años después del incidente y <u>tuvo</u> que usar todo su ingenio para representar a personajes y un paisaje que nunca <u>había visto</u>. Pero, ¡qué sorpresa! No es típico de las pinturas militares porque <u>evita</u> la violencia, la guerra y el orgullo nacional para evocar, en cambio, <u>un sentido</u> de tranquilidad y compasión humana.

Translation:

Today, with the ease of photography, we tend to forget *about* the importance that painting had in the past as a means of preserving *memories* of historic moments. The enormous *painting The Surrender of Breda* was painted to commemorate the Spanish military victory of 1625 against the Dutch. Velázquez painted *it* ten years after the incident and *had* to use all his genius to represent people and a landscape that he *had* never *seen*. But, what a surprise! It is not typical of military paintings because *it avoids* violence, war, and national pride to evoke instead *a sense* of tranquility and human compassion.

50. **C** (A) with
         (B) at
         (C) about
         (D) in

To forget about is an idiomatic expression that requires the use of **de** (C). Remember, idiomatic expressions don't necessarily have rules: You either know them or you don't.

51. **B** (A) the garbage
         (B) the memories
         (C) the music
         (D) the deaths

What exactly is the *garbage* of an historic moment? How does a painting preserve *music?* Do we actually preserve the *deaths* of historic moments or the moments themselves? Interesting questions all, but (A), (C), and (D) are all wrong because they are not answered in this passage. An historic painting is a representation of a *memory,* so (B) is correct.

52. **A** **(A) painting**
         (B) hug
         (C) Spaniard
         (D) event

Notice that *La rendición de Breda* is italicized. Generally, names of books, movies, ships, and, yes, paintings are italicized. Hugs, Spaniards, and events are not accorded this same special treatment, so (A) is the answer.

53.   C   (A)   to him/her
          (B)   it (feminine, singular)
          (C)   it (masculine, singular)
          (D)   himself

What did he paint? The *painting*, which is a direct object, thus eliminating (A). (He did not paint himself, although that would have been interesting, so eliminate (D) as well.) **Cuadro** is masculine, so (C) is the answer.

54.   A   **(A)   had (preterite indicative)**
          (B)   had (imperfect subjunctive)
          (C)   would have
          (D)   would have had

Choice (D) suggests that Velázquez *didn't* use all his genius (he *would* have, but...), but the sentence says just the opposite, so it is wrong. Choice (B) is incorrect because there are no expressions that cue the use of the subjunctive. While (C) might sound correct in English, it is only right as an obscure, dramatic narrative technique in the past. Choice (A) is the clearest way to get the point across.

55.   D   (A)   sees
          (B)   will see
          (C)   will have seen
          (D)   had seen

The painting was dated 1625, long ago, so (A), (B), and (C) are simply not logical. Choice (D) is the answer.

56.   C   (A)   shows
          (B)   delineates
          (C)   avoids
          (D)   adopts

We're looking for something that *wouldn't* be typical of a military painting. Violence and war are the typical themes, and so *showing, delineating,* or *adopting* these themes would not be what we are looking for. Choice (C) is more likely.

57.   D   (A)   some facts
          (B)   an exit
          (C)   a month
          (D)   a sense

Choice (B) doesn't make sense in context, while (A) changes the intended purpose of the painting. Instead of being about a moment of military history, it has become a sort of spiritual self-help painting. It is also highly doubtful that Velázquez only wanted his painting to result in one month of tranquility, and so (D) is correct.

Part C
Passage:

Se marchó y Luisa quedó sola. Absolutamente sola. Se sentó, desfallecida. Las manos dejaron caer el cuchillo contra el suelo. Tenía frío, mucho frío. Por el ventanuco, entraban gritos de los vencejos y el rumor del río entre las piedras. "Marcos, tú tienes la culpa... tú, porque Amadeo..." De pronto, tuvo miedo, un miedo extraño, que hacía temblar sus manos. "Amadeo me quería. Sí: El me quería." ¿Cómo iba a dudarlo? Amadeo era brusco, desprovisto de ternura, callado, taciturno. Amadeo —a medias palabras ella lo entendió— tuvo una infancia dura, una juventud amarga. Amadeo era pobre y ganaba su vida —la de él, la de ella y la de los hijos que hubieran podido tener— en un trabajo ingrato que destruía su salud. Y ella: ¿Tuvo ternura para él? ¿Comprensión? ¿Cariño? De pronto, vio algo. Vio su silla; su ropa allí, sucia, a punto de lavar; sus botas, en el rincón, aún llenas de barro. Algo le subió, como un grito. "Sí, me quería...acaso ¿será capaz de matarse?"

Translation:

He left and Luisa remained alone. Absolutely alone. She sat down, weary. Her hands dropped the knife on the floor. She was cold, very cold. Through the window, the calls of the birds and the mur-mur of the river between the rocks entered. "Marcos, you are to blame...you, because Amadeo..." Suddenly, she was afraid, a strange fear that made her hands shake. "Amadeo loved me. Yes: He loved me." How was she going to doubt it? Amadeo was abrupt, lacking tenderness, quiet, sullen. Amadeo—she understood by reading between the lines—had a tough childhood, a bitter adoles-cence. Amadeo was poor and earned his living—his, hers, and that of the children that they could have had—at an ungrateful job that was destroying his health. And she: Did she have tenderness for him? Understanding? Affection? Suddenly, she saw something. She saw his chair; his clothes there, dirty, ready for washing; his boots, in the corner, still full of mud. Something rose in her, like a shout. "Yes, he loved me...by any chance will he be capable of killing himself?"

58.   A   Translation: What has the narrator always doubted?

(A) **That Amadeo had feelings for her**
(B) That Marcos was to blame for her problems
(C) That Amadeo and she could have children
(D) That Amadeo and she were going to be rich

The narrator spends the majority of the passage convincing herself that Amadeo loved her—**Sí, me quería**—so she must not have believed it in the past. Therefore, (A) is correct.

59.   D   Translation: What type of person is Amadeo?

(A) He is very friendly and extroverted.
(B) He is profoundly cruel and violent.
(C) He is passionate and sensitive.
(D) **He is pretty quiet and is not very well refined.**

Amadeo is described as **brusco** and **callado**, descriptions that are paraphrased nicely in (D).

60. **C**   **Translation:** According to the passage, why is Amadeo's personality like it is?

    (A) The narrator didn't love him.

    (B) He always fought with Marcos.

    (C) He had a difficult life.

    (D) His health is bad.

The narrator speaks of **una infancia dura** and **una juventud amarga**, which are hardly qualities of a happy life. Thus, the best answer is (C).

61. **C**   **Translation:** Where does the narrator think that Amadeo went?

    (A) To the river to fish

    (B) To work to earn money

    (C) Outside the house to kill himself

    (D) To his children's room

The phrase **será capaz de matarse** at the end of the passage is a good clue of what's on the narrator's mind. The answer here is (C).

62. **A**   **Translation:** What is the central point of this passage?

    (A) The narrator hasn't known that Amadeo loves her until this moment.

    (B) Marcos is the cause of the problems between Amadeo and the narrator.

    (C) Amadeo's and the narrator's life is incredibly prosperous.

    (D) Amadeo and Marcos hate each other.

We can look at the reasoning for question 58 to explain why (A) is correct.

Passage:

    Muchos científicos advierten con alarma que la Tierra está calentándose. Explican que esto podría significar un gran peligro debido al efecto invernadero. Un invernadero es un edificio donde se cultivan plantas usando el techo de vidrio (cristal) que permite la entrada de los rayos del sol, pero no deja que salga todo el calor reflejado. Según esta comparación, la atmósfera de nuestro planeta funciona como el techo de vidrio.

    En realidad, el efecto invernadero, en proporciones moderadas, es positivo y aun necesario. Si no tuviera esta función nuestra atmósfera, la Tierra sufriría los radicales cambios de temperatura que ocurren en la luna, con un frío espantoso de noche y un calor insoportable de día. Mirándolo así, debemos darle gracias al efecto invernadero. Sin embargo, algunos expertos temen que la acumulación del dióxido de carbono, del metano y de otros gases producidos por las actividades humanas aumente la eficiencia de nuestro "techo de vidrio" a tal punto que atrape demasiado calor.

    Muchos factores, como los terremotos y las erupciones de volcanes, influyen momentáneamente en el clima, pero el gradual calentamiento de la Tierra parece casi inevitable. De acuerdo con sus cálculos, los científicos afirman que desde el año 1850, el aumento de la temperatura global ha sido de uno a cinco grados centígrados, y que hacia el año 2030, podría llegar a aumentar entre 1,5 a 4,5 grados más. Junto con esta subida, se pronostican consecuencias drásticas en las economías de muchas regiones debido a fluctuaciones en la producción agrícola, pérdida o ganancia en el negocio del turismo y otros cambios.

Translation:

Many scientists warn with alarm that the Earth is warming. They explain that this could mean great danger because of the greenhouse effect. A greenhouse is a building where one grows plants using a glass roof that permits the entry of the sun's rays but doesn't allow all the reflected warmth to leave. According to this comparison, the atmosphere of our planet functions as a glass roof.

In reality, the greenhouse effect, in moderate proportions, is positive and even necessary. If our atmosphere didn't have this function, Earth would suffer the radical temperature changes that occur on the moon, with frightful cold at night and insufferable heat during the day. Looking at it in this way, we should give thanks to the greenhouse effect. However, some experts fear that the accumulation of carbon dioxide, methane, and other gases produced by human activities will increase the efficiency of our "glass roof" to the point that it will trap too much heat.

Many factors, such as earthquakes and volcanic eruptions, momentarily influence the climate, but the gradual warming of Earth seems almost inevitable. In accordance with their calculations, scientists affirm that since the year 1850, the increase in the global temperature has been from one to five degrees centigrade, and that by the year 2030, it could increase between 1.5 and 4.5 degrees more. Along with this increase, they predict drastic consequences in the economies of many regions because of fluctuations in agricultural production, loss or gain in tourism, and other changes.

63.　C　**Translation:** What is the function of a greenhouse effect?

(A) To increase the temperature of Earth
(B) To have positive effects in the planet's atmosphere
(C) To allow the sun to enter but not the heat to leave
(D) To produce gases for the benefit of the atmosphere

The answer, (C), can be found in the second sentence of the passage.

64.　A　**Translation:** What is a positive result of the greenhouse effect?

(A) The temperature of Earth doesn't vary too much.
(B) The cold is frightful and the heat insufferable.
(C) It traps the heat of the sun to heat the planet.
(D) Agricultural production fluctuates.

The passage states that we should really **darle gracias** to the greenhouse effect because we don't have the drastic temperature shifts of the moon. Choice (A) is correct.

65. **B** **Translation:** Why do some experts think that the atmosphere is a "glass roof"?

(A) It allows us to see the stars.
(B) It effectively encloses the planet.
(C) The temperature fluctuates a lot.
(D) It causes economic problems.

This question requires a little careful thinking. Choice (A) is silly, while (D) is not the reason for this expression being coined—rather, it is a result of the phenomenon. Choice (C) looks good only if you misunderstand it—the temperature would only fluctuate if we *didn't* have this "glass roof." Choice (B) is therefore the correct answer.

66. **A** **Translation:** What is the great fear of some scientists?

(A) That the situation will get worse
(B) That the gases produced by human activity will disappear
(C) That one will not be able to see the universe outside of the "glass roof"
(D) That the temperature will drop drastically before the year 2030

The entire last paragraph is dedicated to telling of the "doom and gloom" that the greenhouse effect promises for us in the next 25 years or so; therefore, (A) is correct.

67. **C** **Translation:** What could be the total increase in Earth's temperature by the year 2030?

(A) Between 1 and 5 degrees centigrade
(B) Between 1.5 and 4.5 degrees centigrade
(C) Between 2.5 and 9.5 degrees centigrade
(D) Between 5 and 15 degrees centigrade

The passage states that the temperature has increased from 1 to 5 degrees centigrade since 1850, then states that it could increase an *additional* 1.5 to 4.5 degrees before 2030. The potential totals are given in (C).

68. **B** **Translation:** Why would the economy suffer if the greenhouse effect continued in the future?

(A) Earthquakes and volcanoes would destroy much of the planet.
(B) The quantity of food grown on Earth could drop a lot.
(C) Scientists would need more money to investigate this phenomenon more.
(D) We would need more industries that didn't depend so much on the weather.

The last sentence of the passage speaks of the **consecuencias drásticas** of a continued warming of the planet, and a potential shortage of crops (B) is mentioned.

Advertisement:

**La Cocina de Tomas
Restaurante * Club de Baile**

28 Elf Street, Lee, MA * 432-888-9090

El lugar mas lindo, original y lujoso de Massachusetts.

Comida Hispana con especialidad en: ¡empanadas y margaritas!

¡Venga a probar uno o todos los platos en el menú y quédese a bailar! ¡Música Latina para todos y mucho mas!

¡Abierto todo los días desde las 12 P.M. hasta amanecer!

¡Tenemos muchos grupos musicales que tocan todos los viernes!

La Cocina de Tomas presenta:

Junio 13: Orquesta Orlando—música de Argentina y Colombia
Junio 20: Los Lobos Locos—Mariachi
Junio 27: María Luz Roca—la Cantante Mejicana
Julio 4: Los Independientes—¡un grupo local que viene a festejar el día de la Independencia Americana! ¡Compre 2 entradas antes del 4 de Julio y reciba una margarita gratis!

¡Reserve hoy!
Mesas y asientos limitados.

Translation:

Thomas's Kitchen
Restaurant * Dance Club

28 Elf Street, Lee, MA * 432-888-9090

The most beautiful, original, and luxurious place in Massachusetts.

Hispanic cuisine specializing in empanadas and margaritas!

Come try one or all of our menu items and stay for dancing! Latin music for everyone and much more!

Open every day from 12 P.M. until dawn!

We have a lot of musical groups that play every Friday!

Thomas's Kitchen presents:

June 13: Orlando's Orchestra—Music from Argentina and Colombia
June 20: The Crazy Wolves—Mariachi

June 27: María Luz Roca—the Mexican singer

July 4: The Independents—a local group that is coming to celebrate American Independence Day!

Buy 2 entries before the 4th of July and get a free margarita!

Reserve today!

Tables and seats are limited.

69. **D** **Translation:** What kind of place is Thomas's Kitchen?

(A) A kitchen
(B) A restaurant
(C) A restaurant and bar
(D) A restaurant and place for dancing

The title of the announcement below the restaurant name describes Thomas's as a restaurant and dance club. Choice (D) is the correct answer.

70. **C** **Translation:** Who are The Independents?

(A) A music group from Argentina
(B) A music group from the United States
(C) A local music group
(D) A music group that celebrates everything

The flier lists the music groups that are playing at the venue. The Independents are a local group of musicians who are playing on the Fourth of July to celebrate American Independence Day. Therefore, (C) is the correct answer.

71. **D** **Translation:** When do you have to make a reservation and why?

(A) Whenever, because there are a lot of tables
(B) After dawn, because if not the restaurant will be closed
(C) After the 4th of July, because it's a holiday
(D) Immediately, because there is not a lot of available space

The flier says to *reserve today,* as tables and seating are limited. Choice (A) contradicts this statement, and (B) and (C) do not apply, making (D) the correct answer.

72.   A   **Translation:** How is the establishment described?

(A) **Luxurious**
(B) Ugly
(C) Famous
(D) Far

The flier states that the venue is the *most beautiful, original, and luxurious place in Massachusetts.* Choice (A) is correct.

73.   C   **Translation:** At what time would Thomas's kitchen be closed?

(A) 12:00 A.M.
(B) 2:00 A.M.
(C) **6:00 A.M.**
(D) 12:00 P.M.

According to the flier, Thomas's Kitchen is open from 12:00 P.M. until dawn. The only time that doesn't fall into that range in the given answer choices is 6:00 A.M., so (C) is the correct answer.

74.   B   **Translation:** Is there an advantage to buying the entries early?

(A) Yes, but you have to buy them on the 4th of July.
(B) **Yes, but you have to buy them before the 4th of July.**
(C) No, there isn't an advantage.
(D) No, there's no special offer.

This one requires you to read carefully! Choice (A) may seem correct, but the flier states that you will receive a free margarita if you buy your entries *before* July 4th. So (B) is correct.

Passage:

Un producto de enorme importancia cultural y comercial en el mundo, el café tiene una historia pintoresca y de origen incierto. Según una conocida leyenda, fue en Etiopía, por el año 850, que un pastor observó que su rebaño se agitaba tras ingerir los frutos de un arbusto misterioso, el cafeto. Él mismo probó los frutos, y le gustó tanto la sensación, que compartió los frutos con otros en su poblado.

Varios siglos más adelante, el café llegó a Venecia por medio de los turcos. Desde esta ciudad italiana, el café pasó al resto de Europa, llegando primero a París y, pocos años después, a Londres. En el año 1723, Gabriel de Clieu llevó un cafeto al Caribe, y así llegó esta deliciosa bebida a las Américas. Hoy en día, el café es la bebida más popular del mundo.

Los expertos dicen que hay cuatro factores clave en la producción del café: el clima, es decir, la proporción de sol y lluvia; la altura (cuanto mayor sea, mejor es la calidad); el terreno (el suelo volcánico es el más rico en nutrientes); y el cuidado durante la cosecha. Cada árbol tarda entre tres y cuatro años antes de dar fruto, pero una vez maduro, el árbol permanece activo y productivo durante muchas décadas.

Así, lo que conocemos como el café tuvo que pasar por una interesante historia antes de llegar a la taza que nos tomamos.

Translation:

A product of enormous cultural and commercial importance in the world, coffee has a history that is both picturesque and uncertain. According to popular legend, it was in Ethiopia in the year 850 that a shepherd observed that his flock became excited and energetic after ingesting the berries of a mysterious shrub, the coffee tree. The shepherd tried the berries for himself, and he liked the sensation so much that he shared them with others in his village.

Several centuries later, the Turks brought coffee to Venice. From this Italian city, coffee traveled to the rest of Europe, arriving first in Paris and a few years later in London. In 1723, Gabriel de Clieu took a coffee plant to the Caribbean, and that's how this delicious beverage arrived in the Americas. Nowadays, coffee is the most popular beverage in the world.

The experts say there are four key factors in the production of coffee: the climate, that is to say, the proportion of sun and rain; the altitude (the higher the altitude, the better the quality), the land (volcanic land is richest in nutrients), and the care during the harvest. Each tree takes between three and four years to produce the first berries, but once it's mature, the tree remains active and fruitful for many decades.

So, that which we know as coffee had to go through an interesting history before arriving in our cups.

75. **B**   **Translation:** Where did coffee supposedly originate?

(A) In the Caribbean
(B) In Ethiopia
(C) In Turkey
(D) In Venice

The passage mentions that a shepherd discovered coffee in Ethiopia in the year 850. The passage does indeed also mention Turkey, Venice, and the Caribbean in the second paragraph, but it does so only to show how coffee traveled throughout the world. The correct answer is (B).

76. **C**   **Translation:** Who discovered coffee?

(A) Some wild animals in the desert
(B) Muslim farmers
(C) A shepherd who observed his goats in an animated state
(D) Some uncertain painters

The first paragraph indicates that **un pastor** observed his herd acting strange after ingesting the fruit of the mysterious coffee tree. The passage makes no mention of wild animals, Muslim farmers, or uncertain painters, so (C) is the best answer.

77.   C   **Translation:** What was the initial reaction after trying the berries of the coffee tree?

(A) Disgust
(B) Confusion
(C) **Satisfaction**
(D) Indifference

The end of the first paragraph also indicates that the shepherd who first tried the berries of the coffee tree liked the sensation so much that he shared the berries with others. Therefore, he did not react with (A) *disgust,* (B) *confusion,* or (D) *indifference.* The best answer is (C): *satisfaction.*

78.   D   **Translation:** One can infer that the best place to cultivate coffee would be

(A) the beach
(B) the desert
(C) a big city
(D) **the mountains**

In the third paragraph, experts outline the four keys to the successful production of coffee. One of these is the altitude of the coffee plants. Since mountains have the greatest altitude of the four answer choices, (D) is the best answer.

79.   C   **Translation:** A coffee tree

(A) has a short lifespan
(B) produces a pound of seeds beginning in the first year
(C) **can flourish for more than ten years**
(D) takes several decades to produce its first berries

According to the end of the third paragraph, the coffee tree takes three or four years to produce its first fruit. This helps us eliminate (B) and (D). The author then tells us that the coffee tree can continue to produce fruit for many decades. Now we can eliminate (A) and select (C).

Passage:

Nos gustaba la casa porque, aparte de espaciosa y antigua, guardaba los recuerdos de nuestros bisabuelos, el abuelo paterno, nuestros padres y toda la infancia.

Nos habituamos Irene y yo a vivir solos en ella, lo que era una locura, pues en esa casa podían vivir ocho personas sin estorbarse. Hacíamos la limpieza por la mañana, levantándonos a las siete, y a eso de las once yo le dejaba a Irene las últimas habitaciones por repasar y me iba a la cocina. Almorzábamos a mediodía, siempre puntuales; ya no quedaba nada por hacer fuera de unos pocos platos sucios. Nos resultaba grato almorzar pensando en la casa profunda y silenciosa. A veces, llegamos a creer que era ella la que no nos dejó casarnos. Irene rechazó dos pretendientes sin mayor motivo. A mí se me murió María Esther antes que llegáramos a comprometernos. Entramos en los cuarenta años con la inexpresada idea de que el nuestro simple y silencioso matrimonio de hermanos era una clausura necesaria de la genealogía asentada por los bisabuelos en nuestra casa.

Pero es de la casa que me interesa hablar, de la casa y de Irene, porque yo no tengo importancia. Me pregunto qué hubiera hecho Irene sin el tejido. No necesitábamos ganarnos la vida. Todos los meses llegaba la plata de los campos y el dinero aumentaba. Pero a Irene solamente le entretenía el tejido. Mostraba una destreza maravillosa, y a mí se me iban las horas viéndole las manos. Era hermoso.

Translation:

We liked the house because, aside from being spacious and old, it guarded the memories of our great-grandparents, our paternal grandfather, our parents, and all of childhood.

Irene and I became accustomed to living alone in it, which was a crazy thing since in that house eight people could live without getting in each other's way. We did the cleaning in the morning, getting up at seven, and at about eleven I left the last rooms to Irene to finish and went to the kitchen. We ate lunch at noon, always punctual; there now remained nothing to do aside from a few dirty dishes. We found it pleasing to eat lunch thinking about the deep and silent house. At times, we believed that it was she (the house) that didn't allow us to marry. Irene rejected two suitors for almost no reason at all. María Esther died before we could get engaged. We entered our forties with the unexpressed idea that our simple and silent marriage of brother and sister was a necessary closure of the genealogy laid down by our great-grandparents in our house.

But it is the house about which I am interested in speaking, the house and Irene, because I am not important. I ask myself what Irene would have done without weaving. We didn't need to earn a living. Every month the money arrived from the fields and the money grew. But only weaving entertained Irene. She showed marvelous skill, and watching her hands, the hours flew by for me. It was beautiful.

80. **B** **Translation:** How is the life of the narrator and Irene?

   (A) It is exciting and full of adventure.
   (B) It is repetitive and pretty passive.
   (C) It is sad and very depressing.
   (D) It isn't very prosperous.

The narrator and his sister do *the same thing every day,* which pretty much amounts to nothing. The use of the imperfect tense tells us that all of the actions the narrator describes are habitual. Choice (B) is a nice summary of this description.

81. **D** **Translation:** What is the narrator and Irene's house like?

   (A) It's small and basically comfortable.
   (B) It's badly constructed.
   (C) It's very dirty.
   (D) It's enormous and is pretty empty.

The narrator says **en esa casa podían vivir ocho personas.** Sounds pretty big, huh? Choice (D) is the perfect answer.

82.   **A**   **Translation:** Why did Irene reject her two boyfriends?

(A) **There is no apparent reason.**
(B) The narrator didn't like them.
(C) They didn't want to live in the house.
(D) Irene's parents rejected them also.

The narrator doesn't tell us what he thought of Irene's boyfriends, so (B) is incorrect. He also doesn't say much about the boyfriends themselves, so (C) is wrong. Irene's parents are apparently not living, so their opinion is not relevant in her decision, and therefore (A) is the best answer.

83.   **C**   **Translation:** Who is María Esther?

(A) Another sister of the narrator
(B) The narrator's mother
(C) **The narrator's dead girlfriend**
(D) The narrator's wife

The narrator says that María Esther died before they could **comprometerse**, which means *to get engaged*. This is a pretty serious (and strange) step for brother and sister to take [(A) is wrong], or mother and son [so is (B)]. If she died before they got engaged, they couldn't have been married, so (C) is the answer.

84.   **D**   **Translation:** What is the financial state of the narrator and Irene?

(A) They are very poor because they don't work.
(B) They have a difficult life, but they have few financial problems.
(C) One can't determine their financial state in the passage.
(D) **They are very rich with the money from their property.**

The narrator says **No necesitábamos ganarnos la vida** but that **el dinero aumentaba** anyway. Doesn't sound like too much of a struggle. Choice (D) is correct.

85.   **D**   **Translation:** How does the narrator spend his time?

(A) He goes out with María Esther.
(B) He researches the genealogy of his family.
(C) He weaves.
(D) **He watches Irene do her own work.**

The narrator says in the next to the last line **a mí se me iban las horas viéndole las manos.** Loads of fun, huh? Choice (D) is the answer.

HOW TO SCORE PRACTICE TEST 3

When you take the real exam, the proctors take away your exam and your bubble sheet and send it to a processing center, where a computer looks at the pattern of filled-in ovals on your exam and gives you a score. We couldn't include even a small computer with this book, so we are providing this more primitive way of scoring your exam.

Determining Your Score

STEP 1   Using the answer key, determine how many questions you got right and how many you got wrong on the test. Remember, questions that you do not answer do not count as either right answers or wrong answers.

STEP 2   List the number of right answers here.   (A) _____

STEP 3   List the number of wrong answers here. Now divide that number by 3.   (B) _____ ÷ 3 _____ = (C) _____

STEP 4   Subtract the number of wrong answers divided by 3 (C) from the number of correct answers (A). Round this score to the nearest whole number. This is your raw score.   (A) – (C) = _____

STEP 5   To determine your real score, take the number from Step 4 above and look it up in the left column of the Score Conversion Table on the next page; the corresponding score on the right is your score on the exam.

PRACTICE TEST 3
SCORE CONVERSION TABLE

Raw Score	Scaled Score	Raw Score	Scaled Score	Raw Score	Scaled Score
85	800	47	590	9	360
84	800	46	580	8	360
83	800	45	570	7	350
82	800	44	570	6	350
81	790	43	560	5	340
80	790	42	550	4	340
79	780	41	550	3	330
78	780	40	540	2	320
77	770	39	530	1	320
76	770	38	530	0	310
75	760	37	520	−1	310
74	760	36	520	−2	300
73	750	35	510	−3	290
72	750	34	500	−4	290
71	740	33	500	−5	280
70	730	32	490	−6	270
69	730	31	490	−7	260
68	720	30	480	−8	260
67	720	29	470	−9	250
66	710	28	470	−10	240
65	700	27	460	−11	230
64	700	26	460	−12	220
63	690	25	450	−13	220
62	680	24	450	−14	220
61	680	23	440	−15	210
60	670	22	430	−16	210
59	670	21	430	−17	210
58	660	20	420	−18	200
57	650	19	420	−19	200
56	650	18	410	−20	200
55	640	17	410	−21	200
54	630	16	400	−22	200
53	630	15	400	−23	200
52	620	14	390	−24	200
51	620	13	390	−25	200
50	610	12	380	−26	200
49	600	11	380	−27	200
48	590	10	370	−28	200

The Princeton Review®

Completely darken bubbles with a No. 2 pencil. If you make a mistake, be sure to erase mark completely. Erase all stray marks.

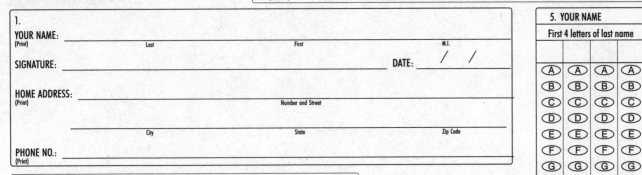

1.

YOUR NAME: _____
(Print)   Last   First   M.I.

SIGNATURE: _____   DATE: ___/___/___

HOME ADDRESS: _____
(Print)   Number and Street

_____
City   State   Zip Code

PHONE NO.: _____
(Print)

IMPORTANT: Please fill in these boxes exactly as shown on the back cover of your test book.

2. TEST FORM

3. TEST CODE

4. REGISTRATION NUMBER

5. YOUR NAME

First 4 letters of last name | FIRST INIT | MID INIT

(bubble grid A–Z)

6. DATE OF BIRTH

Month	Day	Year
JAN		
FEB		
MAR		
APR		
MAY		
JUN		
JUL		
AUG		
SEP		
OCT		
NOV		
DEC		

7. SEX

MALE
FEMALE

The Princeton Review®

1. Ⓐ Ⓑ Ⓒ Ⓓ
2. Ⓐ Ⓑ Ⓒ Ⓓ
3. Ⓐ Ⓑ Ⓒ Ⓓ
4. Ⓐ Ⓑ Ⓒ Ⓓ
5. Ⓐ Ⓑ Ⓒ Ⓓ
6. Ⓐ Ⓑ Ⓒ Ⓓ
7. Ⓐ Ⓑ Ⓒ Ⓓ
8. Ⓐ Ⓑ Ⓒ Ⓓ
9. Ⓐ Ⓑ Ⓒ Ⓓ
10. Ⓐ Ⓑ Ⓒ Ⓓ
11. Ⓐ Ⓑ Ⓒ Ⓓ
12. Ⓐ Ⓑ Ⓒ Ⓓ
13. Ⓐ Ⓑ Ⓒ Ⓓ
14. Ⓐ Ⓑ Ⓒ Ⓓ
15. Ⓐ Ⓑ Ⓒ Ⓓ
16. Ⓐ Ⓑ Ⓒ Ⓓ
17. Ⓐ Ⓑ Ⓒ Ⓓ
18. Ⓐ Ⓑ Ⓒ Ⓓ
19. Ⓐ Ⓑ Ⓒ Ⓓ
20. Ⓐ Ⓑ Ⓒ Ⓓ
21. Ⓐ Ⓑ Ⓒ Ⓓ

22. Ⓐ Ⓑ Ⓒ Ⓓ
23. Ⓐ Ⓑ Ⓒ Ⓓ
24. Ⓐ Ⓑ Ⓒ Ⓓ
25. Ⓐ Ⓑ Ⓒ Ⓓ
26. Ⓐ Ⓑ Ⓒ Ⓓ
27. Ⓐ Ⓑ Ⓒ Ⓓ
28. Ⓐ Ⓑ Ⓒ Ⓓ
29. Ⓐ Ⓑ Ⓒ Ⓓ
30. Ⓐ Ⓑ Ⓒ Ⓓ
31. Ⓐ Ⓑ Ⓒ Ⓓ
32. Ⓐ Ⓑ Ⓒ Ⓓ
33. Ⓐ Ⓑ Ⓒ Ⓓ
34. Ⓐ Ⓑ Ⓒ Ⓓ
35. Ⓐ Ⓑ Ⓒ Ⓓ
36. Ⓐ Ⓑ Ⓒ Ⓓ
37. Ⓐ Ⓑ Ⓒ Ⓓ
38. Ⓐ Ⓑ Ⓒ Ⓓ
39. Ⓐ Ⓑ Ⓒ Ⓓ
40. Ⓐ Ⓑ Ⓒ Ⓓ
41. Ⓐ Ⓑ Ⓒ Ⓓ
42. Ⓐ Ⓑ Ⓒ Ⓓ

43. Ⓐ Ⓑ Ⓒ Ⓓ
44. Ⓐ Ⓑ Ⓒ Ⓓ
45. Ⓐ Ⓑ Ⓒ Ⓓ
46. Ⓐ Ⓑ Ⓒ Ⓓ
47. Ⓐ Ⓑ Ⓒ Ⓓ
48. Ⓐ Ⓑ Ⓒ Ⓓ
49. Ⓐ Ⓑ Ⓒ Ⓓ
50. Ⓐ Ⓑ Ⓒ Ⓓ
51. Ⓐ Ⓑ Ⓒ Ⓓ
52. Ⓐ Ⓑ Ⓒ Ⓓ
53. Ⓐ Ⓑ Ⓒ Ⓓ
54. Ⓐ Ⓑ Ⓒ Ⓓ
55. Ⓐ Ⓑ Ⓒ Ⓓ
56. Ⓐ Ⓑ Ⓒ Ⓓ
57. Ⓐ Ⓑ Ⓒ Ⓓ
58. Ⓐ Ⓑ Ⓒ Ⓓ
59. Ⓐ Ⓑ Ⓒ Ⓓ
60. Ⓐ Ⓑ Ⓒ Ⓓ
61. Ⓐ Ⓑ Ⓒ Ⓓ
62. Ⓐ Ⓑ Ⓒ Ⓓ
63. Ⓐ Ⓑ Ⓒ Ⓓ

64. Ⓐ Ⓑ Ⓒ Ⓓ
65. Ⓐ Ⓑ Ⓒ Ⓓ
66. Ⓐ Ⓑ Ⓒ Ⓓ
67. Ⓐ Ⓑ Ⓒ Ⓓ
68. Ⓐ Ⓑ Ⓒ Ⓓ
69. Ⓐ Ⓑ Ⓒ Ⓓ
70. Ⓐ Ⓑ Ⓒ Ⓓ
71. Ⓐ Ⓑ Ⓒ Ⓓ
72. Ⓐ Ⓑ Ⓒ Ⓓ
73. Ⓐ Ⓑ Ⓒ Ⓓ
74. Ⓐ Ⓑ Ⓒ Ⓓ
75. Ⓐ Ⓑ Ⓒ Ⓓ
76. Ⓐ Ⓑ Ⓒ Ⓓ
77. Ⓐ Ⓑ Ⓒ Ⓓ
78. Ⓐ Ⓑ Ⓒ Ⓓ
79. Ⓐ Ⓑ Ⓒ Ⓓ
80. Ⓐ Ⓑ Ⓒ Ⓓ
81. Ⓐ Ⓑ Ⓒ Ⓓ
82. Ⓐ Ⓑ Ⓒ Ⓓ
83. Ⓐ Ⓑ Ⓒ Ⓓ
84. Ⓐ Ⓑ Ⓒ Ⓓ
85. Ⓐ Ⓑ Ⓒ Ⓓ

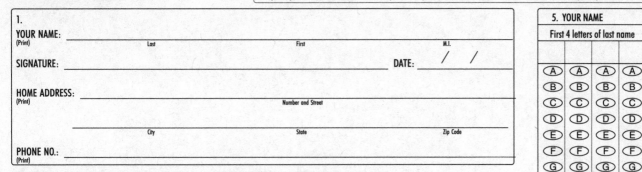

The Princeton Review®

Completely darken bubbles with a No. 2 pencil. If you make a mistake, be sure to erase mark completely. Erase all stray marks.

1.

YOUR NAME:
(Print) _____
　　　　　　　Last　　　　　　　　　First　　　　　　　　　M.I.

SIGNATURE: _____　　DATE: ___/___/___

HOME ADDRESS:
(Print) _____
　　　　　　　　　　　　　　　Number and Street

_____
　　City　　　　　　　State　　　　　　Zip Code

PHONE NO.:
(Print) _____

IMPORTANT: Please fill in these boxes exactly as shown on the back cover of your test book.

2. TEST FORM

5. YOUR NAME

First 4 letters of last name				FIRST INIT	MID INIT
Ⓐ	Ⓐ	Ⓐ	Ⓐ	Ⓐ	Ⓐ
Ⓑ	Ⓑ	Ⓑ	Ⓑ	Ⓑ	Ⓑ
Ⓒ	Ⓒ	Ⓒ	Ⓒ	Ⓒ	Ⓒ
Ⓓ	Ⓓ	Ⓓ	Ⓓ	Ⓓ	Ⓓ
Ⓔ	Ⓔ	Ⓔ	Ⓔ	Ⓔ	Ⓔ
Ⓕ	Ⓕ	Ⓕ	Ⓕ	Ⓕ	Ⓕ
Ⓖ	Ⓖ	Ⓖ	Ⓖ	Ⓖ	Ⓖ
Ⓗ	Ⓗ	Ⓗ	Ⓗ	Ⓗ	Ⓗ
Ⓘ	Ⓘ	Ⓘ	Ⓘ	Ⓘ	Ⓘ
Ⓙ	Ⓙ	Ⓙ	Ⓙ	Ⓙ	Ⓙ
Ⓚ	Ⓚ	Ⓚ	Ⓚ	Ⓚ	Ⓚ
Ⓛ	Ⓛ	Ⓛ	Ⓛ	Ⓛ	Ⓛ
Ⓜ	Ⓜ	Ⓜ	Ⓜ	Ⓜ	Ⓜ
Ⓝ	Ⓝ	Ⓝ	Ⓝ	Ⓝ	Ⓝ
Ⓞ	Ⓞ	Ⓞ	Ⓞ	Ⓞ	Ⓞ
Ⓟ	Ⓟ	Ⓟ	Ⓟ	Ⓟ	Ⓟ
Ⓠ	Ⓠ	Ⓠ	Ⓠ	Ⓠ	Ⓠ
Ⓡ	Ⓡ	Ⓡ	Ⓡ	Ⓡ	Ⓡ
Ⓢ	Ⓢ	Ⓢ	Ⓢ	Ⓢ	Ⓢ
Ⓣ	Ⓣ	Ⓣ	Ⓣ	Ⓣ	Ⓣ
Ⓤ	Ⓤ	Ⓤ	Ⓤ	Ⓤ	Ⓤ
Ⓥ	Ⓥ	Ⓥ	Ⓥ	Ⓥ	Ⓥ
Ⓦ	Ⓦ	Ⓦ	Ⓦ	Ⓦ	Ⓦ
Ⓧ	Ⓧ	Ⓧ	Ⓧ	Ⓧ	Ⓧ
Ⓨ	Ⓨ	Ⓨ	Ⓨ	Ⓨ	Ⓨ
Ⓩ	Ⓩ	Ⓩ	Ⓩ	Ⓩ	Ⓩ

6. DATE OF BIRTH

Month	Day		Year	
◯ JAN				
◯ FEB	⓪	⓪	⓪	⓪
◯ MAR	①	①	①	①
◯ APR	②	②	②	②
◯ MAY	③	③	③	③
◯ JUN		④	④	④
◯ JUL		⑤	⑤	⑤
◯ AUG		⑥	⑥	⑥
◯ SEP		⑦	⑦	⑦
◯ OCT		⑧	⑧	⑧
◯ NOV		⑨	⑨	⑨
◯ DEC				

3. TEST CODE　　　**4. REGISTRATION NUMBER**

⓪	Ⓐ	Ⓙ	⓪	⓪	⓪	⓪	⓪	⓪	⓪	⓪
①	Ⓑ	Ⓚ	①	①	①	①	①	①	①	①
②	Ⓒ	Ⓛ	②	②	②	②	②	②	②	②
③	Ⓓ	Ⓜ	③	③	③	③	③	③	③	③
④	Ⓔ	Ⓝ	④	④	④	④	④	④	④	④
⑤	Ⓕ	Ⓞ	⑤	⑤	⑤	⑤	⑤	⑤	⑤	⑤
⑥	Ⓖ	Ⓟ	⑥	⑥	⑥	⑥	⑥	⑥	⑥	⑥
⑦	Ⓗ	Ⓠ	⑦	⑦	⑦	⑦	⑦	⑦	⑦	⑦
⑧	Ⓘ	Ⓡ	⑧	⑧	⑧	⑧	⑧	⑧	⑧	⑧
⑨			⑨	⑨	⑨	⑨	⑨	⑨	⑨	⑨

7. SEX

◯ MALE
◯ FEMALE

The Princeton Review®

1. Ⓐ Ⓑ Ⓒ Ⓓ
2. Ⓐ Ⓑ Ⓒ Ⓓ
3. Ⓐ Ⓑ Ⓒ Ⓓ
4. Ⓐ Ⓑ Ⓒ Ⓓ
5. Ⓐ Ⓑ Ⓒ Ⓓ
6. Ⓐ Ⓑ Ⓒ Ⓓ
7. Ⓐ Ⓑ Ⓒ Ⓓ
8. Ⓐ Ⓑ Ⓒ Ⓓ
9. Ⓐ Ⓑ Ⓒ Ⓓ
10. Ⓐ Ⓑ Ⓒ Ⓓ
11. Ⓐ Ⓑ Ⓒ Ⓓ
12. Ⓐ Ⓑ Ⓒ Ⓓ
13. Ⓐ Ⓑ Ⓒ Ⓓ
14. Ⓐ Ⓑ Ⓒ Ⓓ
15. Ⓐ Ⓑ Ⓒ Ⓓ
16. Ⓐ Ⓑ Ⓒ Ⓓ
17. Ⓐ Ⓑ Ⓒ Ⓓ
18. Ⓐ Ⓑ Ⓒ Ⓓ
19. Ⓐ Ⓑ Ⓒ Ⓓ
20. Ⓐ Ⓑ Ⓒ Ⓓ
21. Ⓐ Ⓑ Ⓒ Ⓓ

22. Ⓐ Ⓑ Ⓒ Ⓓ
23. Ⓐ Ⓑ Ⓒ Ⓓ
24. Ⓐ Ⓑ Ⓒ Ⓓ
25. Ⓐ Ⓑ Ⓒ Ⓓ
26. Ⓐ Ⓑ Ⓒ Ⓓ
27. Ⓐ Ⓑ Ⓒ Ⓓ
28. Ⓐ Ⓑ Ⓒ Ⓓ
29. Ⓐ Ⓑ Ⓒ Ⓓ
30. Ⓐ Ⓑ Ⓒ Ⓓ
31. Ⓐ Ⓑ Ⓒ Ⓓ
32. Ⓐ Ⓑ Ⓒ Ⓓ
33. Ⓐ Ⓑ Ⓒ Ⓓ
34. Ⓐ Ⓑ Ⓒ Ⓓ
35. Ⓐ Ⓑ Ⓒ Ⓓ
36. Ⓐ Ⓑ Ⓒ Ⓓ
37. Ⓐ Ⓑ Ⓒ Ⓓ
38. Ⓐ Ⓑ Ⓒ Ⓓ
39. Ⓐ Ⓑ Ⓒ Ⓓ
40. Ⓐ Ⓑ Ⓒ Ⓓ
41. Ⓐ Ⓑ Ⓒ Ⓓ
42. Ⓐ Ⓑ Ⓒ Ⓓ

43. Ⓐ Ⓑ Ⓒ Ⓓ
44. Ⓐ Ⓑ Ⓒ Ⓓ
45. Ⓐ Ⓑ Ⓒ Ⓓ
46. Ⓐ Ⓑ Ⓒ Ⓓ
47. Ⓐ Ⓑ Ⓒ Ⓓ
48. Ⓐ Ⓑ Ⓒ Ⓓ
49. Ⓐ Ⓑ Ⓒ Ⓓ
50. Ⓐ Ⓑ Ⓒ Ⓓ
51. Ⓐ Ⓑ Ⓒ Ⓓ
52. Ⓐ Ⓑ Ⓒ Ⓓ
53. Ⓐ Ⓑ Ⓒ Ⓓ
54. Ⓐ Ⓑ Ⓒ Ⓓ
55. Ⓐ Ⓑ Ⓒ Ⓓ
56. Ⓐ Ⓑ Ⓒ Ⓓ
57. Ⓐ Ⓑ Ⓒ Ⓓ
58. Ⓐ Ⓑ Ⓒ Ⓓ
59. Ⓐ Ⓑ Ⓒ Ⓓ
60. Ⓐ Ⓑ Ⓒ Ⓓ
61. Ⓐ Ⓑ Ⓒ Ⓓ
62. Ⓐ Ⓑ Ⓒ Ⓓ
63. Ⓐ Ⓑ Ⓒ Ⓓ

64. Ⓐ Ⓑ Ⓒ Ⓓ
65. Ⓐ Ⓑ Ⓒ Ⓓ
66. Ⓐ Ⓑ Ⓒ Ⓓ
67. Ⓐ Ⓑ Ⓒ Ⓓ
68. Ⓐ Ⓑ Ⓒ Ⓓ
69. Ⓐ Ⓑ Ⓒ Ⓓ
70. Ⓐ Ⓑ Ⓒ Ⓓ
71. Ⓐ Ⓑ Ⓒ Ⓓ
72. Ⓐ Ⓑ Ⓒ Ⓓ
73. Ⓐ Ⓑ Ⓒ Ⓓ
74. Ⓐ Ⓑ Ⓒ Ⓓ
75. Ⓐ Ⓑ Ⓒ Ⓓ
76. Ⓐ Ⓑ Ⓒ Ⓓ
77. Ⓐ Ⓑ Ⓒ Ⓓ
78. Ⓐ Ⓑ Ⓒ Ⓓ
79. Ⓐ Ⓑ Ⓒ Ⓓ
80. Ⓐ Ⓑ Ⓒ Ⓓ
81. Ⓐ Ⓑ Ⓒ Ⓓ
82. Ⓐ Ⓑ Ⓒ Ⓓ
83. Ⓐ Ⓑ Ⓒ Ⓓ
84. Ⓐ Ⓑ Ⓒ Ⓓ
85. Ⓐ Ⓑ Ⓒ Ⓓ

The Princeton Review®

Completely darken bubbles with a No. 2 pencil. If you make a mistake, be sure to erase mark completely. Erase all stray marks.

1.

YOUR NAME:
(Print)

Last   First   M.I.

SIGNATURE: _____ **DATE:** ___ / ___ / ___

HOME ADDRESS:
(Print)

Number and Street

City   State   Zip Code

PHONE NO.:
(Print)

IMPORTANT: Please fill in these boxes exactly as shown on the back cover of your test book.

2. TEST FORM

6. DATE OF BIRTH

Month	Day		Year	
⊘ JAN				
⊘ FEB	⓪	⓪	⓪	⓪
⊘ MAR	①	①	①	①
⊘ APR	②	②	②	②
⊘ MAY	③	③	③	③
⊘ JUN		④	④	④
⊘ JUL		⑤	⑤	⑤
⊘ AUG		⑥	⑥	⑥
⊘ SEP		⑦	⑦	⑦
⊘ OCT		⑧	⑧	⑧
⊘ NOV		⑨	⑨	⑨
⊘ DEC				

3. TEST CODE   4. REGISTRATION NUMBER

7. SEX

⊘ MALE
⊘ FEMALE

The Princeton Review®

5. YOUR NAME

First 4 letters of last name				FIRST INIT	MID INIT

(A–Z bubble grid)

---

1. Ⓐ Ⓑ Ⓒ Ⓓ	22. Ⓐ Ⓑ Ⓒ Ⓓ	43. Ⓐ Ⓑ Ⓒ Ⓓ	64. Ⓐ Ⓑ Ⓒ Ⓓ
2. Ⓐ Ⓑ Ⓒ Ⓓ	23. Ⓐ Ⓑ Ⓒ Ⓓ	44. Ⓐ Ⓑ Ⓒ Ⓓ	65. Ⓐ Ⓑ Ⓒ Ⓓ
3. Ⓐ Ⓑ Ⓒ Ⓓ	24. Ⓐ Ⓑ Ⓒ Ⓓ	45. Ⓐ Ⓑ Ⓒ Ⓓ	66. Ⓐ Ⓑ Ⓒ Ⓓ
4. Ⓐ Ⓑ Ⓒ Ⓓ	25. Ⓐ Ⓑ Ⓒ Ⓓ	46. Ⓐ Ⓑ Ⓒ Ⓓ	67. Ⓐ Ⓑ Ⓒ Ⓓ
5. Ⓐ Ⓑ Ⓒ Ⓓ	26. Ⓐ Ⓑ Ⓒ Ⓓ	47. Ⓐ Ⓑ Ⓒ Ⓓ	68. Ⓐ Ⓑ Ⓒ Ⓓ
6. Ⓐ Ⓑ Ⓒ Ⓓ	27. Ⓐ Ⓑ Ⓒ Ⓓ	48. Ⓐ Ⓑ Ⓒ Ⓓ	69. Ⓐ Ⓑ Ⓒ Ⓓ
7. Ⓐ Ⓑ Ⓒ Ⓓ	28. Ⓐ Ⓑ Ⓒ Ⓓ	49. Ⓐ Ⓑ Ⓒ Ⓓ	70. Ⓐ Ⓑ Ⓒ Ⓓ
8. Ⓐ Ⓑ Ⓒ Ⓓ	29. Ⓐ Ⓑ Ⓒ Ⓓ	50. Ⓐ Ⓑ Ⓒ Ⓓ	71. Ⓐ Ⓑ Ⓒ Ⓓ
9. Ⓐ Ⓑ Ⓒ Ⓓ	30. Ⓐ Ⓑ Ⓒ Ⓓ	51. Ⓐ Ⓑ Ⓒ Ⓓ	72. Ⓐ Ⓑ Ⓒ Ⓓ
10. Ⓐ Ⓑ Ⓒ Ⓓ	31. Ⓐ Ⓑ Ⓒ Ⓓ	52. Ⓐ Ⓑ Ⓒ Ⓓ	73. Ⓐ Ⓑ Ⓒ Ⓓ
11. Ⓐ Ⓑ Ⓒ Ⓓ	32. Ⓐ Ⓑ Ⓒ Ⓓ	53. Ⓐ Ⓑ Ⓒ Ⓓ	74. Ⓐ Ⓑ Ⓒ Ⓓ
12. Ⓐ Ⓑ Ⓒ Ⓓ	33. Ⓐ Ⓑ Ⓒ Ⓓ	54. Ⓐ Ⓑ Ⓒ Ⓓ	75. Ⓐ Ⓑ Ⓒ Ⓓ
13. Ⓐ Ⓑ Ⓒ Ⓓ	34. Ⓐ Ⓑ Ⓒ Ⓓ	55. Ⓐ Ⓑ Ⓒ Ⓓ	76. Ⓐ Ⓑ Ⓒ Ⓓ
14. Ⓐ Ⓑ Ⓒ Ⓓ	35. Ⓐ Ⓑ Ⓒ Ⓓ	56. Ⓐ Ⓑ Ⓒ Ⓓ	77. Ⓐ Ⓑ Ⓒ Ⓓ
15. Ⓐ Ⓑ Ⓒ Ⓓ	36. Ⓐ Ⓑ Ⓒ Ⓓ	57. Ⓐ Ⓑ Ⓒ Ⓓ	78. Ⓐ Ⓑ Ⓒ Ⓓ
16. Ⓐ Ⓑ Ⓒ Ⓓ	37. Ⓐ Ⓑ Ⓒ Ⓓ	58. Ⓐ Ⓑ Ⓒ Ⓓ	79. Ⓐ Ⓑ Ⓒ Ⓓ
17. Ⓐ Ⓑ Ⓒ Ⓓ	38. Ⓐ Ⓑ Ⓒ Ⓓ	59. Ⓐ Ⓑ Ⓒ Ⓓ	80. Ⓐ Ⓑ Ⓒ Ⓓ
18. Ⓐ Ⓑ Ⓒ Ⓓ	39. Ⓐ Ⓑ Ⓒ Ⓓ	60. Ⓐ Ⓑ Ⓒ Ⓓ	81. Ⓐ Ⓑ Ⓒ Ⓓ
19. Ⓐ Ⓑ Ⓒ Ⓓ	40. Ⓐ Ⓑ Ⓒ Ⓓ	61. Ⓐ Ⓑ Ⓒ Ⓓ	82. Ⓐ Ⓑ Ⓒ Ⓓ
20. Ⓐ Ⓑ Ⓒ Ⓓ	41. Ⓐ Ⓑ Ⓒ Ⓓ	62. Ⓐ Ⓑ Ⓒ Ⓓ	83. Ⓐ Ⓑ Ⓒ Ⓓ
21. Ⓐ Ⓑ Ⓒ Ⓓ	42. Ⓐ Ⓑ Ⓒ Ⓓ	63. Ⓐ Ⓑ Ⓒ Ⓓ	84. Ⓐ Ⓑ Ⓒ Ⓓ
			85. Ⓐ Ⓑ Ⓒ Ⓓ

The Princeton Review®

International Offices Listing

China (Beijing)
1501 Building A,
Disanji Creative Zone,
No.66 West Section of North 4th Ring Road Beijing
Tel: +86-10-62684481/2/3
Email: tprkor01@chol.com
Website: www.tprbeijing.com

China (Shanghai)
1010 Kaixuan Road
Building B, 5/F
Changning District, Shanghai, China 200052
Sara Beattie, Owner: Email: sbeattie@sarabeattie.com
Tel: +86-21-5108-2798
Fax: +86-21-6386-1039
Website: www.princetonreviewshanghai.com

Hong Kong
5th Floor, Yardley Commercial Building
1-6 Connaught Road West, Sheung Wan, Hong Kong
(MTR Exit C)
Sara Beattie, Owner: Email: sbeattie@sarabeattie.com
Tel: +852-2507-9380
Fax: +852-2827-4630
Website: www.princetonreviewhk.com

India (Mumbai)
Score Plus Academy
Office No.15, Fifth Floor
Manek Mahal 90
Veer Nariman Road
Next to Hotel Ambassador
Churchgate, Mumbai 400020
Maharashtra, India
Ritu Kalwani: Email: director@score-plus.com
Tel: + 91 22 22846801 / 39 / 41
Website: www.score-plus.com

India (New Delhi)
South Extension
K-16, Upper Ground Floor
South Extension Part–1,
New Delhi-110049
Aradhana Mahna: aradhana@manyagroup.com
Monisha Banerjee: monisha@manyagroup.com
Ruchi Tomar: ruchi.tomar@manyagroup.com
Rishi Josan: Rishi.josan@manyagroup.com
Vishal Goswamy: vishal.goswamy@manyagroup.com
Tel: +91-11-64501603/ 4, +91-11-65028379
Website: www.manyagroup.com

Lebanon
463 Bliss Street
AlFarra Building - 2nd floor
Ras Beirut
Beirut, Lebanon
Hassan Coudsi: Email: hassan.coudsi@review.com
Tel: +961-1-367-688
Website: www.princetonreviewlebanon.com

Korea
945-25 Young Shin Building
25 Daechi-Dong, Kangnam-gu
Seoul, Korea 135-280
Yong-Hoon Lee: Email: TPRKor01@chollian.net
In-Woo Kim: Email: iwkim@tpr.co.kr
Tel: + 82-2-554-7762
Fax: +82-2-453-9466
Website: www.tpr.co.kr

Kuwait
ScorePlus Learning Center
Salmiyah Block 3, Street 2 Building 14
Post Box: 559, Zip 1306, Safat, Kuwait
Email: infokuwait@score-plus.com
Tel: +965-25-75-48-02 / 8
Fax: +965-25-75-46-02
Website: www.scorepluseducation.com

Malaysia
Sara Beattie MDC Sdn Bhd
Suites 18E & 18F
18th Floor
Gurney Tower, Persiaran Gurney
Penang, Malaysia
Email: tprkl.my@sarabeattie.com
Sara Beattie, Owner: Email: sbeattie@sarabeattie.com
Tel: +604-2104 333
Fax: +604-2104 330
Website: www.princetonreviewKL.com

Mexico
TPR México
Guanajuato No. 242 Piso 1 Interior 1
Col. Roma Norte
México D.F., C.P.06700
registro@princetonreviewmexico.com
Tel: +52-55-5255-4495
+52-55-5255-4440
+52-55-5255-4442
Website: www.princetonreviewmexico.com

Qatar
Score Plus
Office No: 1A, Al Kuwari (Damas)
Building near Merweb Hotel, Al Saad
Post Box: 2408, Doha, Qatar
Email: infoqatar@score-plus.com
Tel: +974 44 36 8580, +974 526 5032
Fax: +974 44 13 1995
Website: www.scorepluseducation.com

Taiwan
The Princeton Review Taiwan
2F, 169 Zhong Xiao East Road, Section 4
Taipei, Taiwan 10690
Lisa Bartle (Owner): lbartle@princetonreview.com.tw
Tel: +886-2-2751-1293
Fax: +886-2-2776-3201
Website: www.PrincetonReview.com.tw

Thailand
The Princeton Review Thailand
Sathorn Nakorn Tower, 28th floor
100 North Sathorn Road
Bangkok, Thailand 10500
Thavida Bijayendrayodhin (Chairman)
Email: thavida@princetonreviewthailand.com
Mitsara Bijayendrayodhin (Managing Director)
Email: mitsara@princetonreviewthailand.com
Tel: +662-636-6770
Fax: +662-636-6776
Website: www.princetonreviewthailand.com

Turkey
Yeni Sülün Sokak No. 28
Levent, Istanbul, 34330, Turkey
Nuri Ozgur: nuri@tprturkey.com
Rona Ozgur: rona@tprturkey.com
Iren Ozgur: iren@tprturkey.com
Tel: +90-212-324-4747
Fax: +90-212-324-3347
Website: www.tprturkey.com

UAE
Emirates Score Plus
Office No: 506, Fifth Floor
Sultan Business Center
Near Lamcy Plaza, 21 Oud Metha Road
Post Box: 44098, Dubai
United Arab Emirates
Hukumat Kalwani: skoreplus@gmail.com
Ritu Kalwani: director@score-plus.com
Email: info@score-plus.com
Tel: +971-4-334-0004
Fax: +971-4-334-0222
Website: www.princetonreviewuae.com

Our International Partners

The Princeton Review also runs courses with a variety of
partners in Africa, Asia, Europe, and South America.

Georgia
LEAF American-Georgian Education Center
www.leaf.ge

Mongolia
English Academy of Mongolia
www.nyescm.org

Nigeria
The Know Place
www.knowplace.com.ng

Panama
Academia Interamericana de Panama
http://aip.edu.pa/

Switzerland
Institut Le Rosey
http://www.rosey.ch/

All other inquiries, please email us at
internationalsupport@review.com